Favorite Recipes® of ESA Women International

DESSERTS

© Favorite Recipes Press/NASHVILLE EMS MCMLXXVII
Post Office Box 77, Nashville, Tennessee 37202
Library of Congress Cataloging in Publication Data
Main entry under title:
Favorite recipes of ESA Women International.
Includes index.
1. Desserts.   I. Title: Desserts cookbook.
TX773.F3428   641.8'6   77-22789
ISBN 0-87197-115-1

Recipes on pages 39, 46 and 64.

Recipes on pages 37, 114 and 158.

ESA Women International

It is always my personal pleasure to say . . .

"May I have your recipe," because this is what makes cooking such a joy! And, ESA Women throughout the world are delighted in sharing their recipes, talents and time, as well as an important part of their lives to make a more joyful world.

Every recipe entry in this cookbook represents an enthusiasm to enjoy life to the fullest because that is what every ESA Woman wants for herself and those around her. This beautiful DESSERTS Cookbook will provide funds for children who might have their share of joy through Project Hope and those who might share life through St. Jude Children's Research Hospital. Many other additional educational projects, as well as cultural, social and community needs, will be met with contributions from the sale of this Cookbook.

So let a little "sweetness" into your life with ESA DESSERTS recipes. You can't resist such an outstanding collection of desserts which have been successfully proven by individual ESA members in their own "test" kitchens. You can be sure, whether it's simple or very fancy, each recipe will be distinctive because ESA members are proud to sign each recipe they share with you.

ESA Women honestly enjoy the satisfaction of preparing extra special delicacies for the important people in their lives. Each of you who use this Cookbook will find a challenge to create an unusual dessert for your "special person", or at an impulse you will think of a dear friend who would be delighted with a gift copy of ESA Women's DESSERTS Cookbook.

So, thank you ESA Women who are responsible for this Cookbook, and thank you Friends who purchase it. There will be countless benefits sustained by you and you will make someone's life *sweeter than before.*"

Your Cookbook Editor,

Nicky Beaulieu

Nicky Beaulieu

Contents

Prelude to Beautiful Desserts

No part of cooking and mealtime can be any more expressive, colorful, or memorable than dessert can be. Generally including cakes, cookies, puddings, pastries, and candy, its basic forms are amazingly few and simple. The variety of ingredients, flavors, and textures to be found in desserts, however, is quite myriad. The flavor and texture of a cake, for instance, can be as straightforward as a pound cake, as delicate as angel food, or as luxurious and rich as a holiday fruitcake. A list of favorite desserts further reveals the variety of forms to be found in dessert: rich fudge brownies, steaming apple pies, crisp and spicy gingersnaps, cool and luscious homemade ice cream with fresh fruit, an elegant Baked Alaska or a Charlotte Russe. Truly a rich and varied array!

Almost all countries and their people are noted for their own particular addition of foods and flavors to the endless list of the world's favorite desserts — Italians for fantastic ice creams, the English for their rich puddings, the French for elegant sweets of every description, Austria and Germany for superb tortes, pastries and strudels, and the Scandinavians for delicate cookies, sweet breads, kuchens and coffee cakes. Spices, including ginger, cinnamon, anise, and nutmeg, were probably the main force behind the beginning of world trade, while South America continues to supply the world with most of its chocolate.

Even the American pilgrims and settlers, who were sorely lacking in the basic ingredients for the desserts they loved so well, quickly learned from the native Indians to flavor their corn bread with the many types of berries growing wild all over the countryside. Then, as white sugar and wheat became more easily available, and foodstuffs in general became more abundant, desserts became more common. With the arrival of slaves from Africa and immigrants from all corners of Europe, the sweets and confections from many countries became well known in the kitchens of families throughout the land.

This same delightful diversity is equally true today. Any family's weekly menu might include Devil's Food Cake one evening, American Apple Pie on another night, or even South American Bananas Foster for another meal. Families everywhere love dessert, and appreciate variety. Thanks to the wonders of modern food processing methods, quick desserts are available everywhere so that even the most hurried or inexperienced cook can offer outstanding desserts with some help from a *good cookbook!* Modern transportation also keeps a kaleidoscopic supply of ingredients as well as flavorings and spices available to the homemaker — making dessert preparation easier than ever before. Today, it seems that choosing which dessert to prepare is really the hardest thing of all.

Almost every homemaker or hostess has seen her family and guests brighten when dessert arrives at the end of the meal, no matter how much they might have already eaten. Recipes for sweets and confections are present in the cuisine of just about every country in the world because everyone loves them. Despite a universal taste appeal, desserts and sweets have lost favor in meal planning over the past few years. Weight and health conscious homemakers, knowing that cakes, cookies, pies and other confections are typically high in calories, seemed also to suppose that this meant they were low in nutrition, as well. But, a well planned diet can and should include homemade desserts, as so many are made with eggs, milk, margarine, fresh fruit, various cheeses and nutmeats, as well as rice, oatmeal, and other grains and cereals. Oatmeal and raisin cookies served with a glass of cold milk are an undeniably nutritious afternoon snack for a growing child. Homemade ice cream with fresh fruit is the perfect nutrition and flavor balance to any number of healthful meals. So dessert does have its practical place at the dinner table.

But, the fanciful side of dessert is what everyone really loves best about it. Think how delightful the entire house smells during the year's holidays and special occasions as the family shares in baking cakes and cookies, or in making pies and candy. And how the appetite soars at the sight of an enticing dessert waiting in the background to be served as the finish of the meal. Almost any dessert, but especially cakes and cookies, can be shaped and decorated to fit the theme of an occasion — whether with pastel decorations for Easter, gay circus trim for a birthday party, or beautiful and romantic designs for a wedding reception. Even a cheesecake can be a grand finale for a Fourth of July repast when topped with alternating rows of cherries, blueberries and whipped cream.

The effect of even the most elegant, decorative or delicious dessert will be lost if it is not planned to complement the other foods in the meal. A rich and filling dinner is best balanced by a light and/or cool dessert such as thin, crisp cookies and sherbet, angelfood cake, or most any chilled or frozen dessert such as gelatines and custards. On the other hand, cakes, pies and other filling desserts are the right finish for a light meal. The hot summer months usually call for a light, chilled dessert, even with a light meal; while a heavier dessert is usually preferred in the cold winter months.

For consistently rewarding results in preparing favorite sweets and confections, use only the freshest ingredients of the highest quality, and follow the recipe exactly — add personal touches only after the recipe becomes familiar. Above all, never use sloppy cooking methods when making a dessert. Always think and plan before you act, measure the ingredients accurately, preheat the oven properly, and use clean, shiny utensils and baking pans. Nothing is more heartbreaking than a ruined dessert, as a successful one is often a measure of a cook's more intricate skills.

Many busy homemakers have found that their freezer is an undeniable asset in making dessert preparation doubly easy and far more economical, for both their time and money. From the many, many delicious and favorite dessert recipes available to the homemaker, only custard pies, cream puddings and other cream filled desserts are NOT recommended for freezing. Therefore, the majority of cake, candy, cookie and pie varieties, as well as pastry shells, meringue, whipped cream and fresh nutmeats can be frozen. Recipes for these many sweets can be doubled at baking time, with the extra portions conveniently frozen for later use. Or, if only half the recipe is needed for immediate use, the remainder can be frozen — a real economy aid for the single homemaker, or for the cook who prepares meals for only two or three people. When freezing desserts, remember to allow plenty of space so they are not crushed or mashed, and be sure to wrap them carefully in vapor-proof packaging to fully protect their flavor and texture.

Epsilon Sigma Alpha members have rediscovered the invaluable part desserts can play in planning every meal and party menu. The ESA DESSERTS Cookbook is the result — a delightful collection of delectable recipes that range from simply sweet to simply superb. Add it to your own dessert recipes repertoire, and you will find yourself rediscovering desserts too. Right away!

Dessert Calorie Chart

COMMON DESSERT RECIPE INGREDIENTS

Ingredient	Amount	Calories
Chocolate, semisweet	1 Oz.	150
Chocolate, sweetened	1 Oz.	135
Chocolate Syrup	1 Tbsp.	65
Flour	1 Cup	405
Sugar, granulated	1 Tbsp.	50
Sugar, brown	1 Tbsp.	50
Sugar, powdered	1 Tbsp.	45
Butter or Margarine	1 Tbsp.	100
Corn Syrup	1 Tbsp.	60
Honey	1 Tbsp.	63
Evaporated Milk	1 Tbsp.	60
Sweetened Condensed Milk	½ Cup	504
Cream Cheese	1 Oz.	100
Marshmallows	1 Oz.	94
Sour Cream	1 Cup	800
Vegetable Oils	1 Tbsp.	125
Vanilla Extract	1 Tsp.	8
Almond Extract	1 Tsp.	3
Almonds (whole)	1 Cup	850
Pecans (halves)	1 Cup	750
Walnuts (broken)	1 Cup	790
Heavy Cream	1 Cup	840
Raisins	1 Cup	80

CAKES (average serving or 2" piece without frosting)

Angel Food	104
Caramel	352
Chocolate	252
Fruitcake	250
Pound Cake	250
Strawberry Shortcake	350
Upside-Down Cake	275
Yellow Cake	260

FROSTINGS (2 tablespoons)

Butter	110
Chocolate Butter	106
Lemon Icing	70
Boiled Frosting	85

COBBLERS (average serving)

Apple	256
Blueberry	242
Cherry	261
Peach	255

PIES (1/8 of 9" pie)

Apple	230
Blueberry	255
Cherry	300
Custard	230
Chocolate Meringue	255
Lemon Meringue	275
Strawberry	225
Mincemeat	300
Banana Cream	352
Chiffon	276
Coconut Cream	452
Nesselrode	376

ICE CREAM

8 oz., most flavors	260
average scoop	153
8 oz. sherbet	225
average scoop	105
Banana Split	450
Milk Shake	352
Most Sundaes	375
Hot Fudge Sundae	400

COOKIES (1 average)

Gingersnap	20
Chocolate Chip	21
Macaroon	50
Oatmeal	50
Butter	15

CANDY (average piece)

Fudge	112
English Toffee	25
Peanut Brittle	77
Taffy	45
Chocolate Mints	122

MISCELLANEOUS DESSERTS

Cream Puff	172
Doughnut	200
Chocolate Eclair	276
Mousse	352
Ambrosia, 1 serving	142
Baked Alaska	352
Popcorn Ball	142
Brownie	152
Gingerbread	176

Dessert Cooking Terms

A La Mode: Served or topped with ice cream.

Au Lait: A beverage made or served with cream or milk.

Bake: To cook by dry heat, as in an oven.

Batter: The liquid mixture of flour, eggs, flavoring, etc., of cakes, waffles, or pancakes before they are cooked; also, a coating for food to be fried.

Bavarian: A gelatine and cream based pudding.

Beat: To blend with a spoon, beater, or electric mixer; or to incorporate air into a mixture or food, such as egg whites or whipped cream.

Bisque: A rich frozen mixture of macaroons, nuts, and cream.

Blancmange: A molded milk dessert, thickened and flavored with gelatine, flour, cornstarch or ground almonds.

Blend: To thoroughly combine ingredients.

Bombe: A molded, frozen dessert with an ice cream or sherbet base.

Bonbon: Candy that is made of or dipped into fondant.

Candy: To cook any fruit or its peel in a heavy sugar syrup until it becomes transparent.

Caramel: Typically, burnt sugar syrup, or the flavor of the same.

Caramelize: To heat dry sugar, or a sugary food, until light brown and caramel flavored.

Charlotte: A dessert made by lining a dish with cake, lady fingers or other sweet bread, and then filling it with custard, whipped cream or a fruit combination.

Coat-the-Spoon: To cook or blend ingredients until the mixture coats the spoon in a thin layer.

Cobbler: A pie-like dessert topped with a rich biscuit dough, then baked in a deep dish.

Cream: To work or beat shortening until light and fluffy; sugar, flour or eggs can then be creamed into the shortening.

Crepes Suzette: Paper thin pancakes served in a butter sauce that is flavored with orange, lemon and curacao, then flamed in brandy.

Custard: A mixture of eggs, milk and sugar that is cooked or baked until set.

Cut, or Cut In: To combine shortening with flour or other dry ingredients with a pastry blender, or two knives.

Dissolve: To liquify, or to incorporate a soluable ingredient, like sugar, into a liquid.

Dough: A mixture of flour, other dry ingredients and leavening that is thick enough to knead and bake.

Dredge: To coat with flour before cooking or frying, or with powdered sugar as a garnish or topping.

Fold: To combine ingredients by blending with a spoon or wire whisk by using a gentle up-and-over motion.

Fondant: Candy made with sugar syrup, which is kneaded until creamy.

Frost: To coat, top, or cover with icing.

Glaze: To coat with a thin sugar syrup cooked to the crack stage, or to top with a thin icing.

Grease: To coat a thin layer of fat onto the inside of a baking or cooking pan to keep foods from sticking to it.

Ice: Frozen, sweet dessert made of fruit juice, sugar and water; or to frost, as a cake.

Kisses: Tiny dessert meringues, or any tiny candy, such as chocolate or caramel.

Knead: To prepare dough, or other food, with a pressing, stretching and folding motion.

Macaroons: Small cakes of egg white, sugar, almonds or almond paste, or coconut.

Marzipan: An almond and sugar paste confection, usually shaped and tinted to resemble tiny fruits.

Meringue: Stiffly beaten egg white mixture used as a topping for various desserts, or baked until crisp and eaten topped with ice cream, whipped cream, fruit or sweet sauce.

Mocha: A coffee, or chocolate-coffee flavoring used in various desserts and beverages.

Mousse: Frozen sweet whipped cream combined with fruits and nuts.

Petit Four: Tiny, frosted tea cake of various flavors.

Scald: To heat milk or other liquid to just below the boiling point, indicated by a thin skim forming at the top of the liquid.

Torte: A cake-like dessert made with many eggs, sugar and usually nuts or bread crumbs rather than flour. The batter is baked in large, flat pans, and served in layers filled with whipped cream, custards, jam or frosting.

Whip: To beat air into a mixture with a hand or electric mixer until it is light and fluffy.

Candies

Candy making is one of the true cooking arts. To be a success, favorite candies — including fudge and divinity, taffy and brittle — must have their own characteristic flavor and texture, and probably require more patience, the most exacting methods, and greater attention than any other homemade dessert. Yet, the art of making superior candy is rather easily mastered, as even the most inexperienced cook can perfect it in a very short time.

The most typical problem candy cooks learn to avoid is crystallization. The main ingredient in all candy is, of course, granulated sugar crystals. But, the end product should usually be either creamy, chewy, or brittle — rarely sugary, if ever at all. To avoid crystallized candy, take care that no sugar crystals are introduced into the mixture after it begins cooking, as well as after it starts cooling. Use the butter in a recipe to grease the sides of the pan before adding the other ingredients. Heat any required liquids and then remove the pan from the stove before adding the sugar; then, be sure that the sugar is fully dissolved before returning the mixture to the heat source. Keep the mixture tightly covered until it boils up well, which will keep the sugar crystals washed down. The pan can then be uncovered for evaporation and proper cooking.

The candy is cooked when the sugar mixture reaches the "finish temperature" stated in the recipe. The most reliable guide to this finish temperature is a candy thermometer, although more experienced cooks often rely on the "cold water test" as well. The supplemental *Temperature Test Chart* on page 14 details this information. When the candy is finished cooking and set aside to cool, handle it with care, as jolts and jars may cause it to crystallize. The candy is cool and ready to stir when the pan bottom can be held comfortably in the hand, or about 110° Fahrenheit. To stir, use a wooden spoon in a wide, circular, up-and-over lifting motion. This "stir-beat" method is just right and there is no need to beat furiously.

ESA members are sure they love to make, serve, and enjoy homemade candy as much as you and your family do. Experienced candy makers, as well as those who may not have tried it yet, can both be sure that all the recipes in this section have been well tested, and are well loved, too!

TEMPERATURE TESTS FOR CANDY MAKING

PRODUCT	TEST IN COLD WATER*	DEGREES F. ON CANDY THERMOMETER			
		SEA LEVEL	2000 FEET	5000 FEET	7500 FEET
FUDGE, PANOCHA, FONDANT	SOFT BALL (can be picked up but flattens)	234° - 240° F.	230° - 236° F.	224° - 230° F.	219° - 225° F.
CARAMELS	FIRM BALL (holds shape unless pressed)	242° - 248° F.	238° - 244° F.	232° - 238° F.	227° - 233° F.
DIVINITY, TAFFY AND CARAMEL CORN	HARD BALL (holds shape though pliable)	250° - 268° F.	246° - 264° F.	240° - 258° F.	235° - 253° F.
BUTTERSCOTCH, ENGLISH TOFFEE	SOFT CRACK (separates into hard threads but not brittle)	270° - 290° F.	266° - 286° F.	260° - 280° F.	255° - 275° F.
BRITTLES	HARD CRACK (separates into hard and brittle threads)	300° - 310° F.	296° - 306° F.	290° - 300° F.	285° - 295° F.

* Drop about 1/2 teaspoon of boiling syrup into one cup water, and test firmness of mass with fingers.

MICROWAVE BUTTERMILK PRALINES

2 c. sugar
1 tsp. soda
1 c. buttermilk
3/4 c. margarine or butter
1 tsp. vanilla
2 c. pecans, halved or chopped

Combine all ingredients except vanilla and pecans in buttered glass mixing bowl. Cover with plastic wrap. Microwave on Roast for 15 minutes. Stir and continue cooking on Roast for 13 to 15 minutes or to soft-ball stage. Add vanilla; beat until mixture forms soft peaks. Stir in pecans. Pour into buttered 2-quart glass baking dish. Cool until firm. Cut into pieces. May be dropped from a teaspoon onto waxed paper if desired. Yield: 40-48 pralines.

Bonnie Jordan, Jonquil Girl
Beta Omega No. 4210
Midland, Texas

BUTTERSCOTCH TIDBITS

7 oz. salted peanuts
1 No. 2 can Chinese noodles
2 pkg. butterscotch morsels, melted

Place peanuts and noodles in large mixing bowl. Pour melted morsels over mixture. Blend well. Drop by teaspoonfuls onto waxed paper. Let set for 1 hour.

Charlotte Warren
Zeta Epsilon No. 4614
Seminole, Oklahoma

CREAMY CARAMELS

2 c. cream
1 c. butter
2 c. sugar
1 3/4 c. light corn syrup
1 c. nuts (opt.)
1 tsp. vanilla

Place 1 cup cream, butter, sugar and syrup in saucepan. Bring to a boil; boil for several minutes. Add remaining cream slowly. Cook to hard-ball stage. Add nuts and vanilla. Pour into buttered pan. Cool. Cut and wrap pieces.

Pat Wink
Beta Tau No. 3953
Woodbridge, Virginia

CHOCOLATE CARAMELS

2 c. cream
2 c. sugar
1 c. butter
1 1/2 c. light corn syrup
5 tbsp. cocoa
2 tsp. vanilla
1 1/2 c. chopped nuts

Combine 1 cup cream with sugar, butter, corn syrup and cocoa. Bring to a boil. Add remaining cream. Bring to a boil. Cook slowly to firm-ball stage, about 50 to 60 minutes. Remove from heat. Add vanilla and nuts. Spread on jelly roll pan; cool. Cut into squares and wrap.

Bonnie McAdoo, Chap. Educational Dir.
Alpha Omega No. 4110
Bismarck, North Dakota

CHERRY-CHOCOLATE CANDY

2 c. sugar
2/3 c. evaporated milk
12 marshmallows
1/2 c. margarine
Dash of salt
1 6-oz. package cherry chips
1 tsp. vanilla
1 12-oz. package chocolate chips
3/4 c. peanut butter
1 12-oz. package crushed salted
   peanuts

Combine sugar, milk, marshmallows, margarine and salt in saucepan over medium heat. Boil for 5 minutes. Remove from heat. Add cherry chips and vanilla; set aside. Melt chocolate chips in double boiler. Add peanut butter and crushed peanuts. Spread half the mixture in 9 x 13-inch pan. Pour cherry mix-

ture over this. Top with remaining chocolate mixture. Chill. Cut into bars.

Hazel Kaiser
Alpha Phi Chap. No. 1438
Winner, South Dakota

CREAM CANDY

4 c. sugar
1 c. light corn syrup
2 c. cream
1/8 tsp. salt
1 tsp. vanilla
1 1/2 c. thinly sliced Brazil nuts

Mix sugar, corn syrup and cream in heavy saucepan. Boil to 227 degrees. Add salt and vanilla. Cool. Beat until mixture loses shiny appearance and begins to firm. Add nuts. Turn out into buttered flat pan. Cut into serving pieces. Store in airtight container.

Edith Campbell, Pres.
Zeta Phi No. 2593
Junction City, Kansas

BROWN CREAM CANDY

6 c. sugar
2 c. milk
1/2 c. butter
1/4 tsp. soda
1 tsp. vanilla
2 c. chopped walnuts

Combine 4 cups sugar with milk in a large saucepan. Heat very slowly; stir occasionally until sugar melts. Heat 2 cups sugar in a heavy skillet over very low heat. Stir constantly for 15 minutes or until sugar melts and turns golden brown. Do not cook too fast or too long as it will smoke and taste bitter. Pour the sugar and milk mixture very slowly and carefully into sugar syrup. Cook mixture, stirring occasionally, to soft-ball stage. Stir in butter until melted and blended into candy. Stir in soda. Remove candy from heat. Cool to lukewarm. Add vanilla and walnuts. Beat candy until thick and creamy. Pour into buttered pan. Yield: 3 3/4 pounds.

Dian Krynicki, Treas.
Alpha Epsilon No. 4609
Fort Collins, Colorado

CHOCOLATE-CHERRY CREAMS

1 6-oz. package chocolate chips
1/3 c. evaporated milk
1 1/2 c. powdered sugar
1/3 c. maraschino cherries, well drained
    and cut up
1 1/4 c. coconut

Place chocolate chips and milk in a heavy
2-quart saucepan. Stir over low heat until
chocolate melts. Stir in powdered sugar and
cherries. Chill until cool enough to handle.
Roll into walnut-sized balls. Roll in coconut.
Chill until firm. Yield: 2 dozen.

Janis Disterhaupt, Educational Dir.
Delta Tau No. 3684
Ellisville, Missouri

BONBONS

2 c. powdered sugar
1 1/2 c. crunchy peanut butter
2 c. chopped dates
1 c. chopped nuts
6 tbsp. melted butter
12 oz. chocolate or butterscotch chips
1/2 bar paraffin

Mix together powdered sugar, peanut butter,
dates, nuts and melted butter. Roll into
small balls. Melt chocolate chips and paraffin
in double boiler. Dip balls into melted mixture. Place on waxed paper to harden.

Phyllis Madsen
Alpha Xi No. 1861
West Des Moines, Iowa

HAND-DIPPED CHOCOLATES

1/4 lb. butter
1 can sweetened condensed milk
2 lb. powdered sugar
1 7-oz. can flaked coconut
4 c. ground nuts
2 6-oz. packages chocolate chips
1/2 bar paraffin

Mix first 5 ingredients in a large bowl. Roll
into balls; place on cookie sheet. Combine
next 2 ingredients in double boiler; let melt

completely. Put toothpicks in candy; dip
into chocolate mixture.

Dixie Lamb, Awards Chm., Past Pres.
Alpha Delta No. 1711
Milford, Utah

BUCKEYES

1 lb. peanut butter
1 1/2 lb. powdered sugar
1/2 lb. margarine
8 oz. chocolate chips
1/3 slab paraffin

Mix peanut butter, powdered sugar and
margarine. Form into 1-inch balls; chill. Melt
chocolate chips with paraffin and a small
amount of water in double boiler. Put
chilled peanut butter balls on a toothpick;
dip into chocolate mixture until almost
covered. Refrigerate until set on waxed
paper. They will be shiny. Yield: 50 balls.

Marjorie Dinoff
Beta Tau No. 2949
Trenton, Michigan

MAPLE-NUT CHOCOLATES

3 lb. powdered sugar
1/2 lb. margarine
1 14-oz. can sweetened condensed milk
1 to 2 c. chopped walnuts
1 1/2 tbsp. maple flavoring
1 1/2 tbsp. vanilla
4 1-oz. squares unsweetened baking
    chocolate
1 12-oz. package chocolate chips
1 bar household wax

Mix together first 6 ingredients with hands
until well blended. Roll into balls. Refrigerate overnight. Place next 3 ingredients in
double boiler. Melt together. Dip chilled
balls one at a time into chocolate. May be
frozen for later use. Yield: 250 candies.

Roberta Bell, Pres.
Beta Delta No. 4271
Tucson, Arizona

BUTTERSCOTCH SPOONOODLES

1 3-oz. can chow mein noodles
1 c. coarsely chopped nuts

sugar syrup over beaten egg whites. Beat until stiff. Let stand. Cook 3 cups sugar, 2/3 cup water and light corn syrup to hard-crack stage. Beat into first mixture. Add salt, nuts and vanilla. Drop by spoonfuls onto waxed paper.

Suzan Atkin, Historian
Alpha Delta No. 1711
Milford, Utah

EASY DIVINITY

3 c. sugar
3/4 c. light corn syrup
3/4 c. water
2 egg whites
1 3-oz. package strawberry gelatin
1 c. chopped nuts
1/2 c. shredded coconut

Grease a 9-inch pan thoroughly with butter. Mix sugar, corn syrup and water in saucepan. Bring to a boil, stirring constantly. Reduce heat; continue cooking, stirring occasionally, to hard-ball stage. Beat egg whites in large bowl until soft peaks form; add dry gelatin gradually. Continue beating until mixture holds stiff peaks. Pour syrup mixture into egg white mixture in thin stream, beating constantly, until candy holds shape and loses gloss. Stir in nuts and coconut. Pour quickly into greased pan. Cut with knife dipped in hot water. Yield: 5 dozen pieces.

Blanche M. Boisen, Pres.
Mu Chap. No. 119
Albany, California

1/3 c. honey
1/4 c. sugar
2 tbsp. butter
1/2 tsp. vanilla
1/8 tsp. salt
1 6-oz. package butterscotch-flavored
   morsels

Combine chow mein noodles and nuts in mixing bowl; set aside. Combine honey, sugar, butter, vanilla and salt in saucepan. Bring to a full boil over moderate heat, stirring constantly. Remove from heat. Add butterscotch morsels; stir until melted and smooth. Pour over noodles and nuts; mix gently until coated. Drop by heaping teaspoonfuls onto waxed paper on baking sheet. Let stand until set or chill until firm. Yield: 32 Spoonoodles.

Photograph for this recipe on this page.

TWO-STAGE DIVINITY

4 c. sugar
1 1/3 c. water
4 egg whites
1 c. light corn syrup
Pinch of salt
Nuts to taste
Vanilla to taste

Boil 1 cup sugar and 2/3 cup water to firm-ball stage. Beat egg whites until stiff. Pour

PEANUT BUTTER FUDGE

1 qt. peanut butter
1 lb. margarine
3 lb. confectioners' sugar
3 12-oz. packages chocolate chips

Mix peanut butter, margarine and confectioners' sugar thoroughly. Press into unbuttered pans to a depth of 1/2 inch. Melt chocolate chips. Spread over top of peanut butter mixture about 1/4 inch deep.

Betty Meek, Pres.
Alpha Epsilon No. 414
Vancouver, Washington

CHOCOLATE FUDGE WITH BRAZIL NUTS

15 oz. plain chocolate bars
1   12-oz. package chocolate chips
1   8-oz. jar marshmallow whip
1 1/2 tsp. salt
4 1/2 c. sugar
1 cup evaporated milk
1 c. Brazil nuts, chopped
1 tsp. vanilla

Break chocolate bars into small pieces. Mix with chocolate chips, marshmallow whip and salt in large bowl. Mix sugar and milk. Bring to a boil. Cook over medium heat exactly 4 1/2 minutes, stirring occasionally. Pour 1/2 the sugar mixture over chocolate mixture. Mix thoroughly; repeat. Let stand until cool. Add nuts and vanilla. Pour into large buttered pan. Cool in refrigerator. Cut into pieces.

Helen M. McIntire, Pres.
Alpha Delta No. 3738
Peoria, Illinois

MELODY'S FUDGE

4 c. sugar
1 lg. can evaporated milk
3   6-oz. packages Nestles chocolate
   bits
1/2 lb. margarine
2 tbsp. vanilla
2 c. chopped nuts

Bring sugar and milk to a full boil. Cook for 8 minutes. Remove from heat. Add chocolate bits, margarine, vanilla and nuts. Stir and mix well for about 5 minutes. Pour into large pan greased with butter. Let stand for 6 hours. Remove from pan; cut into squares. Yield: 5 pounds candy.

Melody McKay, Philanthropic Chm.
Alpha Tau No. 2046
Sandston, Virginia

HEAVENLY HASH

6 king-sized plain Hershey bars
1 bag miniature marshmallows
2 c. chopped nuts

Melt chocolate bars over double boiler or on low heat until partially melted. Remove from heat; stir until smooth. Fold marshmallows and nuts into chocolate. Pour into buttered pan. Chill until firm. Cut into chunks.

Terry Lenart, Treas.
Beta Tau No. 2949
Grosse Isle, Michigan

HEAVENLY HASH

2   6-oz. packages chocolate chips
1 c. chunky peanut butter
4 c. small marshmallows

Melt chocolate chips and peanut butter in double boiler. Fold in marshmallows. Spread in 8 or 9-inch pan. Chill. Cut in squares.

Lena M. Gamblin, Pres.
Beta Iota No. 3512
Bellville, Illinois

PANFORTE DI SIENA

1/2 c. sugar
1/2 c. honey
1/2 c. sifted all-purpose flour
2 tbsp. cocoa
1 tbsp. cinnamon
8 oz. diced preserved fruit
2 tbsp. diced citron
3/4 c. almonds
1 1/4 c. filberts
1 tbsp. grated orange rind
Confectioners' sugar

Preheat oven to 275 degrees. Butter 10-inch pie plate. Combine sugar and honey in saucepan. Cook over low heat, stirring constantly. Sift flour, cocoa and cinnamon. Stir into honey mixture. Stir in preserved fruit, citron, nuts and orange rind. Turn mixture quickly into pie plate. Bake for 30 minutes. Cool. Dust thickly with confectioners' sugar. Cut into wedges. Store wrapped in foil. Yield: 12 servings.

Jacqueline Gallo
Gamma Omicron No. 3837
Canoga Park, California

ORANGE CARAMEL FUDGE

1 lg. orange
4 c. sugar
1 tall can evaporated milk
1/4 c. butter
1 c. chopped walnuts

Pare peel from orange leaving very thin layer of white membrane. Cut peel into thin strips, then into small pieces; set aside. Cut enough for 1/3 to 1/2 cup orange peel. Place 1 cup sugar in large, deep aluminum skillet. Place remaining 3 cups sugar, evaporated milk and butter in heavy 3-quart aluminum ssucepan. Place skillet with 1 cup sugar over very low heat; this will warm sugar and skillet for ease in caramelizing at proper time. Cook 3-cup sugar mixture over medium heat, stirring frequently until sugar is dissolved. Continue cooking, stirring occasionally, to 234 degrees; this takes about 25 minutes. Remove from heat. Increase heat to medium under 1 cup sugar in skillet. Stir until sugar is completely melted and turns golden brown. Remove skillet from heat. Stir first mixture gradually into caramelized sugar, blending thoroughly. Temperature of first mixture will still be around 234 degrees; mixture may look separated but it will blend in smoothly. Add orange rind and walnuts to mixture in skillet. Beat until mixture begins to stiffen and looks fudge-like. It will be stiff and hot, but plastic. Turn into lightly buttered 8-inch square pan. Spread evenly with spatula. Cool thoroughly before cutting into squares. Yield: 2 pounds.

Photograph for this recipe on page 13.

ELECTRIC SKILLET PEANUT BRITTLE

1/2 c. water
2 c. sugar
1 c. light corn syrup
Pinch of salt
1 10-oz. package raw peanuts
2 tbsp. margarine or butter
1 tsp. vanilla
1 1/2 tsp. soda

Place water in skillet heated to 340 degrees; bring to a full boil. Add sugar, corn syrup and salt. Cook until mixture spins a thread. Add peanuts; continue cooking until syrup is golden brown. Add margarine and vanilla as you unplug skillet. Add soda. Stir gently and thoroughly. Pour into 18 x 12-inch buttered pan, spreading evenly. Cool. Break into pieces to serve.

Linda Frantz, Pres.
Alpha Mu No. 3348
Copeland, Kansas

PEANUT CUP CANDY

1/3 lb. graham crackers
1 lb. powdered sugar
1/2 lb. margarine or butter
1 c. creamy peanut butter
1 12-oz. package milk chocolate chips, melted

Crush graham crackers very fine in blender. Add powdered sugar, margarine and peanut butter. Mix thoroughly, using hands if necessary. Press into 9 x 13-inch pan. Spread melted chocolate over top. Chill in refrigerator until set. Let stand at room temperature several hours before cutting.

Ernestine Babcock, Pres.
Alpha Omicron No. 1827
Burlington, Iowa

PEANUT PATTIES

2 1/2 c. sugar
1 c. raw peanuts
1 c. milk
2/3 c. light corn syrup
1 c. powdered sugar
3 tbsp. margarine
Few drops of red food coloring

Cook sugar, peanuts, milk and corn syrup to soft-boil stage, stirring constantly. Continue cooking; add powdered sugar, margarine and food coloring. Pour onto oiled waxed paper, making patties about the size of a teacup. Let set until cool. Yield: 20 or more patties.

Pat Bolin, Pres.
Alpha Omicron No. 577
Enid, Oklahoma

OLD-FASHIONED PEANUT PATTIES

2 1/2 c. sugar
1/2 c. light corn syrup
1 c. half and half
Red food coloring
2 1/2 c. raw peanuts
1 tsp. vanilla
2 tbsp. butter

Combine sugar, corn syrup and half and half with enough food coloring to reach desired color. Boil to firm-ball stage. Add peanuts, vanilla and butter. Beat continuously until mixture thickens and loses shiny gloss. Spoon out quickly onto waxed paper. This requires several minutes of beating after cooking, so do not get in hurry.

Alice Barron, 1st V.P.
Rho Theta No. 4093
Irving, Texas

APRICOT PENUCHE

1 1/2 c. sugar
1 c. (firmly packed) light brown sugar
1/3 c. light cream
1/3 c. milk
2 tbsp. butter or margarine

1 tsp. vanilla extract
1/2 c. finely chopped dried apricots
1/3 c. finely chopped pecans
Dried apricots, cut into pieces for garnish

Butter sides of a heavy 2-quart saucepan. Add sugars, cream, milk and butter; stir until well combined. Cook over medium heat, stirring constantly, until sugars dissolve and mixture begins to boil. Continue cooking over medium heat until mixture reaches 238 degrees on candy thermometer or to soft-ball stage. Remove pan from heat; cool mixture to 110 degrees on candy thermometer without stirring. Butter 8 x 8-inch pan; set aside. Add vanilla to cooled mixture. Beat vigorously until candy thickens and starts to lose its gloss. Stir in chopped apricots and pecans quickly; spread evenly in pan. Score into small squares while warm. Garnish each square with apricot piece. Cool; cut when cool and firm. Yield: 64 pieces.

Photograph for this recipe on this page.

ROCKY ROAD CANDY

1   1-lb. package lg. marshmallows
1   8-oz. can walnuts
1 c. raisins
3   8-oz. packages milk chocolate or
      semisweet chocolate

Place marshmallows, walnuts and raisins in a bowl. Place chocolate in double boiler; set over simmering water. Stir until melted. Pour chocolate over marshmallows in bowl. Fold mixture quickly together. Spread evenly in buttered 9 x 13 x 2-inch pan. Chill until firm. Cut into squares to serve.

Romanza O. Johnson, Publicity Chm.
Alpha Theta No. 662
Bowling Green, Kentucky

STRAWBERRIES

2   3-oz. packages strawberry gelatin
1 can sweetened condensed milk
2 to 4 tsp. red food coloring
1/2 tsp. vanilla
Pinch of salt
1 c. coconut

3/4 c. chopped pecans
2 bottles red sugar
Slivered almonds
Green food coloring
Green sugar

Mix gelatin with milk. Add next 5 ingredients. Chill overnight. Shape into strawberries. Roll in red sugar. Tint slivered almonds with green food coloring; roll in green sugar. Place in strawberries for stems. Yield: 36 strawberries.

Helen Duffy
Alpha Delta No. 1711
Milford, Utah

ENGLISH TOFFEE

1 lb. butter
2 c. sugar
1/4 c. water
2 tbsp. light corn syrup
2 c. coarsely chopped walnuts
1 6-oz. package semisweet chocolate bits
1/2 c. finely chopped walnuts

Melt butter over low heat in 4-quart saucepan. Add sugar; stir until sugar is melted. Add water and corn syrup. Continue cooking over low heat, without stirring, to soft-crack stage. This takes about 45 minutes. Remove from heat; stir in coarsely chopped walnuts. Spread in buttered 15 x 10 x 1-inch pan. Let stand until firm. Melt chocolate over hot water; spread evenly on candy. Sprinkle with finely chopped walnuts. Let stand until chocolate is firm; break into pieces. Yield: 2 pounds.

Mary E. Breazeale
Mu No. 119
Oakland, California

PECAN TOFFEE

1 lb. butter
2 c. sugar
6 tbsp. water
2 tsp. vanilla
1 lb. pecans
10 chocolate bars

Cook first 3 ingredients to soft-crack stage or 285 degrees, stirring constantly. Add vanilla. Pour over pecans. Spread on ungreased cookie sheet. Place candy bars over hot tof-fee. Spread chocolate when it softens. Let harden; break into pieces.

Joyce S. Haynes, Treas.
Gamma Beta No. 3939
Dayton, Ohio

PECAN TURTLES

1 pkg. caramels
4 tbsp. milk
2 c. chopped pecans
1 tsp. vanilla
1/2 2-in. square paraffin
1 6 or 8-oz. bar milk chocolate

Melt caramels with milk in double boiler. Stir in pecans. Add vanilla. Drop by spoonfuls onto waxed paper. Let cool. Melt paraffin and chocolate together. Dip cooled candies into chocolate mixture. Place on waxed paper.

Diann Schiessler
Eta Omicron No. 4095
Hoisington, Kansas

WALNUT TURTLES

2 c. walnut halves and lg. pieces
36 caramels
3 tbsp. butter or margarine
1/2 tsp. vanilla extract
2/3 c. semisweet or milk chocolate pieces
1 1/2 tsp. shortening

Cover baking sheets with waxed paper; arrange walnut pieces in 28 to 30 clusters, spaced at least 1 inch apart. Place caramels in top of double boiler with butter. Set over boiling water. Heat until caramels are completely melted, stirring occasionally. Remove from heat. Add vanilla; stir until butter and vanilla are thoroughly mixed with caramels. Drop by teaspoonfuls onto center of each walnut cluster, making sure that caramel touches all the walnut pieces to hold together. Allow to cool. Melt chocolate with shortening over hot, not boiling, water. Spread over caramel on candies. Allow to set before removing from waxed paper. Yield: 28-30 turtles.

Pat Genzlinger, Corr. Sec.
Alpha Phi No. 1438
Winner, South Dakota

Chilled Desserts

When you have that definite feeling that something especially refreshing, elegant and superbly delicious is needed to end a meal, a chilled dessert is usually the perfect choice. Popular refrigerator desserts include an endless variety of ingredients from angel food cake, bourbon and coconut, to rum, whipped cream and zwieback crackers, and its forms are as varied as its flavors. A mousse is an airy-light and luxurious chilled dessert, as are the numerous fruit-flavored gelatine whips, nut and chocolate laced whipped cream souffles, and chilled chiffon whips too numerous to name. Regardless of its form or flavor, whether it's rich or light, simple or elegant, a chilled dessert will be easy on the homemaker. Most any ice box dessert can be prepared well in advance if needed, and kept in the refrigerator until serving time, without losing any of its flavor or appearance.

Some of the most beautiful and imaginative refrigerator desserts include gelatine, both flavored and unflavored, as a base. Gelatine is so popular because it lends itself to almost unlimited combinations with other ingredients, and because it can be prepared in colorful layers and unique decorative molds. What could be prettier or more appetizing than fruit-filled gelatine layered with whipped cream or ice cream in parfait glasses? The ice box cake, often called a *charlotte*, is another chilled dessert as easy to make as it is elegant. For most charlottes, a mold or springform pan is lined with ladyfingers or sponge cake and then filled with alternating layers of whipped cream or pudding and gelatine mixture and more ladyfingers. When set and unmolded, a delicate and heavenly dessert is the result. Whipped cream souffles are another delectable chilled dessert, most often embellished with chocolate shavings, cherries, walnuts, or confetti candy. Just the thought alone will entice you to prepare a chilled dessert today!

ESA members love to serve chilled desserts for the double treat they offer to family or guests — they delight the eye as well as the palate. You will also love the variety that chilled desserts offer, especially when you find that so many of the recipes leave plenty of room for your favorite personal touches.

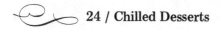

APRICOT ICEBOX CAKE

1 stick butter or margarine
1 c. powdered sugar
2 eggs, separated
1 tsp. vanilla
6 sm. boxes or 1 lg. box vanilla wafers,
 crushed
2 16-oz. cans apricots, drained and
 sieved
1 pt. whipping cream

Cream butter and sugar well. Add beaten egg yolks and vanilla. Beat egg whites until stiff peaks form. Fold egg whites into creamed mixture. Spread half the wafer crumbs evenly on bottom of 6 x 10-inch pan or glass baking dish. Spread the butter mixture over the crumbs. Spoon apricots over butter mixture. Spread whipped cream over the apricots. Top with remaining crumbs. Place in refrigerator for several hours before serving. Yield: 8-10 servings.

Betty M. Smith, State Project Chm. of Chap.
Alpha Omega No. 2060
Winchester, Virginia

APRICOT DESSERT SUPREME

1 lg. box apricot or peach gelatin
2 c. boiling water
1 1/2 c. cold water
2 or 3 sliced bananas
1 No. 1 can crushed pineapple,
 well drained
2 tbsp. butter
2 tbsp. flour
1/2 c. sugar
1 egg
1/2 c. pineapple juice
1 3-oz. package cream cheese
1 pkg. Dream Whip
1/2 c. chopped pecans

Mix gelatin with boiling water. Add cold water. Pour gelatin into glass baking dish. Chill until mixture starts to firm. Add bananas and drained pineapple. Refrigerate again until firm. Combine butter, flour, sugar, egg and pineapple juice in a saucepan. Cook until thick and smooth. Remove from heat. Add cream cheese; mix well. Let mixture cool. Whip Dream Whip according to package directions. Add Dream Whip to cooled mixture; blend. Ice gelatin with this mixture; sprinkle with pecans. Refrigerate until time to serve.

Connie Large
Gamma Omega No. 2910
North Vernon, Indiana

CHILLED FRENCH PASTRY

1 c. butter
4 eggs
2 c. powdered sugar
1 lb. ice cream wafers, crushed
1/4 lb. pecans, chopped
4 c. whipped cream
1 lg. can peeled apricots

Place the butter, eggs and powdered sugar in top of double boiler. Cook to mayonnaise consistency. Place 2/3 the crushed wafers in bottom of a 13 x 9-inch pan. Pour custard over the crumbs. Layer chopped pecans and 1/2 the whipped cream over custard. Place apricots, rounded side up, at proper serving spaces on top of cream. Add layer of remaining cream. Sprinkle with pecans. Place in refrigerator for 24 hours before serving.

Erma R. Kendle
Zeta Phi No. 2593
Junction City, Kansas

BANANA SPLIT CAKE

1 stick margarine, melted
2 1/2 c. confectioners' sugar
2 c. graham cracker crumbs
2 egg whites
1 stick soft margarine
2 pt. fresh strawberries, sweetened and
 drained
3 bananas, sliced lengthwise
Lemon juice
1 lg. Cool Whip
Chopped pecans

Combine melted butter, 1/2 cup confectioners' sugar and graham cracker crumbs. Press into 13 x 9-inch cake pan to form crust. Beat egg whites until stiff; add margarine and 2 cups confectioners' sugar. Beat mixture 10 minutes. Spread over crust. Spread strawberries on top. Dip banana slices in lemon juice; place on top of straw-berries. Spread Cool Whip over top. Garnish with chopped pecans. Chill at least 15 minutes.

Christy Roller
Alpha Kappa No. 3229
Fort Scott, Kansas

BANANA SPLIT DESSERT

2 c. crushed graham crackers
1 stick margarine, melted
2 eggs
2 sticks margarine
2 c. powdered sugar
3 to 5 bananas, sliced
1   20-oz. can crushed pineapple,
*   well drained*
1 lg. container whipped topping
1/2 c. chopped maraschino cherries
3/4 c. chopped pecans

Combine graham cracker crumbs and 1 stick margarine. Pack into a 9 x 13-inch pan. Beat eggs, 2 sticks margarine and powdered sugar together for no less than 15 minutes. Spread over unbaked crumb crust. Add sliced bananas and pineapple. Add a layer of whipped topping. Top with cherries and pecans. Refrigerate overnight. Yield: 15-16 servings.

Dolores Tidd, Rec. Sec.
Beta Eta No. 3431
St. Charles, Missouri

FRENCH BLUEBERRY DESSERT

2 c. flour
2 sticks butter
1/2 c. (firmly packed) brown sugar
1/2 c. chopped pecans or walnuts
1 lg. package cream cheese, softened
1 c. powdered sugar
2 env. Dream Whip
1 can blueberry pie filling

Mix first 4 ingredients. Press on cookie sheet. Bake for 15 minutes at 400 degrees. Cool. Crumble into oblong baking dish, reserving few crumbs for topping. Beat to-gether cream cheese and powdered sugar. Mix Dream Whip according to package direc-tions. Fold together Dream Whip and cream

cheese mixture. Pour over crumbs. Top with pie filling. Sprinkle with remaining crumbs. Chill until ready to serve.

Marie Morgan, V.P.
Alpha Epsilon No. 2069
Hagerstown, Maryland

BUTTER CREAM TORTE

2 c. finely crushed vanilla wafers
1/2 lb. butter, softened
2 c. powdered sugar
4 eggs
1/2 c. finely chopped almonds
1 c. whipping cream
1/4 c. each red and green maraschino
*   cherries, chopped*

Spread 1 cup wafer crumbs in bottom of 9-inch square cake pan. Combine butter with powdered sugar; cream well. Add eggs, one at a time, while beating mixture vigorously until well blended. Stir in chopped almonds. Spoon mixture evenly over crushed wafers. Sprinkle 3/4 cup wafers on top. Beat whip-ping cream until thick. Fold in maraschino cherries. Spread over wafers. Sprinkle remaining 1/4 cup wafers over whipped cream layer. Garnish with whole maraschino cherries. Refrigerate 12 or more hours. May freeze for future use. Cut with knife dipped in water. Yield: 9-12 servings.

Mary M. Hooks, Pres.
Alpha Lambda No. 3592
Alexandria, Virginia

CHERRY DELIGHT

1 box brownie mix
1 lg. carton Cool Whip
1 can cherry pie filling

Mix brownie mix according to package direc-tions. Place in heart-shaped cake pan lined with waxed paper. Bake as directed. Cool. Frost brownie cake with Cool Whip. Top with cherry pie filling. Refrigerate until time to serve. May be frozen.

Marcia Laspada, Pres.
Delta Omega No. 4414
Prescott, Arizona

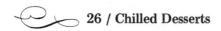

CHERRIES ON A CLOUD

6 egg whites
1/2 tsp. cream of tartar
1/4 tsp. salt
2 1/3 c. sugar
2 3-oz. package cream cheese, softened
1 tsp. vanilla
2 c. whipped cream
2 c. miniature marshmallows
1 20-oz. can cherry pie filling
1 c. fresh strawberries
1 tsp. lemon juice

Beat egg whites, cream of tartar and salt until frothy. Beat in 1 1/3 cups sugar gradually; beat until very stiff and glossy, about 15 minutes. Spread in greased 9 x 15-inch pan. Bake in preheated 275-degree oven for 1 hour. Do not open oven door. Turn off oven. Leave meringue in oven until cool, about 12 hours. Mix cream cheese with 1 cup sugar and vanilla. Fold in whipped cream and marshmallows. Spread over meringue. Refrigerate for 12 hours. Mix remaining ingredients together. Spread on top of dessert. Chill and serve.

Barbara Hansen
Beta Gamma
Oshkosh, Wisconsin

COLD CHERRY SOUFFLE

2/3 c. chopped red maraschino cherries
1/2 c. orange juice or kirsch
2 env. unflavored gelatin
Sugar
1/4 tsp. salt
8 eggs, separated
1 c. milk
1/2 c. water
2 c. heavy cream, whipped

Blend cherries with orange juice in electric blender or food mill; set aside. Mix gelatin, 2/3 cup sugar and salt in top of double boiler. Beat in egg yolks until light. Stir in milk and water gradually. Cook over boiling water, stirring constantly until slightly thickened and gelatin is dissolved, for about 10 minutes. Add cherry mixture. Chill until slightly thickened. Beat egg whites until

foamy. Add 1/2 cup sugar gradually, beating until stiff. Fold with whipped cream into gelatin mixture. Turn into 1 1/2-quart souffle dish with aluminum foil collar. Chill until firm. Remove collar. Garnish with maraschino cherries. Decorate with whipped cream and additional cherries. Yield: 10-12 servings.

Photograph for this recipe on page 23.

CHERRY-PECAN SMOKY MOUNTAINS DESSERT

45 vanilla wafers, finely crushed
3/4 c. butter or margarine
2 c. sifted confectioners' sugar
2 eggs
Rum flavoring to taste
1/2 tbsp. cocoa
1 c. heavy cream
1 c. chopped pecans
1/4 c. sliced maraschino cherries

Combine wafer crumbs with 1/4 cup butter; mix well. Reserve 2 tablespoons. Press remainder into bottom of 9-inch square baking dish. Chill. Cream 1/2 cup butter with 1 1/2 cups confectioners' sugar. Add eggs, one at a time, beating for 2 minutes after each addition. Add rum flavoring. Spread mixture over crumb base. Combine remaining 1/4 cup confectioners' sugar, cocoa and heavy cream. Whip until stiff. Fold in pecans and cherries. Spread over filling mixture. Sprinkle with reserved crumbs. Chill for 24 hours.

Ruth E. Daman, Corr. Sec.
Beta Nu No. 510
Pueblo, Colorado

CHERRY-PINEAPPLE DESSERT

1 9-oz. carton Cool Whip
1 can sweetened condensed milk
1 20-oz. can pineapple chunks
1 can cherry pie filling
1/2 c. chopped nuts

Mix ingredients in order listed. Chill. Serve as dessert.

June Hanna
Gamma Chi No. 834
Comanche, Oklahoma

SHERRY-CHERRY DESSERT

1 sm. package cherry gelatin
3/4 c. boiling water
1 can Bing cherries and juice
1/2 c. chopped nuts
1/4 c. coconut
1/4 c. sherry

Combine gelatin with boiling water; stir until gelatin is dissolved. Cool. Combine remaining ingredients. Let stand for 30 minutes. Mix gelatin mixture with cherry mixture. Chill until firm.

Dee Gazewood, Ed. Dir.
Gamma Kappa
Northglenn, Colorado

VANILLA-CHERRY DESSERT

1 sm. loaf angel food cake, cut into
   cubes
1 can cherry pie filling
1 pkg. instant vanilla pudding mix
1 1/2 c. milk
1 c. sour cream

Place 1/2 the cake cubes in 9 x 13-inch pan. Cover with pie filling. Place remaining cake cubes over pie filling. Mix pudding mix with milk. Add sour cream; stir. Place mixture on top of cake. Refrigerate for several hours.

Joyce Siems
Beta Upsilon No. 1831
Fremont, Nebraska

CHERRY YUM-YUM

3 c. graham cracker crumbs
1 1/2 sticks margarine, melted
1   8-oz. package cream cheese, softened
3/4 c. sugar
1 tsp. vanilla
2 pkg. dessert topping mix
1 c. half and half
2 cans cherry pie filling

Combine cracker crumbs with margarine. Line 9 x 15-inch dish with half the mixture. Blend cream cheese, sugar and vanilla. Whip topping mix with half and half. Fold into cream cheese mixture. Spread half the mixture over cracker crumbs. Top with cherry pie filling. Add remaining cream cheese mix-

ture. Top with remaining crumbs. Refrigerate overnight. Yield: 15 servings.

Mrs. Beverly Kay Bessler, Philanthropic Chm.
Gamma Delta No. 702
Tulsa, Oklahoma

BAVARIAN CREAM

1 pkg. chocolate, milk chocolate or
   vanilla pudding mix
1/4 c. sugar
1 env. unflavored gelatin
Dash of salt
1 egg, slightly beaten
2 c. milk
1 tsp. vanilla
1 env. whipped topping mix

Combine pudding mix, sugar, gelatin and salt in saucepan. Blend egg with milk; gradually add to pudding mixture, blending well. Cook, stirring, over medium heat until mixture comes to a full boil. Remove from heat; add vanilla. Place waxed paper directly on surface of hot pudding; chill thoroughly, at least 2 hours. Prepare whipped topping mix according to package directions. Beat chilled pudding until creamy; blend in topping. Butter 1-quart mold generously. Spoon pudding mixture into mold; chill until firm, at least 2 hours. Garnish with additional prepared whipped topping and chocolate curls. Recipe may be doubled by using 2-quart mold and chilling at least 4 hours.

Photograph for this recipe below.

ROBERTA'S DILEMMA

1 stick margarine
1 1/4 c. flour
1 c. chopped pecans
1 8-oz. package cream cheese
1 c. powdered sugar
1 lg. container Cool Whip
2 3 3/4-oz. boxes chocolate pudding
    mix
3 c. milk
1 tsp. vanilla

Blend margarine, flour and 1/2 cup pecans together. Press into ungreased 9 x 13-inch pan. Bake at 375 degrees for 20 minutes. Let cool. Mix cream cheese, powdered sugar and 1/2 the Cool Whip until creamy. Spoon into crust. Let stand for 1 hour in refrigerator. Mix pudding mix with milk and vanilla. Cook according to package directions. Cool. Pour over cream cheese mixture. Top with remaining Cool Whip. Sprinkle remaining 1/2 cup chopped pecans on top. Refrigerate for several hours.

Roberta J. McDowell, Pres.
Beta Phi No. 0485
Cherokee, Oklahoma

CHOCOLATE AMBROSIA DESSERT

1 c. flour
1 stick margarine
1/2 c. chopped pecans
2 pkg. instant chocolate pudding mix
2 pkg. instant French vanilla pudding
    mix
4 c. vanilla ice cream, softened
3 1/3 c. milk
1 pkg. Cool Whip
Chocolate bar, shaved into curls

Combine flour, margarine and chopped pecans. Press into 9 x 13-inch pan. Bake for 15 to 20 minutes at 350 degrees. Cool. Combine pudding mixes, ice cream and milk. Mix thoroughly. Pour over crust. Chill until firm. Top with Cool Whip. Garnish with chocolate curls.

Sally Swearingen, Pres.
Alpha Rho No. 3451
Lowden, Iowa

ANGEL DESSERT

2 6-oz. packages chocolate chips
2 tbsp. sugar
3 eggs, separated
1 pt. whipping cream, whipped
1 angel food cake
Chopped walnuts or pecans

Melt chips and sugar in double boiler. Add beaten egg yolks quickly; remove from heat. Cool. Beat egg whites until stiff. Fold egg whites into chocolate. Fold in whipped cream. Break cake in bite-sized pieces into 9 x 13-inch pan. Sprinkle walnuts over cake. Cover with chocolate mixture. Chill overnight.

Phyllis M. Alexander, Historian
Beta Omega No. 1081
Blythe, California

CHOCOLATE BAVARIAN CREAM PIE

2 c. crushed Oreo cookies
1/2 c. melted butter
1 tbsp. unflavored gelatin
1/4 c. cold water
3 eggs, separated
1/2 c. sugar
1/4 tsp. salt
1 c. milk, scalded
1 tsp. vanilla
1 c. cream, whipped

Mix cookies and butter together. Pat into serving dish. Soften gelatin in cold water. Combine slightly beaten egg yolks, sugar and salt. Add milk slowly. Cook in double boiler until mixture coats spoon. Add softened gelatin. Stir until dissolved. Cool. Beat egg whites until stiff. Add vanilla. Fold egg whites and whipped cream into cooked mixture. Pour into crust, having reserved some crust crumbs to sprinkle on top. Chill.

Mardell Byrne, Past State Pres.
Alpha Kappa No. 776
Davenport, Iowa

CHOCOLATE DELIGHT SOUFFLE

2 tbsp. unflavored gelatin
2 c. milk
1 c. sugar

1/4 tsp. salt
4 eggs, separated
1   12-oz. package semisweet chocolate
    bits
2 tsp. vanilla extract
2 c. heavy cream, whipped

Soak gelatin in 1/2 cup milk. Place in sauce-pan with remaining milk, 1/2 cup sugar, salt and egg yolks. Stir to mix. Add chocolate. Place over low heat, stirring constantly, until gelatin is dissolved and chocolate melted. Cool. Add vanilla. Beat with rotary beater until chocolate is blended. Chill until partially set. Beat egg whites until stiff but not dry. Beat in remaining 1/2 cup sugar gradually until stiff. Fold into chocolate mixture. Fold in whipped cream. Pour into 2-quart souffle dish with a 3-inch foil collar. Return to refrigerator; chill until set. Remove foil collar; decorate with additional whipped cream if desired. Yield: 12 servings.

Nancy Bowman
Eta Beta No. 2676
Liberal, Kansas

REFRIGERATOR DESSERT

30 marshmallows
1/2 c. milk, scalded
1 c. cream, whipped
1 lg. almond-chocolate bar, grated
1 tsp. vanilla
Graham cracker crumbs

Add marshmallows to scalded milk. Mix until melted. Cool. Fold in whipped cream. Add grated chocolate bar and vanilla. Line bottom of pan with graham cracker crumbs. Add filling. Sprinkle top with crumbs. Chill for several hours before serving. Crushed chocolate wafers may be used in place of graham crackers, if desired.

Bonnie Rock, File Clerk
Beta Theta No. 3818
DeWitt, Iowa

GRAHAM CRACKER-CHOCOLATE DESSERT

18 graham crackers, crushed
3/4 c. melted butter

Powdered sugar
3 eggs, separated
1 tbsp. sugar
1 tsp. vanilla
3/4 pkg. miniature marshmallows
1/2 c. chopped walnuts
1/2 c. Hershey chocolate syrup

Combine graham cracker crumbs, 1/4 cup melted butter and 1 heaping teaspoon powdered sugar. Pat half the mixture in loaf pan. Beat egg whites until stiff. Add sugar, vanilla, marshmallows and walnuts. Spread over crumbs. Combine chocolate syrup, 1 cup powdered sugar and 1/2 cup melted butter. Beat until stiff. Place on top of marshmallow mixture. Top with remaining crumb mixture. Cool. Cut in squares to serve. May be frozen.

Geraldine Bergen
Alpha Theta
Moorhead, Minnesota

FOUR-STEP CHOCOLATE PUDDING CAKE

1 c. flour
1 stick butter
1 c. chopped pecans
1 c. powdered sugar
1 lg. package cream cheese, softened
1 lg. carton Cool Whip
1 pkg. chocolate instant pudding mix
1 pkg. vanilla instant pudding mix
3 c. milk

Mix flour, butter and pecans. Place in bottom of 9 x 13-inch baking dish. Bake at 350 degrees for 20 to 25 minutes. Cool. Cream sugar and cream cheese together. Fold in 1 cup Cool Whip. Spread over crust in pan. Whip pudding mixes with milk until thick. Pour over mixture in pan. Spread remaining Cool Whip over top. Chill 6 to 8 hours or longer.

Barbara Cannon, W. and M. Chm.
Beta Iota No. 4634
Richardson, Texas
Charlyn Ocker, Sec.
Delta Delta No. 3602
San Angelo, Texas

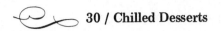

CHARLEY'S COFFEE DESSERT

1 c. butter
4 c. sifted powdered sugar
2 1/2 tbsp. powdered coffee
4 eggs, separated
1 tsp. vanilla
1 tsp. Kahlua (opt.)
1 c. ground pecans
3 c. crushed vanilla wafer crumbs

Line a 9 x 5 x 3-inch loaf pan with plastic wrap. Cream butter. Combine sugar and coffee powder. Add sugar-coffee mixture gradually to butter. Beat until fluffy. Add egg yolks, one at a time, beating well after each addition. Add vanilla, Kahlua and ground pecans; beat well. Beat egg whites until stiff. Fold gently into sugar-butter mixture. Spread 1 cup wafer crumbs in bottom of pan. Spread half the coffee mixture on crumbs. Layer another cup of crumbs; add the remainder of coffee mixture. Sprinkle remaining crumbs on top. Press down with fingertips. Cover with plastic wrap. Chill 24 hours. Unmold and slice.

Leona M. Woeber
Alpha Epsilon No. 4609
Fort Collins, Colorado

MOCHA ICEBOX CAKE

3 doz. ladyfingers
3 pkg. Dream Whip
3 tsp. instant coffee
3 tbsp. cocoa
1 1/2 c. cold milk

Line a springform pan around sides and on bottom with split ladyfingers. Combine in small mixer bowl Dream Whip, coffee and cocoa. Blend in milk following package directions. Spread 1/3 the whipped mixture over ladyfingers. Top with ladyfingers. Spread with second 1/3 of whipped mixture. Top with ladyfingers, then the remaining whipped mixture. Cover loosely. Refrigerate overnight.

Bessie Burnett
Alpha Theta No. 4472
Columbia, Missouri

COCONETTE

1 1/2 c. flour
1 1/2 sticks margarine
3/4 c. chopped nuts
1 c. powdered sugar
1 lg. carton Cool Whip
1 8-oz. package cream cheese, softened
2 boxes coconut instant pudding mix
3 c. milk

Mix first 3 ingredients. Press into 9 x 13-inch baking dish. Bake at 350 degrees for 35 minutes. Cool. Mix powdered sugar, 1/2 carton Cool Whip and softened cream cheese together. Spread over flour and nut mixture. Whip coconut pudding mixes with milk. Spread over cheese and Cool Whip mixture. Top with remaining Cool Whip. Let set in refrigerator for several hours. Also good with chocolate, butterscotch and lemon instant pudding mixes.

Sharon Ferguson, Ed. Dir., Publ. Chm.
Alpha Zeta No. 2710
Anchorage, Alaska

CRANBERRY-GRAPE DESSERT

1 lb. cranberries
1 1/2 c. sugar
1 lb. white grapes
1 lb. marshmallows
1 c. chopped nuts
1 pkg. Dream Whip

Grind cranberries. Sprinkle with sugar. Refrigerate overnight. Cut white grapes into quarters. Cut marshmallows into quarters. Whip Dream Whip according to package directions. Mix all ingredients together. Refrigerate until set. May be served with an additional serving of whipped cream on top.

Bessie L. Towson, Pres.
Central Missouri City Council, ESA
Columbia, Missouri

CROWN JEWEL DESSERT

1 3-oz. package each orange, cherry
   and lime gelatin
1 3-oz. package lemon gelatin
1/4 c. sugar

1/2 c. pineapple juice
1 1/2 c. graham cracker crumbs
1/3 c. melted butter or margarine
2 env. Dream Whip or 4 c. whipped
    cream

Prepare gelatins separately, using 1 cup boiling water and 1/2 cup cold water for each. Pour each flavor into a separate 8-inch square pan. Chill until very firm. Combine lemon gelatin, sugar and 1 cup boiling water. Stir until gelatin and sugar are dissolved. Stir in pineapple juice. Chill until slightly thickened. Mix crumbs and melted butter; press into bottom of 9-inch springform pan. Cut firm gelatins into 1/2 inch squares. Prepare Dream Whip according to package directions. Blend with lemon gelatin. Fold in gelatin cubes. Pour into springform pan. Chill at least 6 hours. Remove sides of pan. Spread additional topping or whipped cream on sides and top if desired. May also be prepared in a pie pan or mold. Yield: 16 servings.

Jennie Mann, Philanthropic-Ed. Chm.
Gamma Beta No. 3939
Dayton, Ohio
Karen Talley
Alpha Chi No. 871
Deming, New Mexico

DATE PUDDING DELIGHT

3 eggs, separated
3/4 c. sugar
1 c. bread crumbs
2 tsp. baking powder
1 c. chopped dates
1 c. chopped pecans
1 pt. whipping cream, whipped
Red and green maraschino cherries,
    drained

Beat egg yolks until light. Add sugar; mix well. Mix together bread crumbs and baking powder. Stir in dates and pecans. Mix with creamed egg yolks and sugar. Beat egg whites until stiff; fold into first mixture. Pour into greased baking pan. Bake for 20 to 25 minutes at 350 degrees. Let cake cool. Cake may be made ahead of serving time or even frozen until needed. Break cake into medium pieces. Whip cream. Fold into chunks

of cake, being careful to coat all pieces. Mix pudding lightly, very important not to over-stir. Garnish with maraschino cherries or mix in pudding.

Jeanne Williams, Pres.
Alpha Mu No. 346
Muncie, Indiana

FRUIT COCKTAIL SURPRISE

1 pkg. instant banana cream pudding mix
1 No. 2 can fruit cocktail
1 No. 2 can crushed pineapple
3 med. bananas, sliced
1 pt. strawberries, cut up
1 tsp. lemon juice
Pecans
Marshmallows

Prepare pudding mix according to package directions. Pour fruit cocktail and crushed pineapple into serving bowl; do not drain. Add pudding; mix well. Add bananas, strawberries and lemon juice. Add chopped pecans and marshmallows to taste. Chill for several hours. Can be kept in refrigerator for about 2 days.

Sallie Laufer, Treas.
Gamma Kappa No. 3544
Slidell, Louisiana

LEMON FLUFF

1 tall can evaporated milk
1 pkg. lemon gelatin
1 3/4 c. hot water
1/4 c. lemon juice
1 c. sugar
2 1/2 c. vanilla wafer crumbs

Chill unopened evaporated milk in refrigerator until icy cold, about 3 to 4 hours. Dissolve gelatin in hot water. Chill until partially set. Whip until light and fluffy. Add lemon juice and sugar. Whip chilled milk. Fold into gelatin mixture. Line 9 x 12-inch pan with part of crumbs. Pour in gelatin mixture. Top with remaining crumbs. Chill until firm.

Gail Sabean, Corr. Sec.
Alpha Sigma No. 637
Madison, Wisconsin

THAT LIGHT AND LEMONY DESSERT

1 stick margarine
1 c. flour
1/2 to 1 c. chopped nuts
1 8-oz. package cream cheese
1 c. powdered sugar
1 lg. carton Cool Whip
2 pkg. instant lemon pudding mix
3 c. milk
1 tsp. lemon juice (opt.)

Melt margarine; stir in flour and nuts. Press in bottom of 9 x 11 1/2-inch pan. Bake at 325 degrees for 10 minutes. Let cool. Beat cream cheese, powdered sugar and 1 cup Cool Whip together. Spread on top of first layer. Mix pudding mix and milk together; add lemon juice. Beat until thick. Pour over second layer. Chill thoroughly. Top with additional Cool Whip. Sprinkle with additional chopped nuts. Chill. Cut into squares and serve.

Iris DeWilde, Pres.
Delta Rho No. 2397
Rantoul, Illinois
Mrs. Gordon Kunkle
Beta Kappa No. 4484
Hazleton, Iowa

LEMON CHIFFON DESSERT WITH BUTTERCRUNCH CRUST

1/2 c. butter
1/4 c. (firmly packed) brown sugar
1 c. flour
1/2 c. chopped pecans
1 c. sugar
1 env. unflavored gelatin
2/3 c. water
1/3 c. lemon juice
4 eggs, separated
1 tbsp. grated lemon rind
1/2 tsp. cream of tartar
Whipped cream

Preheat oven to 400 degrees. Mix first 4 ingredients. Spread in 13 x 9 x 2-inch pan. Bake for 15 minutes. Remove from oven; stir with spoon. Reserve 3/4 cup for topping. Press rest of mixture immediately against sides and bottom of 9-inch pan. Cool. Blend 1/2 cup sugar, gelatin, water, lemon juice and slightly beaten egg yolks in saucepan. Cook over low heat, stirring constantly, just until mixture comes to a boil. Stir in lemon rind. Place pan in cold water. Cool until mounds slightly when dropped from spoon. Beat egg whites, cream of tartar and 1/2 cup sugar until stiff and glossy. Fold egg whites into lemon mixture. Pour over crust. Top with whipped cream and reserved nut topping.

Mary Lou Graves, Pres.
Delta Gamma No. 3749
Bloomington, Indiana

FRESH NECTARINE LADIES' DELIGHT

1 1/2 lb. fresh nectarines, peeled
1 1/2 c. fresh orange juice
2 tbsp. cornstarch
1/4 c. flour
1 c. (firmly packed) brown sugar
1/4 tsp. salt
2 c. milk
6 lg. egg yolks, beaten
2 tbsp. butter or margarine
1 tsp. ground nutmeg
1 tsp. vanilla extract
2 pkg. ladyfingers
1 tbsp. grated orange peel

Slice nectarines into eighths. Place in bowl with orange juice; set aside. Add next 4 ingredients to top of double boiler. Add milk; cook over boiling water, stirring constantly, until thick. Cover; cook about 10 minutes longer. Blend a little of the hot mixture into egg yolks; stir into bulk of mixture. Cook 3 minutes longer. Add butter, nutmeg and vanilla; stir into custard. Cover. Remove top part of double boiler; cool. Alternate ladyfingers with nectarine slices around sides of 1 1/2-quart serving bowl. Reserve remaining slices for garnish. Blend orange peel and juice into custard. Ladle into bowl. Garnish top with nectarine slices. Chill until served. Yield: 8 servings.

Photograph for this recipe on opposite page.

ORANGE CHIFFON MOLD

1 env. unflavored gelatin
3/4 c. sugar
1/8 tsp. salt
2 eggs, separated
1/2 c. cold water
1 6-oz. can frozen orange juice
   concentrate
1 c. heavy cream, whipped

Mix gelatin, 1/2 cup sugar and salt in medium saucepan. Beat together egg yolks and water; stir into gelatin mixture. Place over low heat; stir constantly until gelatin dissolves and mixture thickens slightly, about 5 minutes. Remove from heat. Add frozen orange juice concentrate; stir until melted. Mixture should mound slightly when dropped from spoon. Chill a few minutes if needed. Beat egg whites until stiff but not dry. Gradually add remaining 1/4 cup sugar; beat until stiff. Fold into gelatin mixture. Fold in whipped cream. Turn into 5-cup mold. Chill until firm. Yield: 6 servings.

Marie Muraoka
Alpha Alpha No. 1657
North Salt Lake, Utah

ORANGE DREAM

1 lg. package orange gelatin
2 c. boiling water
1 sm. can frozen orange juice, undiluted
1 lg. can crushed pineapple

1 can mandarin oranges, drained
1 sm. package instant vanilla pudding mix
1 c. cold milk
1 pkg. Dream Whip, prepared according
   to package directions

Dissolve orange gelatin in boiling water. Add orange juice, crushed pineapple with juice and mandarin oranges. Chill until set. Mix vanilla pudding with cold milk. Fold vanilla pudding mixture into prepared Dream Whip. Top gelatin mixture with pudding mixture. Refrigerate for at least 3 minutes. Yield: 12 servings.

Joanne S. Perry, Ed. Dir.
Alpha Beta No. 1408
Roanoke, Virginia

PEANUT BRITTLE BAVARIAN RING

2 tbsp. unflavored gelatin
1 c. milk
1 c. strong coffee
1 c. sugar
2 egg whites
1/2 tsp. salt
2 c. heavy cream
1 c. coarsely broken peanut brittle

Soak gelatin in milk. Bring coffee to a boil. Stir in softened gelatin until dissolved. Stir in sugar. Chill until nearly set. Whip egg whites and salt until stiff. Whip cream until soft peaks form. Whip gelatin mixture; fold in egg whites and whipped cream. Sprinkle bottom of 6-cup mold with peanut brittle. Pour Bavarian mixture into mold. Chill until set. Unmold and serve. Yield: 8 servings.

Photograph for this recipe on cover.

PISTACHIO-PINEAPPLE DESSERT

1 pkg. pistachio pudding mix
1 20-oz. can crushed pineapple
1 9-oz. tub whipped topping
1 c. chopped nuts

Mix all ingredients well. Refrigerate for several hours.

Mary A. Powell, Treas.
Beta Iota No. 1972
Winter Park, Florida

PEPPERMINT STICK DELIGHT

1/4 lb. vanilla wafer crumbs
2 tbsp. sugar
3 tbsp. margarine
5 sticks peppermint candy
1/2 c. chopped walnuts
16 marshmallows
1 1/2 c. whipping cream

Combine first 3 ingredients. Press into bottom of 8 x 8 x 2-inch pan. Set aside. Crush peppermint sticks coarsely. Combine with walnuts and marshmallows. Set aside. Whip cream in a chilled bowl until of medium-thick consistency. Fold walnuts, candy and marshmallows into whipped cream. Pour over crumb crust. Chill about 12 hours. Yield: 8 servings.

Sarah Jones, State 1st V.P.
Alpha Omega No. 4334
Smyrna, Georgia

PINEAPPLE ANGEL DELIGHT

1 env. unflavored gelatin
1/2 c. cold water
1/2 c. boiling water
Sugar
1 can crushed pineapple
1 pt. whipping cream
Vanilla to taste
1 lg. angel food cake
Slivered walnuts
Cherries

Soften gelatin in cold water; let stand for 5 minutes. Stir in boiling water. Add 3/4 cup sugar and pineapple. Chill until set. Whip cream until stiff flavored with vanilla and additional sugar to taste. Fold into pineapple mixture. Break cake into bite-sized pieces. Place a layer in bottom of 8 x 12-inch dish. Cover with half the pineapple mixture. Add remaining cake. Top with pineapple mixture. Garnish with walnuts and cherries. Chill overnight.

Doris L. North, Rec. Sec.
Alpha Epsilon No. 1999
North Las Vegas, Nevada

PINEAPPLE REFRIGERATOR CAKE

1 20-oz. can crushed pineapple
1 env. unflavored gelatin
1/2 c. sugar
1/8 tsp. salt
1 c. heavy cream
Ladyfingers
Whipped cream
Pecans

Drain syrup from pineapple into measuring cup; add water to make 1 cup. Sprinkle gelatin over syrup mixture in medium saucepan. Place over low heat; stir constantly until gelatin dissolves, about 2 to 3 minutes. Remove from heat; stir in sugar and salt. Add pineapple. Chill, stirring occasionally, until mixture mounds slightly when dropped from spoon. Whip cream; fold into pineapple mixture. Line sides of a 6-cup mold with split ladyfingers. Turn pineapple mixture into mold. Chill until firm. Unmold on serving platter. Garnish with whipped cream and pecans. Place additional ladyfingers and pecans around base of mold if desired. Yield: 6 to 8 servings.

Photograph for this recipe on page 6.

FRENCH CREAM PUDDING

1/3 c. butter
1 c. confectioners' sugar
2 eggs, well beaten
1/2 pt. cream
1 No. 2 can crushed pineapple, drained
1/2 c. chopped nuts
1 lb. vanilla wafers, crushed

Cream butter and sugar well. Add beaten eggs. Whip cream; add pineapple and nuts. Combine with butter mixture. Place half the crumbs in bottom of loaf pan. Cover with cream mixture; spread evenly. Add remaining crumbs; spread evenly over top of cream mixture. Chill for several hours.

Mrs. Lindy Lybarger
Theta No. 598
North Manchester, Indiana

Recipe on page 48.

PINEAPPLE DELIGHT

1 sm. package white cake mix
1 8-oz. package cream cheese, softened
2 c. milk
1 pkg. instant pineapple pudding mix
1 20-oz. can crushed pineapple,
    drained
1 pkg. Dream Whip

Bake cake according to package directions in 9 x 13-inch pan for 10 to 15 minutes. Let cool. Beat together cream cheese, milk and pineapple pudding mix. Spread over cake. Spread crushed pineapple on top. Prepare Dream Whip according to package directions and spread on top. Top with nuts or cherries, if desired. Yield: 12 to 15 servings.

Ruth E. Hunt
Alpha Omicron No. 1827
Burlington, Iowa

SNOWBALLS

1/2 c. butter
1 c. sugar
2 eggs, separated
1 c. crushed pineapple, drained
1 c. chopped pecans
12 oz. vanilla wafers
1 pt. whipping cream
2 tbsp. powdered sugar
1 tsp. vanilla
1 c. flaked coconut

Cream butter and sugar. Add egg yolks; beat well. Beat egg whites; fold in. Add pineapple and pecans. Stack 4 wafer layers with filling in between. Chill. Whip cream flavored with powdered sugar and vanilla. Cover stacks with whipped cream. Sprinkle coconut on top.

Helen Long
Gamma Phi No. 1839
Junction City, Kansas

A BOWLFUL OF JELLY

1 6-oz. package lemon gelatin
1 c. seedless grapes
1 c. sliced fresh plums

Recipe on page 174.

1 c. halved strawberries
1 c. sliced fresh peaches
1 fresh pear, peeled and sliced or
    1 8-oz. can pear halves, drained

Prepare gelatin according to package directions. Chill until syrupy. Rinse a 2-quart bowl with cold water. Pour layer of syrupy gelatin into bowl. Arrange a few pieces of fruit decoratively. Mix together remaining gelatin and fruits; pour on top of fruit. Chill until firm. Dip bowl in warm water for 5 seconds. Invert onto serving plate. Cut in wedges. Yield: 8 to 10 servings.

Photograph for this recipe on page 2.

PUMPKIN TORTE

2 pkg. graham crackers, crushed
Sugar
1/2 c. melted margarine
1 8-oz. package cream cheese, softened
5 eggs
1 tsp. vanilla
1 env. unflavored gelatin
1 16-oz. can pumpkin
1/2 c. milk
1 tsp. salt
1 tbsp. cinnamon
1/2 c. powdered sugar
Whipped cream, flavored to taste

Mix graham cracker crumbs with 1/4 cup sugar and melted butter. Press into bottom of baking pan. Bake at 350 degrees for 5 minutes. Mix cream cheese with 2 eggs, 1/2 cup sugar and vanilla; beat well. Pour over crust. Bake at 350 degrees for 15 minutes. Soften gelatin in 1 cup cold water; set aside. Stir occasionally. Combine pumpkin with 3 egg yolks, 2/3 cup sugar, milk, salt and cinnamon; mix well. Add softened gelatin. Cook until thick over low heat, about 20 minutes. Remove from heat. Cool. Beat 3 egg whites until stiff. Add powdered sugar. Fold into pumpkin mixture. Pour over cream cheese mixture. Refrigerate until chilled. Top with whipped cream.

Sharon Hopper
Beta Gamma
Oshkosh, Wisconsin

ROCKY ROAD RAISIN CAKE

1 1-lb. package fudge brownie mix
1/2 c. seedless raisins, coarsely
   chopped
1 tsp. instant coffee powder
1 tsp. rum extract
Rocky Road Filling

Prepare brownie batter according to package
directions. Stir in raisins, coffee powder and
rum extract. Turn batter into greased 9-inch
square pan. Bake according to package directions. Do not overbake. Cool thoroughly.
Cut square into 3 equal strips. Stack strips
together with Rocky Road Filling, spreading
some of the filling on top. Chill 4 to 5 hours
or overnight. Yield: 8 to 10 servings.

Rocky Road Filling

1 c. whipping cream
2 tbsp. cocoa
1/8 tsp. salt
3 tbsp. sugar
1/4 c. coarsely chopped seedless raisins
1/4 c. coarsely chopped walnuts

1/2 tsp. rum extract
8 to 10 marshmallows, cut in sm. pieces

Beat whipping cream to soft peaks; beat in
cocoa, salt and sugar. Fold in raisins, walnuts, rum extract and marshmallows.

Photograph for this recipe above.

RASPBERRY TOPPER

1 1/4 c. graham cracker crumbs
1/4 c. chopped walnuts
1/4 c. melted butter
1 c. milk
50 lg. marshmallows
2 c. whipping cream, whipped
2 10-oz. packages frozen raspberries,
   thawed
1/2 c. sugar
1/4 c. cornstarch
2 tsp. lemon juice

Mix first 3 ingredients. Press into 9 x 12-inch
baking pan. Bake about 7 or 8 minutes at
350 degrees. Cool. Heat milk and marshmallows in saucepan over medium heat until

marshmallows melt, stirring often. Let cool. Fold whipped cream into marshmallow mixture gently. Spread on crumb crust. Combine thawed raspberries with juice, 1 cup water and sugar in saucepan. Mix cornstarch and 1/4 cup water until no lumps remain. Add to berry mixture. Cook over medium heat, stirring constantly, until thick and clear. Cool slightly. Add lemon juice. Spread over creamy mixture. Chill. Yield: 12-15 servings.

Carolyn Jones, Treas.
Epsilon Epsilon No. 3475
Portland, Oregon

MOUSE' (MOOS)

1 sm. package raspberry gelatin
1 c. hot water
45 to 50 miniature marshmallows
1 lg. can evaporated milk, chilled and
    whipped
1/2 c. sugar
1 sm. can crushed pineapple

Dissolve gelatin in hot water. Add marshmallows; stir until melted. Add whipped milk, sugar and pineapple; stir until mixed well. Let chill until set.

Shirley Brice, W. and M. Co.-Chm.
Alpha Xi No. 1610
Virginia Beach, Virginia

SUMMERTIME DESSERT

1 6-oz. package strawberry-banana
    gelatin
1 env. whipped topping
2 bananas, sliced
2 c. fresh strawberries, sliced

Prepare gelatin according to package directions, using 1 1/2 cups cold water. Pour into deep mold. Chill until set. Stir until lumpy. Prepare whipped topping according to package directions. Add bananas, strawberries and prepared topping to gelatin. Stir until well mixed. Chill.

Jean Miller
Beta Zeta No. 2556
Madison, Wisconsin

RUSSIAN CREAM WITH STRAWBERRIES ROMANOFF

1 c. plus 3 tbsp. heavy cream
1/2 c. sugar
1 env. unflavored gelatin
1/2 pt. sour cream
1/2 tsp. vanilla
Strawberries Romanoff

Mix together cream, sugar and gelatin in saucepan. Heat gently until gelatin is thoroughly dissolved. Chill until slightly thickened. Fold in sour cream; flavor with vanilla. Whisk until mixture is quite smooth. Pour mixture into serving bowl or 3-cup metal mold. Cover; chill until set, at least 4 hours. Dip container in hot water until edges just begin to liquify to unmold. Turn mold onto serving dish. Surround liberally with Strawberries Romanoff.

Strawberries Romanoff

4 c. fresh strawberries
1/2 c. confectioners' sugar
1 1/2 oz. vodka
1 1/2 oz. Triple Sec
1 1/2 oz. rum

Wash and hull strawberries. Toss with sugar. Place in bowl. Pour vodka, Triple Sec and rum over berries. Chill.

Nora Nordeen
Gamma Kappa No. 3265
Northglenn, Colorado

NUT AND SPICE BALL

2 8-oz. packages cream cheese,
    softened
1 4-oz. package blue cheese, crumbled
1 tbsp. shredded orange peel
1 c. chopped peanuts
3/4 tsp. cinnamon
1/8 tsp. nutmeg
1/8 tsp. cloves

Whip cream cheese and blue cheese until light and fluffy. Stir in orange peel. Shape into a ball; chill. Toss together peanuts, cinnamon, nutmeg and cloves. Roll cheese ball in peanut mixture. Serve with assorted fresh fruits and crackers.

Photograph for this recipe on page 1.

Puddings

Puddings are a delicious and "smooth" way to end a meal, as well as a satisfying and nutritious snack. They may be as smooth as a cup of cold, delectable vanilla pudding, or as scrumptious and elegant as a Christmas plum pudding. The temperature at which a pudding is served determines its character. Steamed puddings, as well as baked puddings with a crust or dough topping are not usually served chilled, or they will usually taste soggy and lifeless. The same holds true for souffles, which must be carefully served straight from the oven, as they begin to lose their puffiness right away. There are puddings whose texture and flavor are enhanced by refrigeration — the gelatine-based puddings, as well as the egg and cream-based puddings are examples.

Puddings lend themselves quite easily to the addition of most any favorite fruits, nuts, cookies and cakes, jams and jellies, candies and confections, as well as bread, noodles and rice. So puddings, like any other tasty and practical dessert, are varied in nature and can be served quite often without repetition. The number of good variations for puddings, once their basic cooking techniques are understood and perfected, are limited only by the imagination of the cook. For homemakers who include puddings in their menu planning quite regularly, a variety of attractive pudding molds can be a wise investment. A delicious pudding seems far tastier when it arrives at the table in a pretty shape, or handsome baking dish rather than in an ordinary baking utensil. These pudding molds, which come in a marvelous variety of sizes, shapes and colors, can also double for use with gelatine salads and desserts.

Custard puddings have been a favorite dessert for generations because they are smooth, rich, flavorful, and nutritious. A baked custard pudding should not be allowed to cook too long, or it will become tough and unappealing. It is ready to be removed from the oven when a knife inserted into the edge comes out clean. The custard will finish cooking all the way through as it cools. Boiled custard, prepared in the top of a double boiler, is ready when the egg and liquid mixture coats a metal or silver spoon. It is never really *boiled*, as too high a temperature will cause the eggs to separate. This soft, creamy custard is the kind used in banana or strawberry puddings, or to fill eclairs, pies, and other pastries.

ESA members think puddings (and custards) should be a regular dessert in every family's menu planning. Not only do they make a nourishing and delightful dessert, they also serve as the perfect afternoon snack because they satisfy without spoiling the appetite. But homemakers love them so much because they are simplicity itself!

FRESH APPLE CHIFFFON PUDDING

1 lb. sliced peeled tart apples
2 tbsp. water
2 tbsp. fresh lemon juice
1/4 c. butter or margarine
1/2 c. sugar
2 eggs, separated
1/2 tsp. grated lemon rind
Grated nutmeg

Place apples, water and lemon juice in saucepan. Cover; cook until apples fall apart. Push through a sieve. Place in top part of double boiler. Add butter, 1/3 cup sugar and egg yolks. Mix well. Stir; cook over hot water until mixture has thickened. Beat egg whites until soft peaks form. Beat in remaining sugar gradually. Fold into apple mixture. Add grated lemon rind. Serve warm or chilled, topped with sprinkling of grated nutmeg. Yield: 8 servings/148 calories per serving.

Photograph for this recipe above.

SPANISH FLAN

Sugar
3 tbsp. water
6 egg yolks
2 c. milk
1 tsp. vanilla

Bring 6 tablespoons sugar and water to a boil. Cook until syrup becomes well browned, but do not burn. Line bottom and sides of mold evenly with hot syrup, forming a thin solid crust as it cools. Beat 2/3 cup sugar with remaining ingredients. Strain mixture through fine strainer into mold lined with caramelized sugar. Cover. Place mold in large pan filled with water. Cook over hot water for about 1 hour. Test by inserting needle in Flan; when needle comes out completely dry the Flan is done. Cool. Remove from mold. Serve with whipped cream.

Carmen Pratarelli, Corr. Sec.
Gamma Beta No. 4513
San Diego, California

BOILED CUSTARD

2 eggs
2 tbsp. sugar
2 c. milk
1 tsp. vanilla

Beat eggs and sugar together. Add milk; beat well. Cook in double boiler until mixture coats a spoon. Beat well. Cool. Add vanilla.

Elizabeth Braden
Alpha Chi No. 871
Deming, New Mexico

COCONUT CUSTARD

2 c. milk
3/4 c. sugar
1/2 c. Bisquick
4 eggs
1/4 c. butter
1 1/2 tsp. vanilla
1 c. flaked coconut

Combine milk, sugar, Bisquick, eggs, butter and vanilla in blender. Blend at slow speed for 3 minutes. Pour into greased 9-inch pie pan. Let stand 5 minutes. Sprinkle with coconut. Bake at 350 degrees for 40 minutes.

Marian J. McCastle, Rec. Sec.
Beta Delta No. 4271
Tucson, Arizona

BAKED CUSTARD

3 eggs, slightly beaten
1/3 c. sugar
Dash of salt
1 tsp. vanilla
2 1/2 c. milk, scalded
Nutmeg to taste

Blend eggs, sugar, salt and vanilla. Stir in scalded milk gradually. Pour into six 6-ounce custard cups. Sprinkle with nutmeg. Place cups in 13 x 9 x 2-inch baking pan. Pour enough very hot water into baking pan to reach halfway up the cups. Bake in pre-heated 350-degree oven about 45 minutes or until knife inserted halfway between center and edge comes out clean. Remove cups from water. Serve warm or chilled. Garnish custard with raspberries or blueberries. Yield: 6 servings.

Pam Miller, V.P.
Beta Alpha Chap.
Milwaukee, Wisconsin

NEVER-FAIL CUSTARD

4 eggs
4 tbsp. (heaping) sugar
Pinch of salt
2 1/2 c. milk
1 tsp. vanilla
Nutmeg to taste

Beat 4 eggs slightly; add sugar and salt. Mix together until blended. Add milk; whip until blended. Add vanilla. Fill 6 custard cups. Sprinkle with nutmeg. Set custard cups in baking pan. Pour enough boiling water in baking pan to make 1 1/2 inches water on custard cups. Bake 45 minutes at 350 degrees.

Leta Bouchey, Soc. Chm.
Epsilon Beta No. 1653
Stockton, Kansas

SPANISH CUSTARD

5 or 6 eggs, well beaten
1/8 tsp. salt
1 lg. can sweetened condensed milk
1 milk can water
1/2 tsp. vanilla
1/2 tsp. almond extract
3 tbsp. sugar

Beat eggs with salt until foamy. Mix milk with water and flavorings. Add to eggs; blend well. Heat sugar slowly in small skillet over low heat stirring constantly. Divide melted sugar into 6 custard cups. Add egg mixture to each cup. Set cups in pan of water. Bake at 325 degrees until firm in center, about 1 hour. Remove from water. Cool.

Marybelle Comparato, V.P.
Gamma Phi No. 2561
Haines City, Florida

LEMON SPONGE CUPS

2 tbsp. butter or margarine, softened
1 c. sugar
4 tbsp. all-purpose flour
1/4 tsp. salt
5 tbsp. lemon juice
Grated rind of 2 lemons
3 eggs, separated
1 1/2 c. milk
Whipped cream or Cool Whip
Cherries

Cream butter; add sugar, flour, salt, lemon juice and lemon rind. Beat egg yolks; mix with milk. Add to lemon mixture. Beat egg whites until stiff peaks form. Fold into lemon mixture. Pour into 6 greased custard cups. Set cups in pan of hot water. Bake at 350 degrees for 45 minutes. Each cup will contain lemon custard at bottom of cup and sponge cake on top. Cool. Unmold. Top each with whipped cream and a cherry.

Brenda Haselden
Beta Sigma No. 2904
Savannah, Georgia

PEACH CUSTARD

1 1/2 c. sifted flour
1/2 c. butter or margarine, softened
1/2 tsp. salt
1 1-lb. can sliced peaches
1/2 c. sugar
1/2 tsp. cinnamon
1 egg, slightly beaten
1 c. evaporated milk

Mix flour, butter and salt with pastry blender or two knives until mixture looks like coarse meal. Press mixture into bottom of 8-inch square baking dish. Drain peaches, saving 1/2 cup syrup. Arrange peaches on crust. Combine sugar and cinnamon. Sprinkle over peaches. Bake at 375 degrees for 20 minutes. Mix egg, evaporated milk and reserved peach syrup. Pour over peaches. Bake 30 minutes more until custard is firm except in center. Remove from oven. Let stand until firm. Serve warm or cool.

Peggy Sparkman, Bike Ride Chm.
Kappa Theta No. 4343
Gainesville, Texas

APPLE-NUT PUDDING

1 egg
3/4 c. sugar
1/2 c. flour
1/2 tsp. salt
1 tsp. baking powder
1 tsp. vanilla
1/2 c. chopped nuts
1 c. cubed tart apples

Beat egg well; add sugar gradually while beating. Add next 3 ingredients; mix well. Add vanilla, chopped nuts and apples. Pour into greased and floured 8-inch square pan. Bake for 40 to 50 minutes in 350-degree oven. Serve in squares with ice cream. Delicious.

Hilda Franz, Pres.
Alpha Rho No. 3735
Biloxi, Mississippi

BANANA PUDDING

1/3 c. sugar
1/4 c. cornstarch
1/8 tsp. salt
2 3/4 c. milk
2 eggs, beaten
2 tbsp. margarine or butter
1 tsp. vanilla
Vanilla wafers
Bananas

Mix together sugar, cornstarch and salt. Gradually stir in milk, eggs and margarine. Bring to a boil, stirring constantly. Cook for 2 minutes. Remove from heat. Add vanilla. Line a 2-quart casserole or baking pan with vanilla wafers. Cover wafers with part of pudding. Slice layer of bananas over pudding. Alternate 2 layers until dish is full. Sprinkle fine wafer crumbs on top. Chill in refrigerator; serve.

Joan Shepardson, Sec.
Beta Alpha No. 4068
Dubois, Wyoming

COCONUT-BANANA PUDDING

3 eggs, separated
Sugar
1 lg. can evaporated milk
1/4 c. (or more) fresh or frozen coconut
1 pkg. vanilla wafers
3 lg. bananas

Beat egg yolks well. Add 1/4 cup sugar; cream together. Combine with milk and water used to rinse out can of milk. Heat to almost boiling point. Reduce heat; continue cooking until desired thickness. Stir in coconut. Alternate layers of wafers and bananas in deep dish. Pour hot mixture over bananas and wafers. Whip egg whites until stiff peaks form. Add small amount of sugar if desired. Spread over top of pudding. Bake in oven until golden brown.

Martha D. Gray
Alpha Iota No. 1098
Jackson, Tennessee

EASY BREAD PUDDING

1 egg
2 c. scalded milk
2 tbsp. butter, melted
2 tbsp. sugar
1/2 tsp. salt
1/2 c. raisins
1 tsp. vanilla
1 c. stale bread, cut in 1/2-in. cubes

Beat egg slightly. Add milk, butter, sugar, salt, raisins and vanilla. Add bread cubes. Pour into a well-buttered baking dish. Set dish in pan of hot water. Bake until firm, about 30 minutes, in 350-degree oven. Serve with cream or hard sauce.

Carolyn Blanchard, Sec.
Beta Upsilon No. 2127
Myrtle Creek, Oregon

RAISIN BREAD PUDDING

8 slices raisin bread, cubed
2 eggs
1/2 c. sugar
2 c. scalded milk
1/2 tsp. vanilla
Nutmeg
1/4 tsp. salt
Butter

Place raisin bread in 2-quart casserole. Beat eggs with sugar. Add scalded milk, vanilla, 1/2 teaspoon nutmeg and salt; stir well. Pour mixture over bread, mashing down to soak well. Sprinkle with additional nutmeg; dot with butter. Place casserole in pan of water. Bake one hour at 350 degrees. Cool to room temperature. Refrigerate for several hours or overnight for flavors to blend. May be served plain or topped with ice cream, whipped cream or hot vanilla sauce.

Estelle J. Finn, V.P.
Beta Theta No. 1252
Tulsa, Oklahoma

CHOCOLATE-BREAD PUDDING

3 c. stale bread
1 c. milk, scalded
2 sq. chocolate
2 1/4 c. milk
1 1/2 c. sugar
Pinch of salt
3 tsp. vanilla
2 eggs, slightly beaten
1/2 c. butter

Soak bread in scalded milk. Melt chocolate in 2 cups milk in double boiler. Add to bread mixture. Combine 1 cup sugar, salt, 2 teaspoons vanilla and eggs. Add to hot milk mixture; stir well. Pour in glass baking dish. Place in pan of hot water. Bake at 350 degrees for 1 hour and 15 minutes to 1 hour and 30 minutes. Remove from oven. Chill. Combine remaining ingredients. Heat, stirring constantly. Serve warm sauce over pudding.

Linda Girow
Alpha Sigma No. 3084
New Orleans, Lousiana

CARAMEL PUDDING

1 c. sugar
1 c. flour
2 tsp. baking powder
1 tsp. mace
1 c. seedless raisins
1 c. milk
2/3 c. (firmly packed) brown sugar
1 3/4 c. boiling water
1 tbsp. butter

Sift sugar, flour, baking powder and mace. Add raisins and milk. Pour into greased 2-quart casserole. Mix brown sugar, boiling water and butter. Pour over mixture in casserole. Bake at 375 degrees for 40 minutes.

Margaret Swinehart, Pres.
Gamma Tau No. 811
Elk City, Oklahoma

FUDGE PUDDING

1 c. flour
2 tsp. baking powder
1/2 tsp. salt
3/4 c. sugar
6 tbsp. cocoa
1/2 c. milk
1 tsp. vanilla
2 tbsp. melted shortening
3/4 c. chopped nuts
1 3/4 c. hot water
3/4 c. (firmly packed) brown sugar

Sift together flour, baking powder, salt, sugar and 3 tablespoons cocoa. Stir together milk, vanilla and shortening. Add dry ingredients and nuts to milk mixture. Pour into greased 9 x 12-inch pan. Mix 3 tablespoons cocoa, hot water and brown sugar. Pour over cake mixture. Bake for 30 minutes at 350 degrees. Serve as upside-down cake. Good with whipped topping.

Nelva Lee Just, Ed. Dir.
Epsilon Gamma No. 1563
Manhattan, Kansas

CHOCOLATE PUDDING

1/2 c. sugar
2 tbsp. (heaping) flour
1 tbsp. (heaping) cocoa
1 1/2 c. hot water
1 tsp. vanilla
1 lump butter

Mix sugar, flour and cocoa in skillet. Add hot water; stir. Bring to a boil; cook until thick. Add vanilla and butter. Yield: 3 servings.

Carol Main
Alpha Mu No. 763
Des Moines, Iowa

CHOCOLATE POTS DE CREME

1/2 c. milk
2 1-oz. squares unsweetened chocolate
1 tsp. butter
3/4 c. confectioners' sugar

1/2 c. peanut butter
1 tsp. vanilla extract
2 egg yolks, separated
1/2 c. whipping cream, whipped

Place milk, chocolate and butter in saucepan. Warm over low heat, stirring occasionally until chocolate is melted and mixture is blended. Stir in sugar, peanut butter and vanilla until smooth. Spoon a small amount of hot chocolate mixture into beaten egg yolks; combine with the other ingredients in saucepan. Continue to heat until just hot. Cover; cool. Beat egg whites until stiff but not dry. Fold into peanut mixture. Fold in whipped cream. Proportion mixture evenly into 6 individual Pot de Creme cups. Chill. Garnish each with a dollop of whipped cream and chopped peanuts. Yield: 6 1/2-cup servings.

Photograph for this recipe on page 1.

DATE-NUT PUDDING

4 egg whites
1 c. sugar
1 tbsp. flour
1 pkg. chopped dates
1 c. broken nuts
1/2 pt. whipping cream
1 tsp. lemon extract

Beat egg whites until stiff peaks form. Sift together sugar and flour. Fold into egg whites. Mix in chopped dates and broken nuts. Pour in buttered 12 x 9 x 2-inch pan. Bake in 250-degree oven for 1 hour. Whip cream stiff. Flavor with lemon extract. Serve with pudding.

Peggy Olsson
Zeta Phi No. 2593
Junction City, Kansas

DATE PUDDING

1 c. flour
1 c. sugar
Pinch of salt
2 tsp. baking powder

1 c. chopped dates
1 c. chopped nuts
1/2 c. milk
2 c. (firmly packed) brown sugar
2 c. boiling water
1/4 c. butter

Combine first 7 ingredients; mix well. Place in greased 8 x 8-inch baking dish. Bring remaining ingredients to a boil. Pour over cake mixture. Bake at 350 degrees for 25 to 30 minutes. Cool. Serve with Cool Whip and cherry on top.

Genie Gilliland, Pres.
Kappa Theta No. 4343
Gainesville, Texas

WALNUT SPOON PUDDING

1 c. soft dried dark or golden figs
1/4 c. soft butter or margarine
2/3 c. (firmly packed) brown sugar
1/4 tsp. cinnamon
1/8 tsp. each cloves and nutmeg
1 egg, beaten
3/4 c. sifted all-purpose flour
1/4 tsp. soda
1/2 tsp. salt
1 c. chopped walnuts
Fluffy Bourbon Sauce

Clip stems from figs; cut fruit into small pieces. Cream butter, brown sugar, spices and egg together until well blended and fluffy. Resift flour with soda and salt. Add to creamed mixture; beat until blended. Stir in fruit and walnuts. Turn into buttered 8 or 9-inch square pan. Bake at 350 degrees for 20 to 25 minutes. Spoon, while warm, into serving dishes. Serve warm with Fluffy Bourbon Sauce. Yield: 8 servings.

Fluffy Bourbon Sauce

2 egg yolks
1 c. sifted powdered sugar
Pinch of salt
3 or 4 tbsp. bourbon
1 c. whipping cream

Beat egg yolks, powdered sugar and salt together until thick and lemon colored. Stir in bourbon. Beat whipping cream until stiff; gently fold into sauce. Chill until ready to serve; stir before spooning on pudding.

Photograph for this recipe on page 41.

BROILED BUTTERSCOTCH RICE PUDDING

1/2 c. uncooked rice
1 c. water
1/4 tsp. salt
1 tsp. maple extract
1   3 1/4-oz. package butterscotch
    pudding mix
2 c. milk
1 tbsp. butter or margarine
2 tbsp. melted butter or margarine
1/3 c. maple syrup
1 c. shredded coconut

Combine rice, water, salt and maple extract. Bring to a boil over high heat. Stir once. Cover; reduce heat. Simmer for 15 minutes. Blend pudding mix with milk and butter; cook over medium heat, stirring constantly, for about 5 minutes. Fold in cooked rice. Spoon into ovenproof serving dishes; chill. Combine melted butter, maple syrup and coconut. Spread mixture over rice pudding. Broil slowly until golden, 2 to 3 minutes. Watch carefully so as not to burn. Yield: 6 servings.

Photograph for this recipe below.

CREAMY RICE PUDDING

1/3 c. uncooked white rice
1/3 c. sugar
1 qt. milk
1/2 tsp. salt
1 tsp. vanilla
1/2 c. raisins (opt.)
1/2 c. light cream

Combine rice, sugar, milk, salt, vanilla and raisins in 1 1/2-quart greased casserole. Bake in 325-degree oven for 1 hour and 30 minutes, stirring occasionally. Add light cream. Bake 30 minutes longer without stirring. Let cool. Yield: 6 servings.

Jacqueline Jackson, Soc. Chm.
Zeta Gamma No. 4333
Denton, Texas

RICE PUDDING WITH KIRSCH FROSTING

3 c. cooked rice
3 c. milk
1/3 c. sugar
1/4 tsp. salt
2 tbsp. butter or margarine
2 egg yolks, beaten
1 tsp. vanilla
Kirsch Frosting
1/2 c. chopped maraschino cherries

Combine rice, milk, sugar, salt and butter. Cook over medium heat, stirring occasionally, until rice is thick and creamy. Blend a little hot mixture into egg yolks. Stir egg yolk mixture into rice; mix well. Add vanilla. Chill. Spoon into serving dish. Top with Kirsch Frosting. Garnish with chopped cherries. Yield: 6 to 8 servings.

Kirsch Frosting

3/4 c. sugar
1/4 tsp. cream of tartar
Dash of salt
1/4 c. maraschino cherry juice
2 egg whites
2 tsp. kirsch

Bring first four ingredients to a boil. Cook mixture to soft-ball stage. Beat egg whites until stiff but not dry. Pour hot syrup gradually into egg whites, beating constantly. Add kirsch.

Photograph for this recipe on page 35.

RAISIN-RICE PUDDING

2 tbsp. uncooked rice
2 c. milk
1/4 c. sugar
1/2 c. raisins
1/4 tsp. salt
1 tsp. vanilla

Wash rice. Place in greased baking dish. Pour in milk. Bake for 1 hour and 30 minutes at 250 degrees, stirring occasionally. Add remaining ingredients; mix well. Bake 30 minutes longer or until brown. Do not stir. Yield: 6 servings.

Dee Tallman
Gamma Omicron No. 1595
Omaha, Nebraska

RICE PUDDING

1/2 c. Minute rice
2 c. milk
1 c. sugar
2 tbsp. cornstarch
2 eggs
1/2 c. white raisins
2 tsp. vanilla

Cook Minute rice according to package directions. Scald milk; do not boil. Combine sugar, cornstarch and eggs; beat until smooth. Add a small amount of hot milk to egg mixture; mix well. Add egg mixture to hot milk. Stir constantly until thickened. Remove from heat. Pour boiling water over raisins; drain. Add vanilla, rice and raisins to custard. Allow to cool. Serve with Cool Whip topping.

Alice Wyman, Hon. Mem.
Alpha Alpha No. 599
Columbia, South Carolina

PERSIMMON PUDDING

1 1/2 qt. persimmons
1 c. grated sweet potatoes

2 eggs
1 c. sugar
2 c. milk
1 tsp. each cinnamon, nutmeg, cloves
    and lemon extract
1 c. flour
4 tbsp. melted butter
1 tbsp. soda, dissolved in water

Press persimmons through sieve. Add grated sweet potatoes. Set aside. Beat eggs lightly in large mixing bowl. Add sugar and milk; mix well. Add spices and extract to flour. Add flour mixture to egg mixture. Add butter and soda; mix well. Stir in persimmon mixture; place in greased baking pan. Bake 1 hour in 250-degree oven. Cool. Serve with whipped cream or rich cream.

Viola L. Reavis, Pres.
Beta Pi No. 433
Miami, Oklahoma

CHRISTMAS SUET PUDDING

3 1/2 c. flour
1 1/2 tsp. salt
1/2 tsp. each cinnamon, cloves, nutmeg
1 tsp. (heaping) soda
1 c. molasses
1 c. milk
1 c. finely chopped suet
1 c. chopped raisins

Sift together the first 3 ingredients. Combine soda and molasses. Add molasses and milk to suet. Combine mixtures. Add raisins. Turn into buttered mold. Cover tightly. Steam for 4 hours. Serve with whipped cream.

Jayne Weber
Rho Chi No. 2988
St. Charles, Missouri

OVEN-STEAMED CRANBERRY PUDDING

2 c. boiling water
2 c. fresh cranberries, halved
1 9-oz. package mincemeat, crumbled
1/4 c. butter or margarine
1 c. (firmly packed) brown sugar

1 c. molasses
3 1/2 c. flour
1/2 tsp. salt
2 tsp. soda

Combine water, cranberries and mincemeat. Let stand 10 minutes. Cream butter. Stir in brown sugar and molasses. Sift dry ingredients together. Stir into butter alternately with cranberry mixture. Pour mixture into greased 2 1/2-quart pudding mold. Cover tightly with foil. Bake at 350 degrees for about 1 hour and 30 minutes or until tester inserted in middle comes out clean. Cool in mold about 15 minutes. Unmold onto serving platter carefully. Serve warm with hard sauce.

Marjorie Sherwood, Pres.
Alpha Delta No. 1711
Milford, Utah

PLUM PUDDING

1/3 c. butter or margarine, softened
1 1/3 c. sugar
2 eggs
1 c. applesauce
1 2/3 c. flour
3/4 tsp. soda
3/4 tsp. salt
3/4 tsp. cinnamon
1/2 tsp. nutmeg
1/4 tsp. allspice
4 oz. candied cherries, chopped
4 oz. candied pineapple, chopped
1/4 c. chopped seedless raisins
3/4 c. chopped pecans

Grease and flour 6-cup mold. Cream butter and sugar together. Add eggs and applesauce; mix well. Sift next 6 ingredients together. Blend into butter mixture, mixing well. Add remaining ingredients; mix well. Pour into prepared mold. Bake in preheated 350-degree oven for 1 hour and 45 minutes. Invert mold onto foil-lined plate. Tap mold gently on all sides to loosen; do not remove mold for 20 minutes. Top with whipped cream or hard sauce.

Lee Williams
Zeta Alpha
Dallas, Texas

Fruit Desserts

It is common practice in most European countries for fresh fruit to be served at the end of a meal, rather than rich cakes, pies, or other fancy and filling dessert foods. We know this is a wise practice, as fruit is quite nourishing, and tends to refresh the palate after a big meal. But, the many kinds of fruit also make delicious desserts when combined fresh with other ingredients, or when cooked in any of the familiar ways. And, like any good dessert food, fruit can be prepared either very simply or very richly, to suit the menu.

The flavor of so many fruits — apples, cherries, oranges, peaches, pears — is greatly complemented by the fruit's being marinated, cooked, or flamed in a liqueur. Oranges with Cognac is a famous example; flamed dates or bananas are equally elegant and delicious. The combination of any fresh fruit with other ingredients is at its best when kept simple. For example, strawberries or grapes bathed in sweetened yogurt, topped only with a slight sprinkling of light brown sugar, or melon balls in creme de menthe. But combinations that are both fancy and unforgettably delicious are also possible if the ingredients, as a rule, are kept light in both flavor and texture. The flavor of most fruits is not strong, and strong combinations will often ruin it. Even the recipes for cooked fruit desserts are, for the most part, rather simple — especially dumplings, cobblers and crunches. Many homemakers and their families would agree that some fruit is at its best when baked whole, with only a sprinkling of brown sugar or sugar and cinnamon for flavoring.

In this health and calorie conscious age, ESA members recommend fruit desserts as a regular part of your everyday and party menu planning. Their cost is rarely a strain on any budget, whether bought fresh while in season, or frozen or canned from the supermarket. Because it is naturally sweet and loaded with vitamins and minerals, fruit is a natural for dessert. ESA members are sure that this marvelous collection of fruit dessert recipes will become your favorite — quickly and permanently.

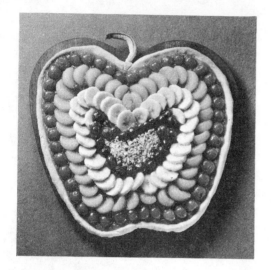

crust on large platter or bread board. Spread with 1 1/2 cups chilled apple mixture. Starting at outer edge, arrange red maraschino cherries, cut side down. Add mandarin orange sections, bananas, green cherries and pecans. Cut into wedges to serve. Top with whipped cream, frozen whipped topping or ice cream, if desired. Yield: 10-12 servings.

Photograph for this recipe on this page.

APPLE DESSERT PIZZA

1   10-oz. package pie crust mix
3 tbsp. lemon juice
4 c. canned applesauce
1 c. (firmly packed) brown sugar
1 tbsp. vinegar
1 tsp. cinnamon
1/2 tsp. ground cloves
1/4 tsp. allspice
1/4 tsp. salt
1 c. red maraschino cherries, drained
1/2 c. green maraschino cherries,
   drained
1 c. mandarin oranges
2 lg. bananas, sliced
1/4 c. chopped pecans or walnuts

Prepare piecrust mix according to directions. Draw outline of large apple about 15 inches in width and 13 inches high. Trace onto cardboard. Cut out. Cover both sides with several layers of aluminum foil. Roll out pastry 1/2 inch larger than apple pattern. Fold excess pastry to make a standing edge around outer rim of apple. Prick the flat surface of pastry with a fork. Bake in 425-degree oven for 20 minutes. Cool. Combine 1 tablespoon lemon juice and next 7 ingredients in 3-quart saucepan. Simmer, stirring occasionally, for 1 hour. Remove from heat. Cool in refrigerator to chill. Cut cherries in half. Drain oranges. Place fruits on layers of paper toweling to remove excess moisture. Place banana slices in bowl; sprinkle with 2 tablespoons lemon juice. Place

APPLE CUSTARD TORTE

6 med. apples, pared and cored
1/4 c. butter
1 1/2 tbsp. flour
Sugar
1/2 tsp. salt
1/2 c. sour cream
6 eggs, separated
1 tsp. cinnamon
1/4 c. fine bread crumbs
1/4 c. sliced almonds

Slice apples 1/8 inch thick. Place apples and butter in heavy pan; cover. Cook over low heat for 10 to 20 minutes, stirring occasionally. Apples should be tender but not mushy. Mix flour, 1 cup sugar, salt and sour cream. Add to slightly beaten egg yolks. Combine with apples. Continue cooking until thickened. Cool. Beat egg whites until stiff peaks form. Fold egg whites into apple mixture. Spread in greased and floured 9 x 12-inch pan. Combine 1 tablespoon sugar with remaining ingredients. Sprinkle over top of pan. Bake in 325-degree oven for 40 minutes. Serve warm or cold with whipped cream.

Ruth Hemann, Publ. Chm.
Alpha Omicron No. 1827
Burlington, Iowa

APPLE GOODIE

3 c. diced apples
1 tbsp. lemon juice
2 tsp. cinnamon
1 c. sugar
3/4 c. (firmly packed) brown sugar

1/2 c. shortening
3/4 c. rolled oats
1 tsp. baking powder
1/2 c. flour
1/4 tsp. soda

Place apples in greased dish. Sprinkle with lemon juice, cinnamon and sugar. Mix remaining ingredients together until crumbly. Sprinkle over apples. Bake at 350 degrees for 45 minutes or until apples are tender and top is browned. Serve with ice cream.

Sydney Feraco
Delta Omega No. 4369
Loveland, Colorado

CRISPY APPLE CRUNCH

4 lg. apples, peeled and cored
1 tsp. cinnamon
1/2 tsp. nutmeg
1/2 c. sugar
1/2 tsp. salt
1/3 c. water
2 tsp. lemon juice
1 tsp. lemon rind
1/2 tsp. soda
1/3 c. butter
1/2 c. chopped walnuts
1 c. rolled oats

Slice apples in 2-quart baking dish. Sprinkle with spices, sugar and 1/2 of the salt. Mix water, lemon juice and lemon rind; pour over apples. Add soda, remaining salt, butter and walnuts to oats. Work into crumbs. Spread over apple mixture. Bake at 375 degrees for 40 minutes. Serve with whipped cream or vanilla ice cream. Yield: 4-6 servings.

Phyllis Cummins, Fin Chm., Yearbook Chm.
Delta Tau No. 4264
Yakima, Washington

APPLE KUCHEN

1/2 c. butter or margarine, softened
1 pkg. yellow cake mix
1 20-oz. can pie-sliced apples, well
    drained, or 2 1/2 c. sliced apples
1/2 c. sugar

1 tsp. cinnamon
1 c. sour cream
2 egg yolks or 1 whole egg

Cut butter into dry cake mix until crumbly. Pat lightly into ungreased 13 x 9 x 2-inch pan, building up the edges slightly. Bake in preheated 350-degree oven for 10 minutes. Arrange apple slices on warm crust. Mix sugar and cinnamon; sprinkle on apples. Blend sour cream and egg yolks; drizzle over apples. Bake in preheated 350-degree oven for 25 minutes or until edges are light brown. Do not overbake. Serve warm or cold.

LaWanda Wiens
Beta Gamma No. 611
Newton, Kansas
Glessie Willingham, Member at Large
Prattville, Alabama

APPLE-SPICE STRUDEL QUICKIE

Sugar
2 c. flour
3 tsp. baking powder
3/4 tsp. salt
1/4 c. shortening
2/3 to 3/4 c. milk
Melted butter
3 c. chopped apples
3/4 tsp. cinnamon
1/2 tsp. nutmeg
Powdered sugar
Butter
Chopped nuts

Combine 2 tablespoons sugar with next 3 ingredients. Cut in shortening. Add milk to make soft dough. Roll dough out to 1/4 inch thickness. Brush with melted butter. Cover with chopped apples. Combine cinnamon, nutmeg and 1/2 cup sugar. Sprinkle over apples. Roll up jelly roll fashion. Place on greased cookie sheet. Shape as crescent roll. Bake at 400 degrees for 20 to 25 minutes. Combine enough powdered sugar, butter and additional milk for an icing. Cover roll with icing. Top with chopped nuts.

Dorothylee Walker, W. and M. Chm.
Delta Xi No. 3038
Clearwater, Florida

APPLE CRUNCH

6 to 8 apples
1 tbsp. cinnamon
3/4 c. flour
1 c. (firmly packed) brown sugar
1/4 lb. butter

Slice apples in buttered baking dish. Sprinkle with cinnamon. Work flour, brown sugar and butter until crumbly. Sprinkle over apples. Bake about 30 minutes in 350-degree oven.

Jean Riggs, Chaplain
Beta Alpha No. 4068
Dubois, Wyoming

AUNT GEORGIA'S APPLE CRISP

4 to 6 c. sliced apples
1 c. sugar
1/2 c. rolled oats
1/2 c. flour
1 tsp. cinnamon
1/2 c. melted butter

Place apples in greased baking dish. Combine dry ingredients; work in butter. Sprinkle mixture over apples. Bake at 350 degrees for about 30 minutes or until topping is brown and crisp.

Angelique J. Cross
Delta Gamma No. 4494
Webb City, Missouri

APPLE DUMPLINGS

1 1/2 c. flour
1/2 tsp. salt
1/2 c. shortening
6 apples, pared and cored
Sugar
3/4 tsp. cinnamon
Butter

Combine first 3 ingredients with 4 1/2 tablespoons water according to directions for plain pastry. Roll out; cut into 6-inch squares. Place apple on each square. Add 1 tablespoon sugar, 1/8 teaspoon cinnamon and 1/8 teaspoon butter to each apple. Fold dough around apple. Prick with fork. Place in baking dish. Combine 1/2 cup sugar, 1 cup water and 1 cube butter. Heat to dissolve sugar and butter. Pour syrup around dumplings. Bake at 425 degrees for 35 to 40 minutes.

Dorothy Winger, State Pres.
Beta Epsilon No. 2669
Idaho Falls, Idaho

APPLE ROLL

2 c. flour
1 tsp. baking powder
1 tsp. salt
6 tbsp. shortening
3/4 c. milk
Sugar
2 c. water
4 (or more) med. apples, peeled and cored
Margarine
Cinnamon

Sift flour, baking powder and salt together. Cut in shortening. Add milk to make a soft dough. Roll out to 1/4-inch thickness. Place 1 1/2 cups sugar and water in 13 x 9 x 2-inch pan. Cook about 5 minutes over low heat. Chop apples onto rolled out dough. Roll jelly roll fashion. Cut into 1 1/2-inch slices. Place in pan of syrup. Dot with margarine; sprinkle with additional sugar and cinnamon. Bake at 450 degrees for about 25 minutes. Serve with ice cream or cream.

Phyllis Gordon, V.P.
Beta Upsilon No. 2127
Myrtle Creek, Oregon

APPLE-OAT DESSERT

4 c. sliced apples
1 tbsp. lemon juice
1/3 c. flour
1 c. rolled oats
1/2 c. (firmly packed) brown sugar
1/2 tsp. salt

1 tsp. cinnamon
1/3 c. melted butter

Place apples in greased shallow baking dish. Sprinkle with lemon juice. Combine dry ingredients. Add melted butter, mixing until crumbly. Sprinkle crumb mixture over apples. Bake for 30 minutes at 375 degrees. Top with whipped cream.

Sue Johnston, Publ. Chm., Awards Chm.
Beta Alpha No. 4068
Dubois, Wyoming

TASTY APPLE-OATMEAL BARS

1 1/2 c. rolled oats
1 c. (firmly packed) brown sugar
2 c. flour
3/4 c. butter or margarine
4 to 5 lb. apples
1 c. sugar
1 c. water
1 tbsp. cornstarch
1 tsp. cinnamon

Combine first 4 ingredients until crumbly. Press 1/2 crumbs in bottom of 9 x 13-inch pan. Slice apples on top until pan is filled. Combine remaining ingredients. Bring to a boil. Boil until thick. Cool. Pour syrup over apples. Add remaining crumb mixture on top. Bake in 350-degree oven for 1 hour and 15 minutes. Cool. Cut into bars.

Mrs. Caroline Moore, Pres.
Alpha Upsilon No. 3337
New Berlin, Wisconsin

SOUR CREAM-APPLE SQUARES

2 c. flour
2 c. (firmly packed) brown sugar
1/2 c. butter or margarine, softened
1 c. chopped nuts
1 tsp. cinnamon
1 tsp. soda
Salt to taste
1 c. sour cream
1 tsp. vanilla
1 egg

2 1/2 c. apples, peeled and finely chopped

Combine flour, brown sugar and butter. Blend at low speed until crumbly. Add nuts. Press 2 3/4 crumb mixture in 9 x 13-inch pan. Add cinnamon, soda, salt, sour cream, vanilla and egg to remaining mixture. Blend well. Stir in apples. Spread over base. Bake in preheated 350-degree oven 25 to 35 minutes. Serve with ice cream or whipped cream.

Brenda Nokes, Pres.
Gamma Zeta No. 2179
McCook, Nebraska

APPLE-CHAMPAGNE COMPOTE

Golden Delicious apples
1 1/2 c. champagne
2 c. sliced strawberries
1 c. powdered sugar

Pare, core and slice apples into very thin circles. Place in bowl; cover with champagne and strawberries. Sprinkle with powdered sugar. Let chill 3 hours. Serve in clear glass compote dishes; garnish with shredded coconut or nuts. Accompany with a light, creamy cheese or a coeur a la creme.

Photograph for this recipe below.

BANANAS FOSTER

1/4 c. butter
1 c. (firmly packed) brown sugar
1 tsp. cinnamon
3 bananas
1/3 c. rum
Ginger brandy or banana liqueur to taste
Vanilla ice cream

Place butter, brown sugar and cinnamon in skillet or chafing dish; melt. Add bananas. Simmer for several minutes, turning once. Mix rum with ginger brandy. Pour over bananas. Ignite. Spoon slightly softened vanilla ice cream over bananas while flaming.

Jean Johnson, Pres.
Gamma Delta No. 3767
Atlanta, Georgia

BLUEBERRY DELIGHT

2 c. crushed graham crackers
1/2 c. powdered sugar
1/2 c. melted margarine
2 eggs
1/2 c. sugar
1   8-oz. package cream cheese
1 can blueberry pie filling

Mix together graham crackers, powdered sugar and margarine. Press in bottom of 9 x 13-inch. pan. Beat together eggs, sugar and cream cheese. Pour over crust. Bake for 15 minutes at 350 degrees. Cool. Pour blueberry pie filling over top. Top with Dream Whip if desired.

Jolene Corkle
Alpha Phi No. 1438
Winner, South Dakota

CHERRY DESSERT

1 c. shortening
3 c. flour
1 c. sugar
1 tsp. baking powder
1 tsp. soda
1/2 tsp. salt
3 eggs
1 c. milk
1 tsp. vanilla
1 can cherry pie filling

Combine shortening and flour. Add sugar, baking powder, soda and salt. Combine eggs, milk and vanilla. Add to sugar mixture. Spread in a large greased and lightly floured cookie sheet with sides. Spread with cherry pie filling. Bake at 350 degrees for 35 to 40 minutes. Excellent served with ice cream or whipped cream.

Kathryn Fredley, State Treas.
Beta Delta No. 4271
Tucson, Arizona

CHERRY DESSERT

6 lg. or 24 sm. soda crackers, rolled
   fine
2 tbsp. sugar
2 tbsp. flour
1 stick margarine, melted
1/2 pkg. coconut
1 lg. can cherry pie filling

Mix first 5 ingredients together. Place 2/3 the mixture in ungreased 13 x 9-inch pan. Spread with cherry pie filling. Top with remaining mixture. Bake at 375 degrees for 20 minutes. Serve with Cool Whip.

Alice N. Fryer, Publ. Chm.
Delta Rho No. 4547
Williamston, Michigan

CHERRIES JUBILEE CREPES

4 eggs
1 c. flour
1/2 c. water
1/2 c. milk
1/2 tsp. salt
2 tbsp. melted margarine
1 tsp. vanilla
Sugar
1   8-oz. package cream cheese
3/4 c. sour cream

Place first 7 ingredients with 2 teaspoons sugar into blender. Cover; process until smooth. Let stand for 1 hour. Bake according to directions for Crepe Maker. Combine cream cheese, sour cream and 1/3 cup sugar; mix well. Fill each crepe with 3 tablespoons filling. Fold sides of crepe over mixture.

Place crepes in buttered baking dish. Bake at 350 degrees for 15 minutes. Keep warm.

Cherries Jubilee Sauce

1 can pitted Bing cherries
1/3 c. sugar
2 tbsp. cornstarch
1/8 tsp. salt
2 tsp. lemon juice
1/4 tsp. grated lemon peel or dried
    orange peel
1/3 c. orange curacao
1/3 c. toasted slivered almonds (opt.)

Drain cherries, reserving 1 cup cherry juice. Combine sugar, cornstarch, salt and cherry juice in saucepan. Cook until sauce is clear and slightly thickened, stirring constantly. Stir in cherries, lemon juice, lemon peel and 2 tablespoons curacao. Heat remaining curacao. Pour sauce into chafing dish. Pour curacao over sauce; ignite. Spoon sauce over crepes as flame dies down. Sprinkle with almonds.

Jackie Ohlson
Eta Beta No. 2286
Arvada, Colorado

CHERRY-RHUBARB FANCY

4 c. diced rhubarb
1/2 c. sugar
2 tbsp. cornstarch
1 c. water
1 1-lb. 8-oz. can cherry pie filling
4 or 5 drops of red food coloring
1 tsp. almond extract
3/4 c. quick-cooking oatmeal
3/4 c. (firmly packed) brown sugar
3/4 c. flour
Dash of salt
1/3 c. butter or margarine
1/2 c. chopped walnuts

Place rhubarb in 11 x 7 x 1 1/2-inch baking dish. Combine sugar and cornstarch in small saucepan. Stir in water slowly. Cook, stirring constantly, over medium heat until thickened. Stir in pie filling, food coloring and almond extract. Pour over rhubarb. Combine oatmeal, brown sugar, flour, salt and butter; mix until crumbly. Add walnuts. Sprinkle over fruit. Bake in 350-degree oven for 45

minutes or until golden brown and rhubarb is tender. Garnish with whipped cream. Yield: 6-8 servings.

Martha Brough, V.P.
Delta Tau No. 4264
Yakima, Washington

L'IL COBBLER SEXTET

1/3 c. sugar
2 tbsp. cornstarch
1 1-lb. can red pitted tart cherries
1/4 tsp. almond extract
1/2 c. pancake mix
3 tbsp. (firmly packed) brown sugar
3 tbsp. melted butter or margarine
Vanilla ice cream

Combine sugar and cornstarch in medium saucepan. Drain cherries, reserving liquid. Add cherry liquid to cornstarch mixture; stir until cornstarch is dissolved. Add cherries and almond extract. Cook over medium heat, stirring constantly until mixture comes to a boil and is thickened. Spoon into six 5-ounce ovenproof custard cups. Combine pancake mix and brown sugar. Add butter; toss with a fork until evenly blended. Sprinkle over base. Bake in preheated 350-degree oven for about 30 minutes. Serve warm topped with a spoonful of vanilla ice cream. Yield: 6 servings.

Photograph for this recipe below.

CHERRY SUPREME

1 No. 2 can cherry pie filling
1 No. 2 can crushed pineapple
1 pkg. yellow cake mix
1 1/2 sticks butter or margarine, melted
1 c. chopped nuts

Spread cherries over bottom of 10 x 14 x 2-inch baking dish. Top with pineapple. Spread cake mix over all. Spoon melted butter over cake mix. Sprinkle nuts over top. Bake for 45 minutes at 350 degrees. This may be served with topping. Do not stir; layer each ingredient and bake.

Mrs. Brenda S. Carpenter, Pres.
Beta Gamma
Garner, North Carolina

CHERRY TORTE

2 1/4 c. sugar
1 c. flour
1 tsp. soda
1 tsp. cinnamon
3/4 tsp. salt
1/2 c. chopped nuts
1 beaten egg
2 c. drained sour cherries
2 tbsp. melted butter
1 tbsp. cornstarch

Sift 1 1/4 cups sugar, flour, soda, cinnamon and 1/4 teaspoon salt into large bowl. Add chopped nuts. Mix egg, cherries and 1 tablespoon melted butter in separate bowl. Pour cherry mixture into dry ingredients. Let stand without mixing for 5 minutes. Mix together. Pour into lightly greased 8 x 8-inch pan. Bake for 45 minutes at 350 degrees. Combine cornstarch, 1/2 teaspoon salt, 1 cup sugar and 1 tablespoon butter. Cook on medium heat, stirring constantly until thickened. Serve in squares topped with whipped cream and sauce.

LaDena Cotten, Treas.
Gamma Delta No. 2302
Lincoln, Nebraska

PEACH CRISP

1 c. (firmly packed) brown sugar
1/2 c. flour

1/2 tsp. each cinnamon and nutmeg
1/4 c. margarine, softened
5 or 6 ripe peaches, sliced
1/4 c. sugar
1 tbsp. lemon juice

Mix brown sugar, flour, spices and margarine until coarse and crumbly. Slice peaches into 8 x 8-inch baking dish. Sprinkle with sugar and lemon juice. Spread topping over peaches. Bake at 375 degrees for 30 minutes, until lightly browned. Serve with whipped cream.

Emily Knight
Gamma Delta No. 2302
Lincoln, Nebraska

PEACH DUMPLINGS

3 c. fresh sliced peaches
2 c. water
1 c. sugar
2 tbsp. lemon juice
1 c. pancake mix
1/4 c. (firmly packed) brown sugar
1/4 tsp. ground nutmeg
1/2 c. milk
2 tbsp. melted margarine

Combine peaches, water, sugar and lemon juice in 3-quart saucepan. Bring to a boil. Combine pancake mix, brown sugar, nutmeg, milk and margarine; stir lightly. Drop batter from tablespoon into boiling peach mixture. Reduce heat; cover saucepan. Cook for 15 minutes without lifting cover. Serve warm with ice cream.

Mary Frances Ledbetter
Beta Pi No. 2225
Benton, Arkansas

PEACHES IN LEMON SAUCE

1 1-lb. 4-oz. can sliced peaches in syrup
1 egg
2 tbsp. lemonade concentrate
1 tbsp. sugar
Dash of salt
1 3-oz. package cream cheese

Drain peaches; reserve 1/2 cup syrup. Spoon peaches into 6 dessert dishes. Beat egg; add undiluted lemonade concentrate, peach syrup, sugar and salt. Beat well. Cook over low heat, stirring constantly, until thick and smooth. Add cream cheese. Beat with rotary beater until smooth. Spoon liquid cheese mixture over peaches. Serve with crisp cookies.

Bernadette Irwin, Ed. Dir.
Alpha Tau No. 4340
York, Pennsylvania

SHERRIED PEARS

1 can pear or peach halves
1 tbsp. butter
2 tbsp. brown sugar
1/2 c. sherry or other sparkling wine
Nutmeg to taste

Drain pears; reserve 1/4 cup juice. Melt butter over low heat; stir in brown sugar. Add sherry and reserved juice. Add pears; sprinkle with nutmeg. Simmer for 5 to 10 minutes or until pears are warmed through. Serve warm with ice cream. May be garnished with prune or cherry in each pear half.

Maisie Maclean, Corr. Sec.
Alpha Tau
Proserpine, Queensland, Australia

WALNUT-CHOCOLATE-PEAR CREAM

1 6-oz. package semisweet chocolate
    morsels
1/2 c. light corn syrup
1 c. coarsely chopped walnuts
1 c. whipping cream
1/2 c. sour cream
2 tsp. vanilla
3 c. drained canned pears, cut into lg. pieces

Melt chocolate morsels and corn syrup together in top of double boiler. Stir in chopped walnuts. Set aside to cool slightly. Whip cream stiff; fold in sour cream and vanilla. Mix in cooled chocolate-walnut mixture and pears. Chill for several hours before serving. Spoon into individual dessert dishes; decorate with toasted walnut halves. Yield: 8-10 servings.

Photograph for this recipe on page 51.

PINEAPPLE AND CRANBERRY DESSERT

1 c. ground cranberries
1 c. chopped apples
1 c. sugar
1 c. crushed pineapple, drained
1/4 c. soft butter
Powdered sugar
2 eggs
1 lb. vanilla wafers, crushed
1 pt. prepared Dream Whip or whipped
    cream

Combine first 4 ingredients. Let stand. Cream butter and 1 1/2 cups powdered sugar. Add unbeaten eggs; beat with mixer or egg beater until creamy. Layer crushed wafers into 9 x 13-inch pan, reserving some for topping. Pour butter mixture over crumbs. Pour cranberry mixture over butter mixture. Whip Dream Whip with 2 tablespoons powdered sugar. Cover cranberry mixture with Dream Whip. Sprinkle remaining crumbs on top. Refrigerate for several hours.

Janice Hespen, Nebraska State Ed. Dir.
Beta Upsilon No. 1831
Fremont, Nebraska

RHUBARB TORTE

2 1/4 c. flour
2 c. plus 2 tbsp. sugar
1 c. butter
6 egg yolks
1 c. half and half
1/2 tsp. salt
6 c. diced rhubarb

Combine 2 cups flour, 2 tablespoons sugar with butter. Mix well. Place in 9 x 13-inch pan. Bake at 350 degrees for 15 minutes. Beat egg yolks together. Add 2 cups sugar, 1/4 cup flour, half and half and salt all at once. Add rhubarb. Pour over baked crust. Bake at 350 degrees about 50 minutes, until custard is set.

Arlene Givens
Gamma Omicron No. 1595
Omaha, Nebraska

STRAWBERRY FLUFF DESSERT

2 env. Dream Whip
3 bananas, sliced thin
1 diced sweet apple
1 c. chopped pecans
1 lg. package marshmallows
1 lg. package frozen sweetened
   strawberries, separated

Prepare Dream Whip according to package directions, using a little less milk. Whip very stiff. Fold in bananas, apple and pecans. Place in serving dish. Chill to serve. Separate marshmallows. Add with frozen strawberries to banana mixture. Drop in; do not blend.

Ruth Gilger, Historian
Gamma Chi No. 834
Comanche, Oklahoma

STRAWBERRIES ROMANOFF

6 tbsp. butter
2 tbsp. sugar
1 qt. strawberries, sliced
6 tbsp. kirsch
Juice and grated rind of 1 orange
Juice and grated rind of 1 lemon
6 tbsp. brandy
Vanilla ice cream

Melt butter and sugar until sugar dissolves. Add strawberries, kirsch and juice of orange and lemon, stirring constantly. Add rind to mixture; stir constantly over low heat. Add brandy; ignite. Pour over generous servings of vanilla ice cream.

Ginny French
Beta Eta No. 3696
Fairfield, Illinois

STRAWBERRY SHORTCAKE

2 c. sifted flour
3 tsp. baking powder
1/2 tsp. salt
1/3 c. (scant) shortening
3/4 c. milk
Butter
Strawberries, sweetened to taste

Sift flour with baking powder and salt. Blend shortening into dry ingredients. Stir in milk to form soft dough. Turn onto floured board. Pat into one large layer on baking sheet. Bake for 15 to 18 minutes in 425-degree oven. Split into 2 layers carefully; butter each layer. Place strawberries between layers and on top of shortcake. Serve warm with thick cream or cover with lightly whipped, unsweetened cream. Garnish with whole strawberries.

Winifred Gilbert, Pres.
Gamma Omega No. 4408
Kingman, Kansas

STRAWBERRY SHORTCAKE BOWL

2 pt. fresh strawberries, sliced
Sugar
1 1/2 tsp. ground cinnamon
1/4 c. butter or margarine, melted
1 can refrigerated flaky biscuits
1/2 c. chopped pecans
1 pt. vanilla ice cream

Sweeten strawberries to taste; chill about 30 minutes. Combine 1/4 cup sugar and cinnamon; set aside. Brush baking sheet with melted butter. Separate each biscuit into 2 thinner biscuits by pulling apart between layers. Brush both sides of each biscuit lightly with butter. Dip both sides in sugar-cinnamon mixture. Place on baking sheet.

Leave 1 inch between biscuits. Sprinkle chopped pecans over biscuits; press pecans into biscuit tops. Bake in 400-degree oven for 10 to 12 minutes or until biscuits are done. Line large serving bowl with about 15 biscuits. Spoon half the strawberries over biscuits. Spoon ice cream into bowl; spoon remaining strawberries over ice cream. Top with remaining biscuits. Serve immediately. Yield: 10 servings.

Photograph for this recipe on opposite page.

MICROWAVE SPICY FRUIT COMPOTE

2 med. apples, peeled and cut into
    eighths
1 No. 1 can pears, cut into eighths
1/2 c. whole cranberry sauce
1/4 tsp. cinnamon
1/4 tsp. cloves
1/4 tsp. allspice
1 tbsp. pear syrup

Layer apples and pears in 1 quart casserole. Combine whole cranberry sauce with spices and syrup. Spoon over fruit. Cook, uncovered, in microwave oven on High for 9 minutes or until apples are tender. Serve warm or chilled. Yield: 6-8 servings.

Thelma Belcher
Contact Chm., W. and M. Chm.
Alpha Psi No. 1883
Port Orford, Oregon

EASY DESSERT

1 No. 2 can crushed pineapple
1 can apple pie filling
1 box yellow cake mix
2 sticks margarine
1 c. coconut

Combine pineapple and pie filling. Pour in bottom of large oblong cake pan. Spread dry cake mix over fruit. Place margarine on top, one stick on each end. Place in 350-degree oven to melt margarine completely. Spread over top of cake mix. Bake 30 minutes longer. Spread coconut on top. Bake 20

more minutes. Serve plain or with whipped cream.

LaDonna Boettcher
Alpha Theta No. 3879
Mankato, Minnesota

FRUIT PUDDING

1 c. flour
1/2 c. sugar
1 tsp. soda
Dash of salt
1 egg, well beaten
1 lg. can fruit cocktail, thoroughly
    drained
1/2 c. (firmly packed) brown sugar
1/2 c. broken pecans
Whipped cream

Blend flour, sugar, soda and salt. Add egg and fruit cocktail. Mix well. Pour into lightly greased 8 x 12-inch pan. Sprinkle with brown sugar and pecans. Bake in 250-degree oven for 1 hour and 20 minutes. Cut into squares; top with whipped cream. Serve warm or cold.

Connie Jannasch, Pres.
Lambda Xi No. 2709
San Antonio, Texas

FRUIT PIZZA

1 pkg. Pillsbury sugar cookie roll
1 8-oz. package cream cheese
1/2 c. sugar
1 tsp. vanilla
Bananas
1 can mandarin oranges, well drained
1 can chunky fruit, well drained
Orange marmalade

Grease pizza pan well. Slice cookie roll. Place slices close in pan to cover, making crust. Bake according to directions. Cool. Mix cream cheese, sugar and vanilla until smooth; spread over crust. Slice bananas around outer rim of pizza. Arrange mandarin oranges inside banana rim. Place chunky fruit in center. Thin orange marmalade with few drops of water. Pour glaze over fruit. Garnish with strawberries, if desired. Chill, but not overnight.

Lois Wade, Pres.
Alpha Kappa No. 1005
Midwest City, Oklahoma

Cookies

The warm, satisfying aroma of cookies baking in the oven probably reminds many people of those unbearable, endless waiting days just before Christmas when the kitchen is in continuous use, and the house bustles constantly. To others, cookies might bring memories of summer vacation hours spent in grandmother's kitchen, with her standing over a batch of cookie dough, rolling, shaping and cutting. Because cookie recipes are countless in number, they provide families everywhere with a steady source of something enjoyable to accomplish together. Besides, homemade cookies are typically far more delicious than the "store-bought" variety.

Cookies include a great diversity of shapes, flavors, textures, and sizes. Bite-sized buttery crisps are as much all-time favorites as large, chewy chocolate mounds or nut-filled, sugary fruit bars. Moreover, both the cookies and the dough can often be frozen or refrigerated for later use — another point in favor of making cookies a regular part of menu planning. There is also no better gift to send through the mail than cookies. They must be packaged carefully, of course, so they will arrive all in one piece. The cookies should be wrapped in pairs with their backs together. The entire package of cookies should then be insulated with popcorn or marshmallows to serve as shock absorbers. When the outer box is wrapped and tied, it should be marked, "FRAGILE, Handle With Care."

The family's cookies should be stored with equal care, to preserve their freshness and flavor. Remember, if a large batch of cookies is too much for present use, most recipes can be frozen before or after baking, or even kept in the refrigerator, for later enjoyment. In the cupboard, cookies should be stored in a container with a tightly fitting cover; soft cookies may be kept in a covered plastic container. Crunchy cookies can be recrisped in a 300-degree oven for 3 to 5 minutes. If soft cookies become dry, add an apple or piece of bread to the container.

ESA members have found that their families greatly enjoy and even benefit from the time they spend baking cookies. It is perfect for fathers and sons learning to try their hand in the kitchen, and for sisters and brothers of all ages, who can then share the results with their friends. And what could be more instantly rewarding than tasting freshly baked cookies prepared by your own hand?

OLD-FASHIONED PEANUT BARS

1/2 c. butter, softened
1 c. (firmly packed) light brown sugar
1 egg
1 tsp. vanilla extract
1 tsp. rum extract
1 c. crushed graham crackers
1 c. flour
2 tsp. baking powder
1/2 tsp. salt
1 c. milk
1 c. chopped peanuts
1/2 c. seedless raisins
Peanut Velvet Frosting

Beat butter until light and fluffy. Beat in brown sugar. Add egg and vanilla and rum extracts. Fold in crushed graham crackers. Sift together flour, baking powder and salt. Blend into creamed mixture alternately with milk. Stir in peanuts and raisins. Pour batter into greased 9 x 13-inch baking pan. Bake in preheated 350-degree oven 35 to 40 minutes or until cake tester comes out clean. Cool. Frost with Peanut Velvet Frosting. Cut into 24 bars, approximately 2 x 2 1/4 inches.

Peanut Velvet Frosting

1/4 c. butter, softened
2 c. sifted confectioners' sugar
3 tbsp. milk
1 tsp. vanilla extract
Dash of salt
1/2 c. peanut butter

Heat butter in small saucepan over low heat, stirring occasionally until butter turns light amber. Beat in sugar, milk, vanilla and salt. Stir in peanut butter.

Photograph for this recipe on page 1.

BLARNEY STONES

4 eggs, separated
1 c. lukewarm water
2 c. sugar
2 c. flour
2 tsp. baking powder
1/2 tsp. salt
1 tsp. vanilla
Desired frosting
Chopped peanuts

Mix egg yolks and water together. Combine dry ingredients; add to egg mixture. Beat egg whites until stiff peaks form. Fold into first mixture. Add vanilla. Place in 9 x 13-inch greased and floured pan. Bake for 35 minutes or until brown in 350-degree oven. Cool. Remove from pan. Cut into squares. Frost on all sides; roll in chopped peanuts.

Nancy Dunn, Treas.
Gamma Lambda No. 1956
Westerville, Ohio

APPLESAUCE BROWNIES

1/2 c. shortening
2 sq. unsweetened chocolate
1 c. sugar
2 eggs, well beaten
1/2 c. slightly sweetened applesauce
1 tsp. vanilla
1 c. flour
1/2 tsp. baking powder
1/4 tsp. soda
1/2 tsp. salt
1/2 c. chopped nuts

Melt shortening with chocolate. Blend in sugar. Add eggs and applesauce. Add vanilla. Sift together flour, baking powder, soda and salt; add nuts. Stir in applesauce mixture. Place in greased 9 x 13-inch pan. Bake at 350 degrees for 40 minutes.

Supreme Frosting

6 tbsp. margarine
6 tbsp. milk
1 1/3 c. sugar
1/2 c. chocolate chips

Combine margarine, milk and sugar. Boil for 1 minute. Remove from heat. Add chocolate chips. Beat until of spreading consistency. Frost brownies with frosting.

Wess Pravecek, Rec. Sec.
Alpha Phi No. 1438
Colome, South Dakota

APRICOT-NUT BARS

4 eggs, well beaten
2 1/2 c. (firmly packed) light brown sugar
1 tall can evaporated milk
2 tbsp. lemon juice
2 1/2 c. sifted flour
1 1/2 tsp. soda
1 tsp. cinnamon
1/2 tsp. salt
1 c. chopped dried apricots
1 c. chopped walnuts
1 c. flaked coconut
Confectioners' sugar

Combine beaten eggs, brown sugar, evaporated milk and lemon juice in a large mixing bowl. Sift together flour, soda, cinnamon and salt. Add all at once to egg mixture. Stir just until blended. Fold in apricots, walnuts and coconut. Do not overmix. Divide batter; smooth evenly in 2 well-greased jelly roll pans. Bake in preheated 350-degree oven for 20 minutes. Allow to cool in pans. Sprinkle with light topping of confectioners' sugar. Cut into bars. Store in an airtight cookie jar. Yield: 5 dozen bars.

Photograph for this recipe above.

BOURBON BROWNIES

1   15-oz. box brownie mix
2 eggs, beaten
1/3 c. plus 3 tbsp. bourbon
1/2 c. plus 2 tbsp. soft butter
2 c. powdered sugar
16 oz. semisweet chocolate chips

Prepare brownie mix according to package directions, using 2 eggs and 3 tablespoons water. Spread mixture in bottom of greased 13 x 9-inch pan. Bake as directed. Cool. Brush with 1/3 cup bourbon. Mix 1/2 cup butter with 3 tablespoons bourbon and powdered sugar. Spread over bourbon-brushed brownies. Melt chocolate chips with 2 tablespoons butter. Cool. Spread over fondant layer. Slice into finger-sized bars while chocolate topping is warm. Refrigerate or freeze to store.

Gloria Davis, Ed. Dir.
Alpha Delta No. 1138
Cadiz, Kentucky

BROWNIES SUPREME

1 stick margarine
1 c. sugar
4 eggs
1   16-oz can Hershey's chocolate syrup
1 c. flour
1/2 c. chopped nuts (opt.)
Frosting

Combine margarine and sugar; cream well. Add eggs; beat well. Add chocolate syrup, flour and nuts. Beat well. Pour into jelly roll pan. Bake 25 minutes at 350 degrees. Cool. Top with Frosting.

Frosting

6 tbsp. margarine
6 tbsp. milk
1 1/3 c. sugar
1/2 c. chocolate chips

Combine margarine, milk and sugar. Bring to a boil. Boil just 1 minute. Remove from heat. Add chocolate chips. Beat until spreading consistency.

Janet Addington, Sec.
Gamma Omicron No. 3837
Canoga Park, California

FROSTED BROWNIES

1/2 c. margarine
1 c. sugar
2 eggs
1 tsp. vanilla
3/4 c. flour
1/3 c. cocoa
1/2 tsp. baking powder
1/4 tsp. salt
1/2 c. chopped nuts
Miniature marshmallows
Chocolate Frosting

Cream margarine and sugar. Add eggs and vanilla; mix well. Add flour, cocoa, baking powder and salt; mix well. Fold in nuts. Pour into greased 7 x 11-inch pan. Bake in 350-degree oven for 25 to 30 minutes. Cover with miniature marshmallows. Return to oven for 2 to 3 minutes. Cool. Frost with Chocolate Frosting; cut in squares.

Chocolate Frosting

1/4 c. margarine
1/4 c. cocoa
Dash of salt
1 tsp. vanilla
2 c. powdered sugar
2 tbsp. milk

Cream margarine; blend in cocoa, salt and vanilla. Add powdered sugar alternately with milk, beating until light and fluffy.

Judy Shaffer, Indiana State Pres.
Beta Upsilon No. 748
Lebanon, Indiana

GRAMMY'S BASIC BROWNIES

2/3 c. flour
1/2 tsp. baking powder
1/4 tsp. salt
1/2 c. butter or shortening
2 sq. unsweetened chocolate
1 c. sugar
2 eggs, well beaten
1/2 c. chopped walnuts
1 tsp. vanilla

Sift flour once. Add baking powder and salt; sift again. Melt butter and chocolate over low heat. Add sugar gradually to eggs, beating thoroughly. Add chocolate mixture; blend. Add flour mixture; mix well. Stir in walnuts and vanilla. Pour in greased 8 x 8 x 2-inch pan. Bake at 350 degrees for 25 minutes. Yield: 2 dozen.

Mary R. Edwards, Corr. Sec.
Alpha Gamma No. 4426
Bluemont, Virginia

CONGO BARS

2 sticks margarine, melted
1 box dark brown sugar
2 eggs
2 1/2 c. flour
2 1/2 tsp. baking powder
Pinch of salt
3/4 c. chopped nuts
3/4 c. chocolate chips

Combine margarine and brown sugar; blend. Add eggs; beat well. Add flour, baking powder and salt. Mix well. Add nuts and chocolate chips. Spread mixture on ungreased cookie sheet with rim. Bake at 350 degrees for 20 to 25 minutes. Do not overbake. Cut into bars. Yield: 2-3 dozen.

Madith Johnson, V.P.
Beta Eta No. 3431
St. Charles, Missouri

CHOCOLATE-TOPPED OATMEAL BARS

1/2 c. plus 2 tbsp. butter
1/2 c. margarine
1/2 c. (firmly packed) brown sugar
1/2 c. sugar
2 egg yolks
1 c. sifted flour
1 c. quick-cooking oatmeal
1 6-oz. package chocolate chips
1/2 c. chopped pecans or walnuts

Cream together 1/2 c. butter, margarine and sugars. Beat in egg yolks. Combine flour and oatmeal. Add to batter; mix well. Spread in greased and floured 13 x 9-inch pan. Bake at 350 degrees for 25 minutes. Cool. Melt chocolate chips with 2 tablespoons butter. Spread over cooled cookie layer. Sprinkle with pecans. Cut into 1 1/2-inch squares. Yield: 48 cookies.

Debbie Van Dyke
Delta Tau No. 3684
Creve Coeur, Missouri

DOUBLE CHIP SQUARES

1 pkg. white cake mix
1/4 c. sugar
1/4 c. (firmly packed) brown sugar
2 eggs
2 tbsp. milk
1/2 tsp. vanilla
1/2 c. butterscotch chips
3 tbsp. oil
1 c. coconut (opt.)
1 c. chopped nuts (opt.)
1 c. semisweet chocolate chips

Combine all ingredients except chocolate chips in mixer bowl. Blend together at low speed. Spread into greased and floured rimmed cookie sheet. Sprinkle chocolate chips on top. Bake in 350-degree oven about 25 minutes. Cut into squares immediately. Cool. Serve.

Kathleen Boschult, Rec. Sec.
Gamma Omicron No. 1595
Omaha, Nebraska

FRUIT BARS

1 c. margarine
1 3/4 c. sugar
4 eggs
1 tsp. vanilla
1/4 tsp. butter flavoring
1 1/2 tsp. baking powder
3 c. flour
1 can fruit pie filling
Powdered sugar

Cream margarine and sugar together. Add eggs, one at a time, beating well after each addition. Blend in flavorings. Sift dry ingredients; add to egg mixture, mixing well. Spread in 10 x 15-inch cake pan. Spoon fruit pie filling over dough in 16 or more dollops.

Bake at 350 degrees for 30 minutes or more. Remove from oven. Sift powdered sugar lightly over top. Cut into bars. Freezes well.

Janelle Teply
Alpha Lambda No. 618
Vermillion, South Dakota

HOLIDAY FRUIT BARS

1 lb. dates, cut into small pieces
1 c. chopped pecans
1/2 lb. shredded coconut
1 large can sweetened condensed milk
1 tsp. vanilla

Blend all ingredients to form stiff dough. Pack firmly into greased and floured waxed paper-lined 8 x 8-inch pan. Bake in preheated 375-degree oven for 25 minutes or until golden brown. Cool. Slice. Bars keep for several weeks if stored in air-tight container. Yield: 20 bars.

Shelaine Lindley, Ed. Dir.
Beta Sigma No. 2853
Florence, Alabama

FRESH ORANGE CHEWIES

2 med. oranges
1/2 c. (firmly packed) brown sugar
2 eggs
1 1/3 c. all-purpose flour
3/4 tsp. baking powder
1/2 tsp. salt
2/3 c. chopped walnuts
1 pkg. white Jiffy frosting mix

Grate oranges to obtain 1 tablespoon orange rind; set aside. Peel, section and chop oranges; set aside. Beat brown sugar and eggs at high speed for 3 minutes. Fold in flour baking powder, salt, walnuts, oranges and rind. Spread batter in greased and floured 9 x 13-inch pan. Bake in 350-degree oven for 30 to 35 minutes. Prepare frosting mix according to package directions. Frost; cut into bars.

Nancy Raab, Sec.
Alpha Omega No. 886
Gahanna, Ohio

LEMON BARS

2 1/4 c. flour
1 c. margarine
1 c. powdered sugar
1/4 tsp. salt
4 eggs, slightly beaten
2 c. sugar
4 tbsp. lemon juice

Mix 2 cups flour, margarine, powdered sugar and salt. Pat into two 9 x 9-inch pans or 1 large cookie sheet with rim. Bake 10 minutes at 350 degrees. Mix remaining ingredients. Pour over baked crusts; spread evenly. Bake at 325 degrees for 25 minutes or until set.

Anita Witt, Ed. Dir.
Alpha Alpha No. 4347
Bethany, Oklahoma

PECAN PIE BARS

1 pkg. yellow cake mix
1/2 c. melted margarine or butter
4 eggs
1/2 c. (firmly packed) brown sugar
1 1/2 c. dark corn syrup
1 tsp. vanilla
1 c. pecan halves

Measure 2/3 cup yellow cake mix; reserve for topping. Combine remaining cake mix with margarine and 1 egg; mix well. Press into bottom of greased 9 x 13-inch baking pan. Bake in preheated 350-degree oven for 15 minutes. Combine remaining ingredients. Pour over baked crust. Bake 30 minutes longer. Cool. Cut into bars.

Leatrice Sexton, Ed. Dir.
Alpha Omicron No. 3217
Cambridge, Nebraska

PUMPKIN SQUARES

1 c. flour
1/2 c. quick-cooking oats
1 c. (firmly packed) brown sugar
1/2 c. plus 2 tbsp. margarine
2 c. cooked pumpkin
1 13 1/2-oz. can evaporated milk
2 eggs
3/4 c. sugar
1/2 tsp. salt
1 tsp. cinnamon
1/2 tsp. ginger
1/4 tsp. cloves
1/2 c. chopped pecans

Combine flour, oats, 1/2 cup brown sugar and 1/2 cup margarine. Mix until crumbly. Press into 13 x 9 x 2-inch pan. Bake at 350 degrees for 15 minutes. Combine pumpkin, milk, eggs, sugar, salt and spices. Beat well. Pour over crust. Bake at 350 degrees for 20 minutes. Combine pecans, 1/2 cup brown sugar and 2 tablespoons margarine. Sprinkle over pumpkin mixture. Return to oven for 15 to 20 minutes or until set. Yield: 2 dozen.

Delma Paul, Pres.
Zeta Alpha No. 1891
Beatrice, Nebraska
Elaine Broz, Nebraska State 2nd V.P.
Beta Upsilon No. 1831
Fremont, Nebraska

NUT BARS

1/2 tsp. salt
1/2 tsp. baking powder
1/2 tsp. soda
1 box brown sugar
2 tsp. vanilla
3 c. chopped nuts
3 eggs
1 1/2 c. sifted flour
Powdered sugar

Grease 11 x 13-inch baking pan. Combine all ingredients except powdered sugar in order given in large mixing bowl. Mix together. Place in prepared baking pan. Bake in preheated 350-degree oven for 20 minutes or until done. Cool. Sprinkle powdered sugar on top. Cut into bars.

Diana Flynn, Corr. Sec.
Delta Omega No. 3448
Stockton, California

Recipes on pages 74 and 80.

WALNUT TREASURE BARS

1/2 c. shortening
1 c. (firmly packed) brown sugar
1 egg
1/4 c. milk
1/4 c. sherry
1 2/3 c. sifted all-purpose flour
1 tbsp. instant coffee powder
3/4 tsp. salt
1/2 tsp. baking powder
1/2 tsp. soda
1/2 tsp. cinnamon
1 c. coarsely chopped walnuts
1 c. semisweet chocolate morsels
Icing

Cream together shortening, brown sugar and egg. Add milk and sherry. Batter may look curdled at this point, but will smooth out when flour is added. Resift flour with coffee powder, salt, baking powder, soda and cinnamon. Add to creamed mixture; blend to a smooth batter. Stir in walnuts and semisweet chocolate morsels. Spread in greased 10 x 15-inch pan. Bake at 375 degrees about 20 minutes, until top springs back when touched lightly. Cool in pan. Spread with Icing. Decorate tops of bars with additional walnuts and morsels. Cut in squares.

Icing

2 1/4 c. sifted powdered sugar
1 1/2 tbsp. soft butter
2 tbsp. sherry
1 tbsp. milk
1 tsp. instant coffee powder

Combine all ingredients; beat until smooth.

Photograph for this recipe on page 63.

CHOCOLATE CRINKLE COOKIES

1/2 c. salad oil
4 1-oz. squares unsweetened
    chocolate, melted
2 c. sugar

Recipes on pages 72, 77 and 82.

4 eggs
2 tsp. vanilla
2 c. sifted flour
2 tsp. baking powder
1/2 tsp. salt
1 1/2 c. confectioners' sugar

Mix salad oil, melted chocolate, sugar, eggs and vanilla until well blended. Sift flour once. Measure and sift with baking powder and salt. Stir into shortening mixture. Chill overnight. Grease baking sheets. Drop dough by teaspoonfuls into confectioners' sugar; roll in sugar. Shape into balls. Place balls about 2 inches apart on greased baking sheets. Bake in preheated 350-degree oven about 10 minutes. Remove from baking sheet as soon as taken from oven. Yield: 5 dozen.

Jane Hanekamp, V.P.
Gamma Delta No. 3767
Atlanta, Georgia

DATE PINWHEEL COOKIES

2 1/2 c. chopped dates
1 c. water
1 c. sugar
1 c. chopped nuts
2 c. (firmly packed) brown sugar
1 c. shortening
3 eggs, well beaten
4 c. sifted flour
1/2 tsp. salt
1/2 tsp. soda

Cook dates, water and sugar over low heat until thick. Add chopped nuts. Let cool. Cream brown sugar and shortening. Add eggs; mix well. Sift flour, salt and soda. Add to creamed mixture. Divide dough. Roll 1/4 inch thick. Spread date mixture over each portion of dough. Roll up jelly roll fashion. Chill overnight. Slice. Place on greased cookie sheet. Bake at 325 degrees until lightly browned.

Pauline Lenox, Pres.
Alpha Psi No. 1883
Port Orford, Oregon

HOLIDAY SUGAR COOKIES

1 c. butter
1 c. sugar
2 eggs, beaten
1/2 tsp. vanilla
3 c. flour
1/2 tsp. soda
1/2 tsp. salt
1 tsp. baking powder
1/2 c. sour cream

Cream butter. Add sugar; mix well. Add eggs and vanilla. Sift together flour, soda, salt and baking powder. Add to creamed mixture alternately by thirds with sour cream. Chill dough overnight. Roll about 1/2 inch thick. Cut into desired shapes. Place on greased cookie sheet. Bake in 375-degree oven for 8 minutes. Frost and decorate as desired.

Merle Allred, Treas.
Alpha Alpha No. 1657
Salt Lake City, Utah

DOUBLE-SWIRL WALNUT COOKIES

3/4 c. shortening
1 1/4 c. sugar
2 eggs
1 tsp. vanilla
2 1/2 c. sifted all-purpose flour
1 tsp. baking powder
1 tsp. salt
2   1-oz. squares unsweetened chocolate, melted
2 tbsp. milk
2/3 c. finely chopped walnuts

Beat shortening, sugar, eggs and vanilla together until fluffy. Resift flour with baking powder and salt. Blend into creamed mixture. Divide dough in halves. Blend chocolate, milk and 1/3 cup walnuts into one portion. Blend remaining 1/3 cup walnuts into remaining light dough. Wrap each in waxed paper. Chill thoroughly. Roll light dough on lightly floured board to 8 x 12-inch rectangle. Cover with a sheet of waxed paper; top with a baking sheet. Invert board, dough and baking sheet. Remove board; refrigerate dough and baking sheet. Roll chocolate dough to 8 x 12-inch rectangle. Remove light dough from refrigerator. Place over chocolate dough, with shorter sides matching, longer side about 1/4 inch from edge of chocolate. Cut crosswise through center, making two 6-inch sections for easier rolling. Starting from side with chocolate dough showing under light dough, roll the two together to center. Turn over; roll from other side to meet first roll. If dough should start to crack on rolling, allow to stand at room temperature a minute or two to warm up slightly. Cracks may be pinched together. Wrap in waxed paper, plastic wrap or foil. Place in freezer until very firm. Cut in 1/4-inch slices; place on lightly greased baking sheets. Bake at 400 degrees about 8 minutes. Let stand 1 minute. Remove carefully with broad spatula; cool on wire racks. Yield: 40 cookies.

Photograph for this recipe on page 70.

OATMEAL REFRIGERATOR COOKIES

1 c. shortening
1 1/2 c. (firmly packed) brown sugar
2 eggs, well beaten
1 tsp. vanilla
2 1/2 c. flour
1 tsp. soda
1 1/2 c. rolled oats
1 c. raisins, cut fine
1/2 c. chopped nuts

Cream shortening and brown sugar. Add eggs. Add vanilla. Mix flour, soda, oats, raisins and nuts. Add to creamed mixture. Form into rolls. Wrap in waxed paper. Chill in refrigerator. Slice thin. Place on greased cookie sheet. Bake 10 to 12 minutes at 400 degrees. Yield: 4-5 dozen.

Gertrude Kamphaus
Gamma Tau No. 811
Canute, Oklahoma

ORANGE SLICE COOKIES

20 lg. or 40 sm. orange candy slices, cut fine
Flour

1 1/2 c. chopped nuts
3 c. oatmeal
1 1/2 c. coconut
2 c. shortening
1 c. sugar
2 c. (firmly packed) brown sugar
3 eggs
1 1/2 tsp. soda
3 tbsp. water
1/2 tsp. salt

Coat orange slices with flour to keep from sticking together. Mix nuts, oatmeal, coconut and chopped orange slices. Combine shortening and sugars in a large bowl. Cream well. Add eggs, one at a time; beat well. Dissolve soda in water. Add to creamed mixture. Sift together 3 cups flour and salt. Add to creamed mixture. Combine with orange slice mixture; mix well. Divide into 4 parts. Roll in waxed paper; freeze. Slice into 1/4-inch slices. Place on greased cookie sheet. Bake at 325 degrees for about 8 minutes.

Dee Holly, V.P.
Beta Omega No. 4210
Midland, Texas

RUTH'S SUGAR COOKIES

1 c. oil
1 c. butter or margarine
1 c. powdered sugar
1 c. sugar
2 eggs
2 tsp. vanilla
5 c. flour
2 tsp. salt
1 tsp. cream of tartar
1 tsp. soda

Cream oil, butter, sugars, eggs and vanilla. Sift flour. Measure; add salt, cream of tartar and soda. Sift again. Add gradually to creamed mixture; beat well. Chill for several hours. Roll into walnut-sized balls. Roll in additional sugar. Place on cookie sheet. Flatten with glass dipped in sugar. Bake at 350 degrees for 8 to 10 minutes. Colored sugar may be used to roll dough in.

Ruth Hankins, Philanthropic Co-Chm.
Alpha Lambda
Great Falls, Montana

FRUITY GUMDROP COOKIES

2 c. sifted flour
1/2 tsp. salt
2 tsp. baking powder
1/2 tsp. ground cinnamon
1/2 c. shortening
1/2 c. sugar
1 egg, beaten
3/4 c. thick applesauce
1 c. gumdrops, cut in sm. pieces
1 c. raisins

Sift together flour, salt, baking powder and cinnamon. Cream shortening and sugar. Add egg and applesauce; mix well. Add flour mixture; stir until well blended. Stir in gumdrops and raisins. Drop by teaspoonfuls onto lightly greased baking sheet. Bake in 400-degree oven for 10 to 15 minutes, until lightly browned. Transfer to cooling rack. Yield: 4 dozen.

Kathy Mieras
Delta Tau No. 4264
Yakima, Washington

DOUBLE ORANGE COOKIES

2 oranges
2 c. sugar
1 c. mixed butter and shortening
2 eggs
Pinch of salt
1 tsp. soda
1 c. sour milk or buttermilk
5 c. flour
4 tsp. baking powder
1 tsp. butter
1 box confectioners' sugar

Grind 1 orange pulp and peel together. Mix orange, sugar, shortening mixture, eggs and salt. Add soda to sour milk; add to orange mixture. Sift flour and baking powder together. Add to orange mixture. Drop by small teaspoonfuls onto greased cookie sheet. Bake 10 to 13 minutes in 375-degree oven. Let cool. Grind 1 orange pulp and peel. Add butter and confectioners' sugar; blend well. Spread on cookies. Yield: 60 cookies.

Sheryl K. Cooley
Gamma Delta No. 2208
Peru, Indiana

LACE COOKIES

1/2 c. butter or margarine
1/2 c. sugar
1/3 c. sifted all-purpose flour
1/4 tsp. salt
1 c. quick rolled oats, uncooked
2 tbsp. milk

Melt butter in saucepan. Stir in remaining ingredients, mixing well. Drop by 1/2 teaspoonfuls, about 3 inches apart, onto greased and floured cookie sheets. Spread thinly with a spatula. Bake in preheated 375-degree oven for 5 to 7 minutes or until edges are brown. Remove from oven. Let stand 1 minute before removing from cookie sheets. Remove carefully with a wide spatula. Cookies will be very thin and lacy. Cool thoroughly. Yield: 3 1/2 dozen cookies.

Photograph for this recipe above.

CHOCO-NUT CLOUDS

4 egg whites
1/2 tsp. vinegar
1 tsp. vanilla
1/4 tsp. salt
1 c. sugar
1/2 c. chopped chocolate-covered
   peanuts

Place egg whites, vinegar, vanilla and salt in bowl. Beat until soft peaks form. Add sugar very gradually, about 1 tablespoon at a time, beating well after each addition. Continue beating until mixture is glossy and stiff peaks form. Lightly fold in chopped chocolate-covered peanuts. Drop by heaping teaspoonfuls onto paper-lined baking sheets. Bake in 275-degree oven about 30 minutes, or until crisp, dry and lightly browned. Cool a few minutes; remove from paper. May be placed in a preheated oven. Turn off heat and leave cookies in oven overnight. Yield: 5 dozen cookies.

Photograph for this recipe on page 69.

PEANUT LACE ROLL-UPS

1/2 c. sifted flour
1/2 c. sugar
1/4 tsp. salt
1/4 tsp. baking powder
1/4 c. melted butter or margarine
2 tbsp. milk
2 tbsp. dark corn syrup
1/2 tsp. vanilla
1/2 c. finely chopped salted peanuts

Sift together dry ingredients. Add remaining ingredients. Stir until well mixed. Drop by small teaspoonfuls onto greased and floured cookie sheets. Place at least 3 inches apart and no more than 6 cookies to a sheet. Bake 1 sheet at a time in 375-degree oven for 6 to 8 minutes, or until bubbly in center and brown around edge. Remove from oven. Cool about 1 minute on cookie sheet. Remove 1 cookie at a time working very quickly. Roll top side out around a wooden spoon handle or similar implement. Cool on handle until set. Remove to wire rack. Return cookie sheet to oven for about 30 seconds if cookies get too firm to roll up easily. Yield: 2 1/2 dozen cookies.

Photograph for this recipe on page 69.

PEANUT-COCONUT COOKIES

1 1/4 c. sifted flour
1 tsp. baking powder
1 tsp. soda
1/2 tsp. salt
1/2 c. sugar

1/2 c. (firmly packed) brown sugar
1/2 c. butter or margarine, softened
1 egg
1 tsp. vanilla
1 c. chopped peanuts
1 c. flaked coconut

Sift together first 4 ingredients. Stir in sugars. Add butter, egg and vanilla; stir until well mixed. Blend in peanuts and coconut. Drop by teaspoonfuls onto greased cookie sheets. Bake in 350-degree oven for 12 to 15 minutes. Yield: 3 dozen cookies.

Photograph for this recipe on page 69.

PECAN CRISPS

1 c. butter
2 1/2 c. (firmly packed) brown sugar
2 eggs, well beaten
2 1/2 c. sifted flour
1/2 tsp. soda
1/4 tsp. salt
1 c. chopped pecans

Cream butter and brown sugar. Add eggs; mix well. Sift flour, soda and salt together. Add to creamed mixture. Add pecans. Drop from teaspoon onto greased cookie sheet. Bake in 350-degree oven for 15 minutes.

Margaret R. Sandy, Treas.
Alpha Gamma No. 4426
Stephens City, Virginia

PECAN MERINGUES

2 egg whites
1/2 c. (firmly packed) brown sugar
1 c. pecan halves

Beat egg whites. Add brown sugar; beat until stiff. Drop in pecan halves. Spoon onto greased cookie sheet. Bake 30 minutes at 250 degrees. Turn off oven. Let cool in oven for 30 minutes. Remove. Store in airtight container. Will keep for at least 1 week. Do not freeze.

Frances White
North Carolina State Coun. Pres.
Beta Psi No. 3059
Burlington, North Carolina

SOUR CREAM SPICE COOKIES

3 c. flour
1 tsp. soda
1/2 tsp. cloves
1/2 tsp. nutmeg
1 tsp. cinnamon
1/2 tsp. salt
1/3 c. shortening
2 c. (firmly packed) brown sugar
2 eggs, well beaten
1 tsp. vanilla
2/3 c. thick sour cream

Sift flour, soda, spices and salt together 3 times. Cream shortening with sugar until light and fluffy. Add eggs and vanilla; mix well. Add dry ingredients alternately with sour cream in small amounts. Mix well. Drop from teaspoon onto greased baking sheet. Bake in 350-degree oven for 12 minutes.

Oma Jean Westeman, Rec. Sec.
Delta Kappa No. 1193
Syracuse, Kansas

WALNUT-CRANBERRY COOKIES

3 c. white raisins
1/2 c. bourbon
1/4 c. butter
1/2 c. (firmly packed) brown sugar
1 1/2 c. flour
1 1/2 tsp. soda
1 1/2 tsp. cinnamon
1/2 tsp. nutmeg
1/2 tsp. ground cloves
2 eggs
1 c. chopped cranberries
1 c. chopped walnuts

Soak raisins in bourbon for 1 hour. Cream butter and brown sugar until fluffy and light. Sift flour, soda, cinnamon, nutmeg and cloves together. Beat eggs into butter-sugar mixture. Add flour and spice mixture to butter mixture. Stir in cranberries, walnuts and raisins with liquid. Drop by teaspoonfuls onto buttered baking sheet. Bake at 325 degrees for 15 minutes or until firm. Transfer to rack; cool. Yield: 48 cookies.

Jan Reppentine, Pres.
Alpha Omicron No. 2520
Glendale, Arizona

OLD-FASHIONED WALNUT-SOUR CREAM COOKIES

2/3 c. butter
1 c. sugar
2 eggs
1 tsp. grated lemon rind
1 tsp. grated orange rind
1 tbsp. lemon juice
2 c. sifted all-purpose flour
1 tsp. baking powder
1/2 tsp. soda
Salt to taste
1/2 c. sour cream
3/4 c. chopped walnuts
Walnut halves

Cream butter and sugar together; add eggs, grated lemon rind, orange rind and lemon juice. Continue creaming until light and fluffy. Resift flour with baking powder, soda and salt. Add to creamed mixture alternately with sour cream. Mix well. Stir in chopped walnuts. Drop by tablespoonfuls onto greased cookie sheet. Sprinkle with additional sugar; decorate with walnut halves. Bake at 350 degrees for 15 to 18 minutes. Yield: 2 dozen cookies.

Photograph for this recipe above.

SOUR CREAM CASHEW DROPS

1/2 c. soft butter or margarine
1 egg
1 c. (firmly packed) brown sugar
1/2 c. sour cream
1 1/2 c. chopped salted cashew nuts
1 tsp. vanilla
2 c. flour
1 tsp. baking powder
3/4 tsp. salt

Cream butter, egg and brown sugar until fluffy. Add sour cream, nuts and vanilla. Add remaining ingredients; stir well. Drop by teaspoonfuls onto greased cookie sheet. Bake at 375 degrees for 10 minutes or until done. Cool. Frost with desired creamy white frosting.

Kim Hoover
Gamma Kappa No. 3265
Northglenn, Colorado

WILLIAMSBURG COOKIES

1 egg white
1 c. (firmly packed) light brown sugar
1 tbsp. flour
1 c. chopped nuts

Beat egg white until stiff. Add brown sugar slowly. Add flour and nuts. Drop by 1/2 teaspoonfuls onto greased cookie sheet. Bake at 300 degrees for 20 minutes. Cool. Tap pan and cookies will pop off.

Nancy B. Reece
Past Virginia State Pres.
Alpha Xi No 1610
Norfolk, Virginia

JAM THUMBPRINTS

2/3 c. butter or margarine
1/3 c. sugar
2 eggs, separated
1 tsp. vanilla
1/2 tsp. salt
1 1/2 c. sifted all-purpose flour
3/4 c. finely chopped walnuts
1/3 c. jelly

Cream together butter and sugar until fluffy. Add egg yolks, vanilla and salt; beat well. Add sifted flour gradually, mixing well. Shape dough into about thirty-six 3/4-inch balls. Dip in beaten egg whites. Roll in walnuts. Place 1 inch apart on greased cookie sheet. Press down center of each with thumb. Bake in 350-degree oven for 15 to 17 minutes. Cool slightly. Remove from sheet; cool on rack. Fill centers with jelly just before serving.

Norma Knight, Ed. Chm.
Beta Tau No. 2949
Riverview, Michigan

ICE CREAM KOLACHY

4 c. flour
2 c. soft butter or margarine
2 tbsp. sugar
1 pt. vanilla ice cream, softened
Fruit preserves or desired filling
Powdered sugar

Combine flour, butter and sugar as for pie dough. Add vanilla ice cream; blend well. Separate into 4 parts. Wrap each part in Saran Wrap. Chill in refrigerator overnight. Roll each section, one at a time, on floured board to 1/4-inch thickness. Cut into desired size squares. Fill with small amount of fruit preserves. Fold edges together. Place on ungreased cookie sheet. Bake at 350 degrees for 15 minutes. Can be frozen. Dust with powdered sugar; serve.

Dr. Cardine S. Katowicz, Hon. Mem.
Alpha Upsilon No. 3337
South Milwaukee, Wisconsin

WALNUT BONNETS

1 c. butter
3/4 c. sugar
1 egg
1 tsp. vanilla
2 1/2 c. sifted all-purpose flour
1/2 tsp. salt
1/4 tsp. baking powder
1 c. finely chopped walnuts
3 tbsp. apricot jam
Glaze
Candy sprinkles

Beat butter, sugar, egg and vanilla together until light and fluffy. Resift flour with salt and baking powder. Blend into creamed mixture. Divide dough into thirds. Mix walnuts and jam into one third dough. Fill pastry bag fitted with No. 4 star tube with plain 2/3 dough. Press out rings onto lightly greased baking sheets, about 2 1/4 inches in diameter. Fill centers with rounded teaspoon walnut dough. Bake at 350 degrees about 15

minutes, until edges are lightly browned. Cool on wire racks. Brush centers with Glaze. Sprinkle with candy sprinkles. Yield: 3 dozen small cookies.

Glaze

1 c. sifted powdered sugar
1 tbsp. milk
Few drops of vanilla

Combine powdered sugar with milk and vanilla. Blend well.

Photograph for this recipe on page 70.

PECAN PIE COOKIES

1 c. butter or margarine
1/2 c. sugar
1/2 c. dark corn syrup
2 eggs, separated
2 1/2 c. unsifted all-purpose flour
Pecan Filling

Mix butter and sugar on low speed in large bowl. Add corn syrup and egg yolks; beat until thoroughly blended. Stir in flour gradually. Chill several hours. Beat egg whites slightly. Roll 1 tablespoon dough into ball for each cookie. Brush lightly with egg whites. Place on greased cookie sheet, leaving 2-inch space between each cookie. Bake at 375 degrees for 5 minutes. Remove from oven. Roll 1/2 teaspoon chilled Pecan Filling in ball. Press firmly into center of each cookie. Return to oven. Bake 5 minutes longer or until lightly browned. Cool 5 minutes on cookie sheet. Remove; cool completely on rack. Yield: 50 cookies.

Pecan Filling

1/2 c. powdered sugar
1/4 c. butter or margarine
3 tbsp. dark corn syrup
1/2 c. chopped pecans

Combine powdered sugar, butter and corn syrup in saucepan; stir to blend. Cook over medium heat, stirring occasionally, until it reaches full boil. Remove from heat; stir in pecans. Chill.

Joyce House, Pres.
Epsilon Upsilon No.1626
North Manchester, Indiana

BROWNIE SNACK

1 21 1/2-oz. package brownie mix
1 8-oz. package cream cheese
2 tsp. vanilla
1 c. chopped nuts
1 c. chocolate chips
Confectioners' sugar

Prepare brownie mix according to package directions, using 3 eggs. Divide batter in half. Spread half in greased 9 x 13 x 2-inch pan. Beat cream cheese with vanilla. Spread cream cheese mixture over brownie batter in pan. Top with nuts and chocolate chips. Spread remaining batter over all. Bake at 350 degrees for 45 minutes or until wooden pick inserted in center comes out clean. Sprinkle with confectioners' sugar. Cool. Cut into squares.

Mrs. Roberta G. Evans, Treas.
Beta Omicron No. 2997
Madison, Wisconsin

HELLO DOLLIES

1 stick margarine
2 c. crushed graham crackers
1 c. butterscotch chips
1 c. chocolate chips
1 c. flaked coconut
1 c. chopped walnuts
1 can sweetened condensed milk

Melt margarine 9 x 13-inch pan. Add in layers the next 5 ingredients in order listed; do not stir. Pour sweetened condensed milk on top, without stirring or mixing. Bake at 325 degrees for 30 minutes.

Lilah M. Floyd, Mem at Large
Hays, Kansas

MERINGUE SURPRISE

3 eggs, separated
1 1/2 c. (firmly packed) brown sugar
1/2 c. sugar
1/2 c. shortening
1 tbsp. water
1 tsp. vanilla
2 c. flour

1 tsp. salt
1 tsp. baking powder
1/4 tsp. soda
1 pkg. chocolate chips

Combine egg yolks, 1/2 cup brown sugar with next 8 ingredients. Spread into 13 x 9 x 5-inch pan. Sprinkle with chocolate chips. Press chips into batter. Beat egg whites until stiff; beat in remaining 1 cup brown sugar. Spread over batter. Bake at 350 degrees for 30 minutes. Let cool. Cut into 1-inch squares.

Linda Hurt, Pres.
Beta Gamma No. 3994
Council Bluffs, Iowa

SEVEN-LAYER COOKIES

1 stick margarine
1 c. graham cracker crumbs
1 6-oz. package chocolate chips
1 6-oz. package butterscotch chips
1 can coconut
1 c. chopped nuts
1 can sweetened condensed milk

Melt margarine. Mix with cracker crumbs. Place in oblong baking dish. Layer remaining ingredients in order listed. Bake in preheated 350-degree oven for 30 to 40 minutes. Cool. Cut to serve. Cookies will be cake-like in texture.

Phyllis Fullbright
Alpha Theta No. 3511
Anderson, South Carolina

THREE-LAYERED CHOCOLATE-DATE-MINT BARS

3/4 c. flour
1/2 tsp. baking powder
1/3 c. shortening
1 c. plus 2 tsp. sugar
3 eggs, well beaten
2 sq. melted chocolate
1 c. chopped dates
1/2 c. chopped walnuts
1 tsp. vanilla
1/4 c. butter
1 tsp. cornstarch
3 tbsp. evaporated milk
1 tsp. peppermint extract

2 c. powdered sugar
Few drops of green food coloring
1 pkg. chocolate chips

Sift together flour and baking powder; set aside. Beat shortening, 1 cup sugar and eggs together until light and fluffy. Add melted chocolate; blend well. Add sifted ingredients. Add dates, walnuts and vanilla. Pour into greased 9 x 13-inch baking pan. Bake at 350 degrees for 30 minutes. Let cool. Melt butter. Combine cornstarch and 2 teaspoons sugar. Add melted butter and evaporated milk. Cook until smooth and of fudge-like consistency, stirring constantly. Add peppermint and powdered sugar; blend well. Mixture will be stiff. Add food coloring. Spread over first layer. Melt chocolate chips. Spread over creamed layer. Let partially cool. Cut before bars become too firm.

Marian Thomas, Fremont City Coun. V.P.
Beta Upsilon No. 1831
Fremont, Nebraska

FROSTED RAISIN TOASTIES

2 c. rolled oats
1 c. broken walnuts
1/2 c. shortening
1/2 c. butter or margarine
2 c. (firmly packed) brown sugar
3 eggs, beaten
2 1/2 c. sifted flour
1 tsp. soda
1/2 tsp. salt
1 tsp. cinnamon
1/2 c. milk
1 c. chopped seedless raisins
2 c. powdered sugar
2 tbsp. hot water
Raisins

Spread oats and walnuts on baking sheet; toast lightly in 400-degree oven about 8 minutes. Cream shortening, butter and brown sugar together well; beat in eggs. Sift together flour, soda, salt and cinnamon. Add to creamed mixture alternately with milk; stir in 1 cup chopped raisins, toasted oats and walnuts. Divide into 6 parts; chill dough. Roll each piece into long roll 1 inch in diameter and about 15 inches long. Place 2 strips on each lightly greased baking sheet. Press to flat 4-inch strip with rolling pin. Bake in 375-degree oven for 12 to 15 minutes. Combine powdered sugar with hot water. Brush strips with glaze. Sprinkle with raisins; turn raisins to coat with frosting. Cool. Cut each strip into 12 diagonal slices. Yield: 6 dozen.

Photograph for this recipe below.

FROSTED PEANUT BUTTER CRISPIES

5 c. chocolate-flavored crisp rice
  cereal
2 tbsp. butter or margarine
1/3 c. peanut butter
1/4 lb. marshmallows
5 1-oz. milk chocolate bars

Pour cereal into large bowl. Melt butter, peanut butter and marshmallows in top of double boiler over boiling water. Stir until well blended. Pour peanut butter mixture over cereal. Stir with spoon or mix with greased hands until cereal is evenly coated. Pack firmly into greased 9-inch square pan. Lay chocolate bars over top in single layer. Place in moderate oven about 2 minutes until chocolate is melted. Remove from oven. Spread to form frosting. Cool at room temperature or in refrigerator until chocolate is set. Cut into squares. Yield: 3 dozen cookies.

Photograph for this recipe on page 69.

PEANUT BRITTLE CUPS

1/4 c. butter or margarine
1/4 c. crushed peanut brittle
12 maraschino cherries, quartered
1 1/4 c. sifted flour
3/4 c. sugar
2 tsp. baking powder
1/2 tsp. salt
1/4 c. peanut oil
1/2 c. water
2 eggs, separated
1/2 tsp. vanilla
1/4 tsp. cream of tartar
1/2 c. finely crushed peanut brittle

Measure about 1/4 teaspoon butter into each cup of tiny cupcake pans. Place pans in oven for a few seconds to melt butter. Remove from oven. Place in each cup 1/4 teaspoon crushed peanut brittle and 1/4 cherry. Sift together flour, sugar, baking powder and salt. Make a well in center of dry ingredients. Add oil, water, egg yolks and vanilla. Beat with spoon until smooth. Beat egg whites with cream of tartar until stiff and glossy.

Fold into batter. Fold in finely crushed peanut brittle. Spoon into prepared pans. Bake in 325-degree oven about 18 to 20 minutes, or until delicately browned. Remove from pans at once by loosening edges with sharp knife. Invert pan quickly over wire rack. Yield: 4 dozen cookies.

Photograph for this recipe on page 69.

APRICOT-ORANGE BALLS

2 tbsp. orange juice
1 1/2 c. dried ground apricots
2 c. shredded coconut
2/3 c. sweetened condensed milk
Powdered sugar

Mix first 4 ingredients together with enough powdered sugar to hold mixture together. Work with hands. Shape mixture into small balls. Roll in additional powdered sugar.

Jaxine Johnson, Awards Chm.
Kappa Theta No. 4343
Gainesville, Texas

BOURBON BALLS

48 vanilla wafers, crushed fine
2 c. sifted powdered sugar
1/2 tsp. salt
1 c. chopped pecans
3 tbsp. cocoa
1 1/2 tbsp. light corn syrup
3 oz. bourbon

Mix first 5 ingredients together. Combine corn syrup and bourbon. Add to dry ingredients. Form into balls. Roll in additional powdered sugar.

Cheryl Knight, V.P.
Alpha Kappa No. 4604
Savannah, Georgia

CHERRY DELIGHTS

1/2 c. butter
1 1/2 c. powdered sugar
1 tsp. orange juice
1 1/2 c. coconut
1/2 c. chopped nuts

40 cherries, drained
1/2 c. graham cracker crumbs

Cream butter and sugar until creamy. Add orange juice and coconut, mixing well. Add chopped nuts. Mix until mixture is blended completely. Roll each cherry in small amount of mixture, forming round ball with cherry in center. Roll balls in cracker crumbs. Refrigerate overnight. May be stored for several days. Yield: 40 servings.

Jan Scott
Alpha Theta No. 3511
Anderson, South Carolina

BABY RUTH BARS

2 c. sugar
1 c. crunchy peanut butter
1 1/2 c. light corn syrup
7 c. corn flakes
1 c. salted Spanish peanuts
4 tbsp. peanut butter
3 tbsp. butter
1 c. milk chocolate chips

Mix sugar, crunchy peanut butter and corn syrup in saucepan over low heat. Bring to a boil; cook for 1 minute, stirring constantly. Remove from heat. Add corn flakes and peanuts. Pat into well buttered 9 x 13-inch pan. Mix peanut butter, butter and chocolate chips. Melt over low heat until blends well. Spread over peanut mixture; cut into bars while warm.

Myrtle Baumgartner, Pres.
Theta Phi No. 2895
Oakland, California

CHOCOLATE MOUNTAIN BAR COOKIES

1/2 c. butter
1/2 c. cocoa
2 c. sugar
1/2 c. milk
1/4 tsp. salt
3 c. oatmeal
1/2 c. peanut butter
1 tsp. vanilla

Bring butter, cocoa, sugar, milk and salt to a boil. Boil together for 1 minute, stirring constantly. Remove from heat. Add remaining ingredients; stir until thick. Pour into buttered 9-inch pan. Cool. Cut into squares.

Lorraine Thornberry, Sec.
Alpha Epsilon No. 414
Ridgefield, Washington

CHOCOLATE SCOTCHEROOS

1 c. sugar
1 c. light corn syrup
1 c. peanut butter
6 c. Rice Krispies
1 6-oz. package semisweet chocolate chips
1 6-oz. package butterscotch morsels

Bring sugar and light corn syrup to a boil in 3-quart saucepan. Remove from heat. Blend in peanut butter and Rice Krispies. Press into buttered 13 x 9-inch pan. Melt chocolate chips and butterscotch morsels over hot, not boiling, water. Spread over top. Chill for 5 minutes or until top is firm. Cut into squares.

Donna Sullivan, W and M Chm.
Beta Eta No. 3696
Fairfield, Illinois

GRANDMOTHER'S OATMEAL COOKIES

2 c. sugar
1 stick butter or margarine
1/2 c. milk
3 c. quick-cooking oats
3/4 c. crunchy peanut butter

Bring sugar, butter and milk to a rolling boil. Boil for 1 1/2 minutes, stirring constantly. Pour over oats and peanut butter in large bowl. Stir until well mixed. Drop by teaspoonfuls onto waxed paper. Let stand for several hours.

Sandra Davis, Pres.
Beta Pi No. 2076
Pinellas Park, Florida

GERMAN WALNUT CAKES

1 1/4 c. sifted all-purpose flour
1/3 c. sugar
1/2 c. butter
2 tbsp. milk
1/2 tsp. vanilla
1/2 c. chopped walnuts
1 to 1 1/2 c. walnut halves and lg. pieces
Glaze
4 oz. milk chocolate or semisweet
    chocolate

Combine flour and sugar. Cut in butter until particles are very fine. Sprinkle milk and vanilla over mixture. Mix to a stiff dough. Mix in chopped walnuts. Roll 1/4 inch thick on lightly floured board; cut into rounds. Place on ungreased baking sheet. Cover each cookie with walnut halves, pressing lightly into dough. Bake at 350 degrees about 15 minutes, until edges are very lightly browned. Remove to wire rack; set on baking sheet. Drizzle tops with hot Glaze. Cool. Melt chocolate over warm, not hot water. Spread bottom of each cookie with chocolate; place on waxed paper until chocolate is set. Yield: 1 to 3 1/2 dozen cookies.

Glaze

1/3 c. (firmly packed) brown sugar
1/3 c. light corn syrup

Combine brown sugar and corn syrup in small saucepan. Stir over moderate heat until sugar is dissolved. Boil 1 minute.

Photograph for this recipe on page 70.

SNAPPY TURTLE COOKIES

1 1/2 c. flour
1/4 tsp. soda
1/4 tsp. salt
1/2 c. butter
1/2 c. (firmly packed) brown sugar
2 eggs
1/4 tsp. vanilla
Pecans

Sift first 3 ingredients well. Cream butter. Add sugar; cream well. Add 1 egg plus 1 egg yolk and vanilla; beat well. Add dry ingredients; mix thoroughly. Arrange pecans in groups of 3 or 5 on greased cookie sheet. Mold dough in balls; dip ends in egg white. Press lightly on pecans. Dough will be soft. Bake at 350 degrees for 10 to 12 minutes. Frost with favorite chocolate frosting.

Dorothy L. Barton
Alpha Omicron No. 1827
Burlington, Iowa

EASY PEANUT BUTTER COOKIES

1 c. sugar
1 c. peanut butter
1 egg

Combine all ingredients. Cover. Chill for 30 minutes. Roll into small balls. Place on an ungreased cookie sheet. Press each one slightly with tines of fork. Bake at 350 degrees for 10 minutes.

Charlene Walters
Theta No. 598
Claypool, Indiana
Pearl Stock, Ed Chm.
Beta Theta No. 2655
Manitowoc, Wisconsin

SAND TARTS

1/4 lb. butter
2 tbsp. sugar
1 c. flour
Pinch of salt
1 tsp. vanilla
1 c. finely chopped pecans
Confectioners' sugar

Cream butter and sugar. Sift flour and salt twice. Add to creamed mixture; mix well. Add vanilla; mix well. Add pecans. Shape into finger-shaped rolls. Place on greased cookie sheet. Bake 20 minutes at 325 degrees. Roll in confectioners' sugar.

Jackie Jackson, Pres.
Alpha Tau No. 2046
Richmond, Virginia

SNICKERDOODLES

1 1/2 c. plus 2 tbsp. sugar
1 c. soft shortening
2 eggs

2 3/4 c. sifted flour
2 tsp. cream of tartar
1 tsp. soda
1/2 tsp. salt
2 tsp. cinnamon

Combine 1 1/2 cups sugar with shortening and egg. Sift together flour, cream of tartar, soda and salt. Add to egg mixture. Chill dough thoroughly. Roll into balls the size of walnuts. Mix 2 tablespoons sugar and cinnamon. Roll balls in cinnamon mixture. Place 2 inches apart on ungreased cookie sheet. Bake for 8 to 10 minutes in 400-degree oven or until lightly browned. Cool on rack.

Barbara Haygood, Scrapbook Chm.
Beta Xi No. 4153
Gautier, Mississippi
Jan Cain, V.P.
Beta Kappa
Muenster, Texas

PECAN CURLS

1/2 c. sifted all-purpose flour
1/4 tsp. soda

1 c. (firmly packed) brown sugar
3/4 c. butter or margarine, softened
2 eggs
1 tsp. vanilla
3/4 c. finely chopped pecans
3/4 c. rolled oats
2 tbsp. confectioners' sugar

Sift together flour and soda into bowl. Add brown sugar, butter, eggs and vanilla. Beat until smooth, about 2 minutes. Blend in pecans and oats. Drop by teaspoonfuls onto well greased cookie sheets, allowing about 3 inches between cookies. Bake in preheated 350-degree oven for 8 to 10 minutes or until cookies are brown around edges. Cool about 1 minute. Remove cookies carefully from cookie sheets with wide spatula. Turn upside down over rolling pin or several straight-sided glasses which have been wrapped in paper towels or napkins. Allow to cool completely before removing from rolling pin. Sift confectioners' sugar into a small flat bowl. Dip edge of each cooled cookie carefully into sugar to frost. Yield: 4 dozen.

Photograph for this recipe below.

Frozen Desserts

One of the world's most popular desserts is a particular frozen dessert —
available in almost every flavor under the sun. Because there is hardly a
grocery store or supermarket that doesn't carry it, it's available to anyone.
There are even restaurants and parlors famous the world over for the many
flavors they can invent! Of course we mean delicious ice cream. Most people
would agree, however, that homemade ice cream is still the best of all.
Frozen desserts are, of course, not limited to ice cream alone, as they also
include ices, sherbets, and combinations of these with cake, coconut, nuts
and fruit, chocolate, and candy. Each frozen dessert can be very unique in its
flavor, texture and appearance, with very little effort on the part of the
cook.

Imagination does play a very big part in making frozen desserts. For example, the number of recipes for homemade vanilla ice cream is really quite
astounding. But, the success of ice cream parlors featuring dozens of flavors
proves that people like a wild variety in their ice cream flavors — from
daiquiri sherbet to licorice! With imagination and inventiveness, many of
these delightful flavors can be duplicated right at home in frozen desserts
that do not include the traditional ice cream at all. The base of many of
these is heavy cream and egg whites stiffly whipped, flavored, and frozen.
Variations are infinite as the garnishes you might use. Nuts, cookies, candy
or any fruit may be added just before serving. Fruit juices and juice concentrates, and most fruit slices, freeze quite well, and take on a whole new
personality when frozen with combinations of marshmallows, whipped
dessert toppings, and flavor extracts. Try your own inventiveness because
there are many surprises awaiting you.

ESA members serve their favorite frozen desserts all the year around because
they are delectably satisfying on a hot, summer day as well as on a chilly
winter evening. And because a frozen dessert can be as simple or as snazzy as
the hostess desires, there is a recipe to complement almost any favorite
family or party menu. They hope that these recipes will prove that there is a
whole new world of desserts waiting for you and your family — right in your
freezer!

GINGER-PEACH ICE CREAM

1 1/3 c. sweetened condensed milk
3/4 tsp. salt
1 tsp. vanilla
1/4 tsp. almond extract
1/3 c. thinly sliced preserved ginger
    or 3/4 tsp. powdered ginger
1 c. whipping cream, whipped
1 29-oz. can cling peach slices,
    drained

Combine condensed milk, salt, vanilla, almond extract and ginger. Refrigerate until well chilled. Fold in stiffly beaten cream. Turn into freezer trays; set control at lowest temperature. Freeze until firm 1 inch from edge. Coarsely crush 2 cups peaches; reserve remainder for garnish. Turn partially frozen mixture into chilled bowl. Beat quickly until smooth; fold in crushed peaches. Return to trays; freeze until firm, stirring once or twice during freezing to distribute peaches and sliced ginger. Return temperature control on freezer to normal. Yield: 1 quart ice cream.

Photograph for this recipe above.

ALMOND ICE CREAM DESSERT

1 c. unblanched almonds
1/2 c. soft margarine
2 sq. unsweetened chocolate, melted
2 c. powdered sugar
3 eggs, separated
Pinch of salt
1 tsp. vanilla
1 12-oz. package vanilla wafers,
    crushed
1 1/2 to 2 qt. vanilla ice cream

Grind or grate unblanched almonds. Place on a cookie sheet; brown slowly at about 300 degrees. Watch carefully as they brown easily. Mix margarine, melted chocolate and 1 cup powdered sugar. Add egg yolks, one at a time, beating until smooth. Beat egg whites, salt and vanilla until stiff. Add 1 cup sugar. Fold into chocolate mixture. Place half the crumbs in buttered 9 x 13-inch pan. Spread chocolate mixture over crumbs. Sprinkle with toasted almonds. Spread slightly softened ice cream over top. Sprinkle with remaining crumbs. Place in freezer

overnight or until frozen firm. Yield: 12
servings.

Mrs. Helen Rankin, Sec.
Sigma Beta No. 162
Spokane, Washington

FROZEN GREEN APPLESAUCE

1 qt. green apples, peeled and diced
1/3 c. water
Sugar to taste
2 egg whites

Cook apples in water until very tender. Add
sugar to taste. Cover with airtight lid. Chill.
Beat egg whites until stiff. Fold in applesauce. Freeze in ice tray until firm.

Jean Butler, Pres.
Gamma Delta No. 702
Tulsa, Oklahoma

BIG-BATCH DESSERT

4 1-lb. 4-oz. cans crushed pineapple
2 1-lb. cans sliced peaches, drained
*   and cubed*
2 c. fresh white seedless grapes,
*   halved*
1 1/2 c. maraschino cherries, drained
*   and cut in eighths*
1/2 lb. marshmallows, quartered
2 tsp. crystallized ginger, finely
*   chopped*
1 env. unflavored gelatin
1/4 c. cold water
1 c. orange juice
1/4 c. lemon juice
2 1/2 c. sugar
1/2 tsp. salt
2 c. coarsely chopped pecans
2 qt. heavy cream, whipped or 10 pkg.
*   dessert topping mix, prepared*

Drain pineapple, reserving 1 1/2 cups pineapple juice. Combine fruits, marshmallows
and ginger. Soften gelatin in cold water.
Heat pineapple juice to boiling. Add gelatin;
stir to dissolve. Add orange and lemon juice,
sugar and salt; stir to dissolve. Chill until partially thick. Add fruit mixture and pecans.
Fold in whipped cream. Spoon into 1-quart
cylinder cartons. Cover. Freeze until firm.

Cut into 1-inch slices to serve. Top with
additional whipped cream. Yield: 9 quarts.

Helen Judah, Treas.
Delta Alpha No. 2012
Columbia, Missouri

FROZEN CHEESECAKE

Margarine
1 c. vanilla wafer crumbs
2 8-oz. packages cream cheese,
*   softened*
4 eggs, separated
2 c. sugar
2 tsp. vanilla
1/2 pt. whipping cream, whipped

Grease springform pan well with margarine.
Sprinkle cookie crumbs to line pan. Combine cream cheese and egg yolks; beat until
fluffy. Add sugar and vanilla; beat well. Beat
egg whites until stiff. Fold egg whites into
cheese mixture. Add whipped cream. Place
in freezer container. Freeze for 12 to 15
hours. Serve frozen.

Joanne Lintzenich, Rec. Sec.
Alpha Psi No. 2841
Kokomo, Indiana

FROZEN CHOCOLATE JUBILEE

3/4 to 1 box crushed vanilla wafers
4 tbsp. melted butter
3 c. powdered sugar
3/4 c. softened butter
2 sq. unsweetened chocolate, melted
1/2 tsp. vanilla
5 eggs, separated
Vanilla ice cream
Chopped pecans

Mix vanilla wafers and butter; press into 9 x
13-inch Pyrex dish. Mix together powdered
sugar, butter, melted chocolate, vanilla and
beaten egg yolks. Beat egg whites until stiff
peaks form. Fold into first mixture. Spread
over crumbs in pan. Let stand in freezer
until firm. Spread with vanilla ice cream.
Sprinkle with chopped pecans. Freeze.

Kaye Wyly
Gamma Lambda No. 4241
Tulsa, Oklahoma

BLUEBERRY DELIGHT

34 vanilla wafers
1 c. whipping cream
1 8-oz. package cream cheese, softened
1/4 c. powdered sugar
1 can blueberry pie filling

Crush vanilla wafers; place in bottom of 8 x 12-inch pan. Whip cream and cream cheese together. Add powdered sugar. Spoon over vanilla wafers. Spoon blueberry pie filling on top cream mixture. Freeze for 2 hours. Refrigerate until ready to serve.

Jo Becker, Ed. Dir.
Gamma Delta No. 2302
Lincoln, Nebraska

CHERRY FREEZE

1 9-oz. carton Cool Whip
1 can sweetened condensed milk
1 tsp. vanilla
1 6-oz. can crushed pineapple, drained
1 can cherry pie filling
1 c. small marshmallows

Combine all ingredients in bowl; mix well. Pour into 9 x 13 x 2-inch pan. Freeze until firm.

Sandra Hayes
Alpha Omicron No. 577
Enid, Oklahoma

CHOCO-MINT FREEZE

1 1/4 c. crushed vanilla wafers
4 tbsp. margarine, melted
1 qt. peppermint stick ice cream,
    softened
1/2 c. butter
2 sq. unsweetened chocolate
3 eggs, separated
1 1/2 c. powdered sugar
1/2 c. chopped pecans
1 tsp. vanilla

Toss together crumbs and melted margarine. Reserve 1/4 cup crumbs; press remaining crumb mixture into 9 x 9 x 2-inch baking pan. Spread with ice cream. Freeze. Melt butter and chocolate over low heat; gradually stir into egg yolks. Add powdered sugar, pecans and vanilla. Cool thoroughly. Beat egg whites until stiff peaks form. Beat chocolate mixture until smooth. Fold in egg whites. Spread chocolate mixture over ice cream. Top with reserved crumb mixture. Freeze. Yield: 8 servings.

Shirley Fox, Oregon State Editor
Theta Beta No. 3670
Springfield, Oregon

CREME DE MENTHE FRAPPE

1 qt. vanilla ice cream, softened
1/4 c. brandy
1 c. green creme de menthe

Combine all ingredients in a mixer; beat well. Place in ice trays. Let stand in freezer 10 hours. Serve in champagne glasses. Yield: 6 servings.

Carol Breffeilh Smith, Pres.
Alpha Eta No. 4393
Patterson, Louisiana

FROZEN ICE CREAM SUNDAE DESSERT

2 c. graham cracker crumbs
2 or 3 bananas, sliced
1/2 gal. vanilla ice cream
1 c. chopped walnuts
1 c. semisweet chocolate chips
1/2 c. butter
2 c. powdered sugar
1 1/2 c. evaporated milk
1 tsp. vanilla
2 c. whipping cream, whipped

Place 1 cup graham cracker crumbs in bottom of 9 x 13-inch pan. Cover crumbs with sliced bananas. Slice ice cream 1/2 inch thick. Lay ice cream slices on top of bananas. Sprinkle with walnuts. Freeze until firm. Combine chocolate chips, butter, powdered sugar and evaporated milk. Cook until thick and smooth. Add vanilla. Cool. Pour over ice cream layer. Freeze until firm. Cover with layer of whipped cream. Sprinkle with remaining cracker crumbs. Return to freezer until ready to serve.

Beverly Larson, Pres.
Beta Theta No. 2655
Manitowoc, Wisconsin
Robin White
Alpha Eta No. 4269
Davenport, Iowa
Carole King
Delta Omicron No. 1391
Ness City, Kansas

ICE CREAM TORTE

1 4-oz. package German sweet chocolate
1 stick butter
1 sm. can evaporated milk
2/3 c. sugar
1/8 tsp. salt
1 tsp. vanilla
1 pkg. chocolate wafers, crushed
1 stick margarine, melted
1/2 gal. vanilla or nut ice cream
Cool Whip
Chopped pecans

Combine first 5 ingredients. Bring to a boil. Cook for 4 minutes. Add vanilla. Chill thoroughly. Combine wafer crumbs with melted margarine. Line bottom of 9 x 13-inch pan with layer of crumb mixture. Slice vanilla ice cream; put over crumbs. Pour chilled fudge over ice cream. Top with Cool Whip and pecans. Freeze.

Sonjia Olstad, Rec. Sec.
Delta Phi No. 4658
Oregon, Wisconsin

ELEGANT RAINBOW ALASKA

1 1-lb. 1-oz. package pound cake mix
1 pt. strawberry ice cream
1 pt. vanilla ice cream
1 1/2 pt. pistachio ice cream
5 egg whites
1/4 tsp. cream of tartar
1/2 tsp. vanilla extract
2/3 c. sugar
Flaked coconut

Mix pound cake according to package directions. Pour into 2 ungreased 8-inch round cake pans. Bake according to package direc-

tions. Cool. Line a deep 1 1/2-quart bowl with aluminum foil, allowing 1-inch extra to extend over edge of bowl. Spread softened strawberry ice cream in bottom of bowl. Return to freezer until firm. Pack vanilla ice cream on top of strawberry. Return to freezer until firm. Top with pistachio ice cream. Cover with foil. Press with hands to smooth the top. Freeze until firm. Place one cake layer on cookie sheet. Wrap second layer in foil and freeze for future use. Let bowl of ice cream stand at room temperature while preparing meringue. Combine egg whites with cream of tartar and vanilla extract. Beat until soft peaks form. Add sugar gradually, beating until stiff peaks form. Remove foil from top of ice cream. Invert onto cake layer. Quickly cover both completely with meringue. Sprinkle with flaked coconut. Bake at once in preheated 500-degree oven for 3 minutes or until brown. Dessert can be prepared ahead of time and frozen until ready to serve, then popped under broiler to brown. Yield: 10 wedge-shaped servings.

Photograph for this recipe on page 85.

BANANA SPLIT ICE CREAM

4 eggs
1 1/4 c. sugar
1/2 tsp. salt
6 c. milk
1 tbsp. flour
1 can sweetened condensed milk
1 pt. half and half
1 tbsp. vanilla
3 sliced bananas
1 sm. jar maraschino cherries, halved

Beat eggs until lemon colored; add sugar a little at a time. Add salt, milk and flour. Cook until scalded. Remove from heat. Add milk, half and half and vanilla. Stir in bananas and undrained cherries. Freeze according to freezer directions. This is great vanilla ice cream recipe. Omit bananas and cherries and use peaches for peach ice cream.

Deanne Anthony, Sec.
Beta Pi No. 2225
Benton, Arkansas

HOMEMADE ICE CREAM

Milk
4 eggs
2 c. sugar
1/4 tsp. salt
1 tbsp. vanilla
3 c. cream

Heat 2 cups milk to almost boiling. Beat eggs at high speed in large mixer bowl. Add sugar gradually, beating constantly. Add salt and vanilla. Pour hot milk into egg mixture, beating constantly. Add cream. Pour into freezer container. Add enough milk to fill container 2 inches from top. Freeze according to freezer directions. Yield: 1 gallon.

Judy Bartels, Pres.
Beta Kappa No. 4197
Winner, South Dakota

PEANUT BUTTER-CHOCOLATE CHIP ICE CREAM

3 eggs, beaten
2 c. sugar
1 pt. half and half
1 can evaporated milk
1/2 c. crunchy peanut butter
1 c. chocolate chips, chopped

Combine eggs, sugar, half and half and evaporated milk in saucepan. Cook until thickened. Cool. Add peanut butter and chocolate chips. Pour in freezer container; fill with enough milk to meet freezer directions. Freeze as directed.

Rita Fitch, Corr. Sec., Chaplain
Kappa Nu No. 4415
Newton, Kansas

FROZEN APPLE SOUFFLE

4 egg yolks
1 c. sugar
1 env. unflavored gelatin
1/8 tsp. salt
1 c. light cream
2 c. canned applesauce
1 tsp. vanilla
2 c. heavy cream, whipped

Stemmed cherries (opt.)
Walnuts or pecans (opt.)

Beat egg yolks in top of double boiler over hot water until light. Beat in sugar mixed with gelatin and salt gradually. Heat together light cream and applesauce. Add to thick egg mixture gradually, stirring constantly. Continue to cook and stir over hot water until mixture is thick and smooth, or until mixture coats a metal spoon. Empty water from bottom of double boiler; fill with ice cubes. Replace top section of double boiler containing cooked mixture; cool over ice, stirring frequently. Add vanilla to cream; whip until stiff. Fold whipped cream and cooled apple custard together. If mixture is thick and fairly stiff, turn into small 1-quart souffle dish with 3 inch band of foil tied around outside top. Chill in freezer overnight. If mixture is not very thick and tends to be liquid, leave in mixing bowl and chill, folding at intervals, until thick enough to heap in cuffed souffle dish; chill as above. Garnish with cherries and walnuts. Yield: 6-8 servings.

Photograph for this recipe below.

MACAROON ANGEL TARTS

1 env. dessert topping
1 1/2 c. crumbled soft macaroon cookies

1/4 c. chopped walnuts
1 pt. raspberry sherbet

Prepare topping mix according to package directions. Fold in crumbled macaroons and walnuts. Spread 1/3 cup of the mixture in bottom and sides of 8 paper bake cups. Spoon 1 small scoop sherbet into each. Cover loosely. Freeze overnight. Yield: 8 servings.

Betty Burkholder
Alpha Alpha No. 911
Victoria, Texas

RACHEL RAINBOW SPECIAL

1 pt. whipping cream
3 tbsp. sugar
1 tsp. vanilla
1/2 c. chopped nuts (opt.)
24 coconut macaroon cookies, crushed
3 pt. varied flavors sherbet

Whip cream. Add sugar and vanilla. Add nuts and cookie crumbs. Spread half the mixture in 9 x 13-inch cake pan. Cover with sherbet, alternating flavors by small spoonfuls. Top with remaining half cream and cookie mixture. Freeze. Yield: 15 large servings.

Linda M. Klingler
Theta Mu No. 2790
Bakersfield, California
Sandra Fiechtner
Alpha Theta No. 1616
Fargo, North Dakota

FROZEN PEPPERMINT DELIGHT

1 angel food cake
1 qt. peppermint ice cream, softened
1 pkg. Dream Whip
3 drops of peppermint extract
3 or 4 drops of red food coloring
1/2 c. crushed peppermint candy

Slice angel food cake into 2 layers. Spread 1/2 the ice cream on bottom layer. Cover with second layer. Place remaining ice cream in center hole of angel cake. Prepare topping mix, adding peppermint extract and red food coloring. Frost entire cake. Sprinkle top and sides with crushed peppermint.

Freeze until firm. Remove from freezer 5 minutes before serving.

Candi Shelpman
Alpha Chi No. 3171
Merritt Island, Florida

MAMIE'S FROSTED MINT PARTY DELIGHT

1 1-lb. 4-oz. can crushed pineapple
1 env. unflavored gelatin
3/4 c. mint jelly
1 pt. whipping cream
2 tsp. confectioners' sugar

Drain pineapple syrup into small saucepan; place fruit in large bowl. Soften gelatin in pineapple syrup. Add mint jelly. Heat slowly, stirring constantly, until gelatin is dissolved and jelly has melted. Stir into pineapple. Chill about 20 minutes. Whip cream and confectioners' sugar until stiff in medium-sized bowl. Combine with pineapple mixture. Pour into 2 ice trays. Freeze until firm enough to spoon and hold its shape.

Helen M. Haynes, Sec.
Beta Rho No. 4135
Owensboro, Kentucky

FROZEN PEPPERMINT DESSERT

1 No. 2 can crushed pineapple
1 pkg. strawberry or raspberry gelatin
1 10 1/2-oz. package miniature
   marshmallows
1/4 c. cinnamon red hot candies (opt.)
2 c. whipping cream
1/4 lb. butter mints, crushed
Graham cracker crumbs (opt.)

Combine pineapple, gelatin, marshmallows and cinnamon candies in large bowl; mix well. Cover. Chill overnight in refrigerator. Whip cream. Fold whipped cream and mints into pineapple mixture. Line 9 x 12-inch pan with graham cracker crust. Pour mint mixture into pan. Freeze until firm.

Peggy Cunningham, Ed. Dir.
Beta Pi No. 1939
Waterloo, Iowa

APRICOT SHERBET

1 lg. can whole apricots
Juice of 2 oranges
Juice of 1 lemon
3 c. sugar
Milk

Blend apricots with juices and sugar. Pour in freezer container. Add milk to 3/4 full in container. Freeze according to freezer instructions.

Jane Viers, Pres.
Gamma Kappa No. 3265
Northglenn, Colorado

FRUIT SHERBET

3 1/2 c. sugar
3 c. water
1 c. crushed pineapple
3 bananas, mashed
Juice of 3 med. lemons
Juice of 3 med. oranges
1/2 pt. whipping cream

Combine sugar and water; boil for 5 minutes. Chill. Add pineapple, bananas, lemon juice and orange juice; mix thoroughly. Fill freezer tray 3/4 full. Freeze mixture to mushy stage, stirring 3 times. Whip cream. Whip partially frozen mixture thoroughly. Add whipped cream. Whip combined mixture again. Return to freezer to freeze again without stirring. Yield: 2 1/2 quarts.

Mary Stout, Sec.
Alpha Beta No. 165
Lincoln, Nebraska

STRAWBERRY DELIGHT

1/2 c. butter or margarine
1/2 c. (firmly packed) brown sugar
1 c. flour
1/2 c. chopped nuts
1 pkg. frozen strawberries
2 egg whites
1 c. sugar
1 tbsp. lemon juice
1 tsp. vanilla
1 pt. whipped cream

Combine first 4 ingredients; place in baking pan. Bake at 400 degrees for 10 to 15 min-

utes. Stir. Cool. Beat next 5 ingredients for 20 minutes with electric mixer. Fold in whipped cream. Place flour mixture in 13 x 9-inch pan. Layer strawberry mixture and remaining flour mixing alternately, ending with flour mixture. Freeze for 24 hours.

Marjorie Fuller, Sec.
Delta Tau No. 4264
Yakima, Washington

FROZEN FRUIT FLUFF

1 sm. can crushed pineapple
1/3 c. sugar
1 pkg. thawed frozen strawberries
1/2 pt. whipping cream
3 bananas, sliced
1/2 c. chopped pecans (opt.)

Heat pineapple and sugar until sugar is dissolved. Stir in strawberries until broken up. Cool. Whip cream; add bananas and pecans. Mix all together. Pour into round mold. Freeze overnight. Serve sliced in rounds.

Dianne Clegg, Scrapbook Chm.
Kappa Theta No. 4343
Gainesville, Texas

FROZEN STRAWBERRY DESSERT

1 c. melted margarine
1/4 c. (firmly packed) brown sugar
1 c. flour, unsifted
1/2 c. chopped nuts
2 egg whites
1 c. sugar
1 tbsp. lemon juice
1/2 tsp. vanilla
2 10-oz. packages frozen strawberries
1 c. cream, whipped

Mix margarine, brown sugar, flour and nuts in 9 x 13-inch pan until crumbly and well mixed. Spread evenly in pan. Bake at 400 degrees until brown, 5 to 10 minutes. Stir occasionally. Keep crumbled. Reserve 1/3 cup mixture for topping. Beat 2 egg whites until frothy. Add sugar, lemon juice, vanilla and strawberries. Beat 20 minutes at medium speed. Fold whipped cream into beaten mixture. Spread on top of baked crust. Top with remaining crumbled mix. Freeze until firm.

Sally Rowell, Treas.
Alpha Sigma No. 4298
Farmers Branch, Texas

STRAWBERRY FROZEN CUSTARD PARFAIT

1   3-oz. package golden custard mix
2 c. milk
1 egg yolk
1 c. sour cream or plain yogurt
Strawberry Sauce

Blend custard mix, milk and egg yolk in saucepan. Prepare according to package directions. Fold in sour cream. Pour into shallow pan. Freeze until almost firm. Place in mixing bowl. Beat at high speed on mixer until smooth. Spoon alternate layers of custard mixture and Strawberry Sauce into dessert glasses, beginning with custard and ending with sauce. Refreeze. Remove from freezer to thaw slightly fifteen minutes before serving time. Garnish with whipped cream and whole strawberries. Serve at once. Yield: 4 parfait servings.

Strawberry Sauce

1   10-oz. package frozen sliced
   strawberries in syrup, partially thawed
2 tbsp. sugar
1/2 tbsp. cornstarch
2 tsp. lemon juice

Pour strawberries and syrup into saucepan. Mix sugar and cornstarch together. Add to strawberries. Bring to a boil. Cook and stir 2 minutes, or until sauce is slightly thick. Remove from heat. Add lemon juice. Chill. Yield: 1 1/4 cups sauce.

Photograph for this recipe on page 103.

STRAWBERRY PARFAIT PERFECT

1/2 c. sugar
1/2 env. unflavored gelatin
2 egg whites
1 tsp. almond extract
1/4 tsp. salt

1 c. whipping cream, whipped
Strawberry Sauce

Boil sugar and 1/2 cup water in saucepan over medium heat to soft-ball stage. Combine gelatin and 2 tablespoons cold water in small saucepan. Dissolve over low heat; set aside. Beat egg whites in bowl with electric mixer at high speed until stiff peaks form. Beat hot syrup gradually into egg whites. Add dissolved gelatin, almond extract and salt, mixing until well blended. Fold in whipped cream. Spoon alternate layers of cream mixture and Strawberry Sauce into parfait glasses, beginning with cream mixture and ending with sauce. Freeze until firm. Remove from freezer to thaw slightly fifteen minutes before serving time. Garnish with whipped cream and whole strawberries. Serve at once. Yield: 4 parfait servings.

Strawberry Sauce

1   10-oz. package frozen sliced
   strawberries in syrup, partially thawed
2 tbsp. sugar
1/2 tbsp. cornstarch
2 tsp. lemon juice

Pour strawberries and syrup into saucepan. Mix sugar and cornstarch together. Add to strawberries. Bring to a boil. Cook and stir for 2 minutes or until sauce is slightly thick. Remove from heat. Add lemon juice. Chill.

Photograph for this recipe on page 103.

PINK LEMONADE PIE

1 can sweetened condensed milk
1 sm. can frozen pink lemonade
1 sm. carton Cool Whip
Red food coloring
1 graham cracker crust

Blend condensed milk and pink lemonade. Add Cool Whip; stir until smooth. Add a few drops of red food coloring for deeper color. Pour into graham cracker crust. Freeze until firm. Serve frozen. Garnish with whipped cream.

Ann Hartung, Contact Chm.
Alpha Gamma No. 240
Phoenix, Arizona

CHOCOLATE ICE CREAM PIE

20 Oreo cookies with icing, crushed
1/4 c. melted margarine or butter
1 pkg. redi-blend unsweetened chocolate
　or 1 sq. baking chocolate
3/4 c. evaporated milk
3/4 c. sugar
1/4 c. margarine or butter
1 qt. vanilla ice cream
Chopped pecans

Mix cookies with 1/4 cup melted margarine. Press into 9 or 10-inch pie pan to form crust. Mix chocolate, evaporated milk, sugar and margarine in saucepan. Cook until thick. Let cool until lukewarm. Fill pie shell with softened ice cream. Pour cooked topping over ice cream. Sprinkle with chopped pecans. Freeze for 8 hours or more until ready to serve.

Paula Farr, Pres.
Delta Tau No. 4304
Portales, New Mexico

FROZEN LIME PIE

1/4 c. confectioners' sugar
1/4 tsp. cinnamon
1 1/2 c. graham cracker crumbs
1/4 c. melted butter or margarine
2 eggs
1/2 c. sugar
1/2 c. light corn syrup
1 c. cream or top milk
1 c. milk
1/3 c. lime juice
1 tsp. grated lime rind
Few drops of green food coloring

Add confectioners' sugar and cinnamon to graham cracker crumbs. Blend in melted butter. Cover bottom and sides of buttered pie plate with crumb mixture, reserving a small portion of crumb mixture to sprinkle over the top. Press down firmly. Place in freezer. Beat eggs until thick and lemon-colored. Add sugar gradually, continuing to beat. Stir in remaining ingredients, tinting mixture a delicate green with food coloring. Pour into freezing tray; freeze until firm. Remove to chilled bowl. Beat with rotary beater until light and smooth, but not melted. Pour into

graham cracker crust. Top with reserved crumbs. Freeze. Yield: 6 servings.

Viola Bowrey, Treas.
Alpha Kappa No. 776
Davenport, Iowa

LAYERED LEMON PIE

20 chocolate wafers
1/2 c. butter
1/3 c. lemon juice
3/4 c. sugar
Dash of salt
3 eggs, beaten
1 pt. vanilla ice cream

Crumble wafers; mix with 1/4 cup butter. Press into 10 x 10-inch glass baking dish. Bake for 8 minutes at 350 degrees. Set aside. Melt 1/4 cup butter. Stir in lemon juice, sugar and salt. Cook and stir to dissolve. Pour half the mixture into eggs. Return eggs to butter-egg mixture. Cook over medium heat until thick. Cool. Spread half the ice cream over crust. Pour half the lemon mixture over ice cream. Freeze until firm. Repeat layers; freeze until firm. Garnish with wafer crumbs. Let stand 10 minutes before serving.

Judith C. Slaughter
Alpha Epsilon No. 1461
Greenville, South Carolina

FROSTY PUMPKIN PIE

1 1/2 c. gingersnap crumbs
1/4 c. butter or margarine, melted
1 c. mashed cooked pumpkin
1/4 c. (firmly packed) brown sugar
1 tsp. aromatic bitters
1/2 tsp. salt
1/2 tsp. ground ginger
1/4 tsp. ground nutmeg
1/4 tsp. ground cinnamon
1 carton frozen whipped topping, thawed
1 pt. butter pecan ice cream, slightly
　softened
2 tbsp. chopped pecans

Combine gingersnap crumbs and butter. Press evenly in 9-inch pie pan. Bake for 10 minutes at 350 degrees. Cool completely. Mix pumpkin, brown sugar, bitters, salt, ginger, nutmeg and cinnamon. Fold whipped topping into pumpkin mixture. Spoon ice cream onto gingersnap crust; spread to edge of crust. Swirl pumpkin mixture over ice cream. Freeze, uncovered, at least 3 hours. Let stand at room temperature 15 minutes before serving. Sprinkle pecans in circle on pie.

Barbara Rounds
Beta Epsilon No. 4533
Lawton, Oklahoma

FROZEN RASPBERRY PIE

1 recipe pie pastry
1/2 tsp. almond extract
1   10-oz. package frozen raspberries, thawed
1 c. sugar
2 egg whites, at room temperature
1 tbsp. lemon juice
Dash of salt
1 c. whipping cream, whipped
1/4 c. chopped toasted almonds

Prepare pie pastry for 9-inch pie plate, adding almond extract to pastry dough. Bake as directed; cool. Reserve a few raspberries for garnish. Combine remaining raspberries, sugar, egg whites, lemon juice and salt. Beat for 15 minutes or until mixture is stiff. Fold in whipped cream and almonds. Mound mixture in baked pie shell. Freeze until firm. Garnish with reserved raspberries and mint sprigs.

Caral Serres
Delta Tau No. 3684
Creve Coeur, Missouri

MILE-HIGH STRAWBERRY PIE

1   10-oz. package frozen strawberries, thawed
1 c. sugar
2 egg whites
1 tbsp. lemon juice
1 1/2 tsp. salt
1/2 c. whipping cream
1 tsp. vanilla
1   10-in. baked pie shell

Combine strawberries, sugar, egg whites, lemon juice and salt in large mixing bowl. Beat with mixer at medium speed for 15

minutes or until stiff. Whip cream; add vanilla. Fold into strawberry mixture. Pile lightly into pie shell. Freeze for several hours or overnight.

Shari Sutton
Delta Tau No. 4264
Yakima, Washington

SKY-HIGH FUDGE PIE

12 ladyfingers
1 pkg. chocolate instant pudding mix
1 c. milk
1 tsp. vanilla
1 c. whipping cream, whipped
1 qt. vanilla ice cream
1/3 c. coarsely chopped pecans

Reserve 5 ladyfingers for edge of crust. Separate remaining ladyfingers; cover bottom of 9-inch pie pan. Separate reserved ladyfingers; cut each in half crosswise. Stand pieces upright around edge of pie pan. Store in freezer while preparing filling. Combine pudding mix, milk and vanilla; beat according to package directions. Fold in whipped cream. Spoon ice cream and chocolate mixture in layers into pie shell, starting and ending with ice cream. Sprinkle pecans over top. Freeze until chocolate filling is firm. Yield: 8 servings.

Photograph for this recipe below.

Pies

There was a time when pie making was an everyday thing, as colonial families often ate pie for almost every meal. Colonial ovens were sized by the number of pies they could hold, and cooks were known to make as many as 50 to 100 pies at one time. Today's cook may not depend on pie the way her ancestors did, but she still depends on the same basic skills, methods and utensils. Almost any pie, regardless of its filling, is often entirely judged on the delicacy and flakiness of its crust. This kind of perfection is certainly no accident, although it is easy to achieve. The sure key to a layered flaky pie crust is to follow time-proven mixing, handling, and rolling hints.

There are many prize-winning pie makers who insist upon chilling everything required to make a crust — the mixing bowl, the pastry blender, the rolling pin, the water, the flour, the shortening. Chilling insures against softened shortening particles, one of the main causes of a lifeless, tough pie crust. Accurate measuring is also a must: each cup of sifted flour requires at least 1/3 cup of shortening, while the water measure varies from 2-4 tablespoons, depending upon the dryness of the flour and the amount of shortening used. The shortening is then lightly cut into the flour until the mixture resembles cornmeal, with the water added by single tablespoons until the mixture cleans the bowl. The pastry dough can be rolled immediately, or chilled for as long as 12 hours before rolling. Either way, a light hand is the next key to a flaky crust. Too much handling will melt the shortening particles, so holes should be patched with iced fingers and the dough should (preferably!) never be rolled more than once.

The most popular pies are probably fruit-filled pies, although classic chiffon and custard pies are favorites, too. Many of the new instant puddings, packaged whipped toppings and flavored gelatines on the market have added a new dimension to quick and easy pie making, as well.

The great variety of cookie crumb pie crusts are a versatile source of unique flavor for pies. Graham crackers, zwieback cookies, chocolate wafers and gingersnaps are some of the many cookies that can be used to complement a filling, as well as chopped nutmeats, selected spices, and ready-to-eat cereals.

ESA members like to hear their families "exclaim" over the great pies that come from their kitchens, and they know that you too can receive some of the same compliments. Try these delicious recipes soon and see what happens!

APPLE-CHEESE PIE

1 tbsp. cornstarch
Sugar
1/4 c. heavy cream
1/4 c. rum
3 tbsp. butter
1 tbsp. lemon juice
Cinnamon to taste
6 to 8 sliced apples
1   9-in. baked pastry shell
1   8-oz. package cream cheese
1 egg
1 tbsp. vanilla
1/2 c. coconut
1 c. chopped walnuts

Combine cornstarch and 1/2 cup sugar in saucepan. Stir in cream and rum; mix well. Cook over medium heat until boiling. Stir in butter, lemon juice and cinnamon. Add apples. Simmer for 10 minutes, stirring occasionally. Cool. Place in pastry shell, filling 3/4 full. Beat cream cheese and 1/3 cup sugar until fluffy. Add egg; beat well. Stir in vanilla. Spoon over apples. Add coconut and walnuts on top. Bake at 350 degrees for 15 to 20 minutes. Cool before serving.

Kendra Busby, Parliamentarian
Iota Alpha No. 2961
Fremont, California

APPLE PIE CORIANDER

3/4 c. sugar
3/4 tsp. crushed coriander
1/4 tsp. salt
Pastry for 2-crust pie
8 lg. cooking apples, peeled and sliced
4 tbsp. butter

Mix sugar, coriander and salt. Fill pie shell layer by layer with apples and sugar mixture. Dot with butter. Cover with upper crust; prick with fork. Bake at 400 degrees for 10 minutes. Reduce temperature to 350 degrees; bake for 30 to 40 minutes longer or until apples are tender.

Mary Holder, Soc. Chm.
Alpha Kappa No. 1005
Midwest City, Oklahoma

CRUNCH-TOP APPLE PIE

6 med. cooking apples, peeled and sliced
1   10-in. unbaked pastry shell
1 c. sugar
1 c. graham cracker crumbs
1/2 c. flour
1/2 c. chopped walnuts
1/2 tsp. cinnamon
1/4 tsp. salt
1/2 c. butter or margarine
1/2 pt. whipping cream, whipped

Arrange apples in unbaked pastry shell. Mix together sugar, graham cracker crumbs, flour, walnuts, cinnamon and salt; sprinkle over apples. Melt butter; pour evenly over topping. Bake for 1 hour in 350-degree oven or until apples are tender. Serve at room temperature or chilled. Top each serving with whipped cream.

Lorraine Street
Alpha Epsilon No. 414
Vancouver, Washington

CRUNCH-TOP APPLE PIE

3 tbsp. cornstarch
1 c. (firmly packed) brown sugar
1 tsp. cinnamon
1/2 tsp. nutmeg
1/4 tsp. salt
1 tbsp. lemon juice
3/4 c. water
5 to 6 c. canned apple slices with
   juice

Mix cornstarch, brown sugar, spices, salt, lemon juice and water in saucepan. Stir over moderate heat until smooth and slightly thickened. Add apple slices. Cook 10 more minutes. Cool to room temperature.

Crunch Topping

3/4 c. chopped walnuts or pecans
3/4 c. flour
1 c. (firmly packed) brown sugar
1/4 tsp. each cinnamon and nutmeg
1/8 tsp. each ground cloves and salt
1/4 tsp. dried grated lemon peel (opt.)
1 stick butter or margarine
2 unbaked 9-in. pie shells

Mix all ingredients except pie shells. Work with fingers until mixture is crumbly and butter is thoroughly distributed. Pour cooled filling into crusts. Sprinkle topping over filling. Bake at 400 degrees for 15 minutes. Reduce heat to 350 degrees; bake 30 minutes or until brown.

Annis Crawford, V.P.
Kappa Theta No. 4343
Gainesville, Texas

SOUR CREAM-APPLE PIE

1 c. sour cream
3/4 c. sugar
Flour
1/4 tsp. salt
1 tsp. vanilla
1 egg
2 c. diced tart apples
1 8-in. unbaked pie shell
1/2 c. (firmly packed) brown sugar
1/4 c. butter or margarine

Beat together sour cream, sugar, 2 tablespoons flour, salt, vanilla and egg. Add apples. Pour into pie shell. Bake in 400-degree oven for 25 minutes. Mix brown sugar, 1/3 cup flour and butter together. Sprinkle evenly over baked pie. Continue baking 20 minutes longer.

Lucille Gross, Awards Chm.
Beta Iota No. 3512
O'Fallon, Illinois

APPLE-MARMALADE PIE

1 10 to 11-oz. package piecrust mix
7 c. thinly sliced pared tart apples
3 tbsp. butter or margarine
3/4 tsp. ground cinnamon
3/4 tsp. ground ginger
1/2 tsp. ground nutmeg
1 tbsp. lemon juice
3/4 c. orange marmalade
1 egg yolk
1 tsp. water

Prepare piecrust mix according to package directions. Roll out 2/3 the pastry to form 12-inch circle; line 9-inch pie plate. Cover and chill remaining pastry. Saute apples in large

skillet in butter with cinnamon, ginger, nutmeg and lemon juice until tender, about 5 minutes. Remove from heat; toss apples with marmalade. Turn into pie shell. Roll out remaining pastry to form 10-inch circle. Cut 10 strips 1/2 inch wide with knife or pastry wheel. Beat egg yolk with water; brush over pastry strips. Arrange 5 strips across filling; form lattice by weaving remaining strips in opposite direction. Press ends to rim of pie shell, trimming off ends if necessary. Crimp pastry edge. Bake in 425-degree oven for 35 to 40 minutes or until pastry is golden. Serve pie slightly warm. Yield: 9-inch pie.

Photograph for this recipe above.

BLUEBERRY PIE

1 8-oz. package cream cheese
1 c. sugar
2 env. Dream Whip
2 9-in. baked pie shells
3 bananas (opt.)
1 can blueberry pie filling

Blend cream cheese with sugar. Prepare Dream Whip according to package directions. Blend with cheese mixture. Line shells with bananas. Layer with cheese mixture and pie filling mixture, ending with cheese mixture. Other pie fillings can be used. Chill.

Neva Williford, Treas.
Beta Delta No. 349
Port Neches, Texas

BRANDIED MINCE PIE

1 recipe 2-crust 9-in. pie pastry
1/3 c. finely chopped walnuts
2 c. prepared mincemeat
1/2 c. orange marmalade
1 c. peeled diced apple
2 tbsp. brandy
2 tbsp. flour
1 egg white, beaten with sm. amount of
　　water

Prepare pastry according to recipe instructions, adding walnuts after blending flour and shortening. Proceed as usual. Mix together mincemeat, marmalade, apple and brandy. Sprinkle flour over all; stir well. Pour into pie shell. Cut remaining pastry with small decorative cookie cutter. Arrange on surface of pie. Brush pastry cutouts and edges with beaten egg white. Bake in 425-degree oven for 35 to 40 minutes until crust is golden and filling is bubbly. Serve with hard sauce or ice cream. Yield: 8 servings.

Mrs. Leona Thorpe, Sec.
Beta Omicron No. 2112
Los Alamos, New Mexico

BUTTERSCOTCH PIE

3/4 c. sugar
3/4 c. flour
2 c. milk
3 tbsp. margarine
3/4 c. (firmly packed) brown sugar
2 eggs, separated
1/4 tsp. salt
1 tsp. vanilla
1 baked pie shell

Combine sugar, flour and milk in double boiler. Cook until thick and smooth. Cook margarine and brown sugar in small skillet until bubbly. Add to thickened mixture. Add egg yolks; cook about 2 minutes. Add salt and vanilla. Cool. Beat well. Pour into cooled pie shell. Beat egg whites stiff; sweeten to taste. Spread meringue over filling. Bake until brown. Yield: 6-8 servings.

Mary Hill
Gamma Lambda No. 4241
Tulsa, Oklahoma

BUTTERMILK PIE

1/2 c. margarine
5 eggs
1 c. buttermilk
1 tsp. vanilla
1 tsp. lemon extract
3 tbsp. flour
3 c. sugar
2 8-in. unbaked pie shells

Cream margarine. Add eggs and buttermilk. Beat together well. Add flavorings. Combine flour and sugar. Add to creamed mixture. Mix well. Pour into unbaked pie shells. Bake at 350 degrees for 45 minutes.

Faith Akey, Publ. Chm.
Alpha Upsilon No. 333704
South Milwaukee, Wisconsin

CARAMEL PIE

3 eggs, separated
2 c. (firmly packed) med. brown sugar
1 c. milk
1 c. hot water
7 tbsp. flour
1/4 stick butter or margarine
1 baked pie shell
1 tsp. cream of tartar
6 tbsp. sugar
1/2 tsp. vanilla

Combine egg yolks with next 5 ingredients; mix thoroughly in medium saucepan. Cook until thick over medium heat. Spread into pie shell. Beat egg whites and cream of tartar until foamy. Beat in sugar, 1 tablespoon at a time; continue beating until stiff and glossy. Beat in vanilla. Spread over pie. Bake 10 minutes at 400 degrees.

Ann Haskins
Alpha Xi No. 1610
Chesapeake, Virginia

CHERRY PIE SUPREME

1 can cherry pie filling
1 9-in. unbaked pie shell

4 3-oz. packages cream cheese,
  softened
1/2 c. sugar
2 eggs
1/2 tsp. vanilla
1 c. sour cream

Spread half the cherry pie filling in pie shell. Bake in preheated 425-degree oven for 15 minutes or just until crust is golden. Remove from oven. Reduce oven temperature to 350 degrees. Place cream cheese, sugar, eggs and vanilla in small bowl; beat until smooth. Pour over hot cherry pie filling. Bake for 25 minutes longer. Filling will be slightly soft in center. Cool completely on wire rack. Spoon sour cream around edge of pie. Fill center with remaining cherry pie filling.

Georgia Givens
Beta Alpha No. 4068
Dubois, Wyoming

GLAZED CHERRY-CHEESE PIE

22 graham crackers
1/4 lb. butter or margarine, melted
3/4 c. plus 1 tbsp. sugar
3/4 lb. cream cheese, softened
2 eggs
1 tsp. vanilla
3/4 pt. sour cream
1 tsp. vanilla
1 lg. can pitted Bing cherries
1 tbsp. cornstarch
1/4 tsp. almond extract

Drizzle with butter. Mix 1/2 cup sugar with next 3 ingredients with mixer for 10 minutes. Pour into graham cracker-lined pie plate. Bake in 350-degree oven for 20 minutes. Cool. Whip sour cream, 1/4 cup sugar and vanilla with mixer for 10 minutes. Pour over cream cheese mixture. Bake in 375-degree oven for 5 minutes. Cool. Drain cherries, reserving juice. Heat juice with cornstarch and 1 tablespoon sugar until thickened. Add almond extract. Cool. Arrange cherries on top of pie; spoon thick-

ened juice over all. Refrigerate overnight, preferably 2 nights. Yield: 8-10 servings.

Sally Richison, Treas.
Gamma Beta No. 4513
San Diego, California

CHESS PIE

3 3/4 c. sugar
1/2 tsp. salt
1/2 c. flour
6 eggs
2 sticks margarine, melted
1 c. buttermilk
1 tsp. vanilla
2 9-in. unbaked pie shells

Combine sugar, salt and flour. Set aside. Beat eggs until light and fluffy; add sugar mixture slowly, beating constantly. Add margarine, buttermilk and vanilla; beat well. Pour into pie shells. Bake in preheated 350-degree oven for about 1 hour or until knife inserted in center comes out clean.

Charlotte Smith
Kappa Nu No. 4377
Norman, Oklahoma

BUTTERNUT BROWNIE PIE

4 lg. egg whites, at room temperature
1/2 tsp. baking powder
1/4 tsp. salt
1 c. sugar
1 c. graham cracker crumbs
1 c. broken pecans
1 tsp. vanilla
Whipped cream

Combine egg whites, baking powder and salt. Beat until fluffy; add sugar, a small amount at a time, beating until stiff. Fold in graham cracker crumbs, pecans and vanilla. Pour into greased 9-inch pie pan. Bake in preheated 350-degree oven for 30 minutes. Cool; top with whipped cream. Refrigerate until serving time.

Elizabeth Westfall, Treas. Service Chm.
Kappa Mu No. 2737
Harlingen, Texas

Melt chocolate morsels over hot water. Blend in egg yolks and water until smooth. Spread 3 tablespoons chocolate mixture over cooled meringue; chill remainder until begins to thicken. Beat together heavy cream, sugar and cinnamon until thick. Spread 1/2 the whipped cream mixture over chocolate layer in pie shell. Fold chilled chocolate mixture into remaining whipped cream mixture. Spread over whipped cream in pie shell. Chill pie at least 4 hours before serving.

Photograph for this recipe on this page.

HEAVENLY CHOCOLATE PIE

1 c. sifted all-purpose flour
3/4 tsp. salt
1/3 c. shortening
3 or 4 tbsp. cold water
2 egg whites
1/2 tsp. vinegar
1/4 tsp. cinnamon (opt.)
1/2 c. sugar

Combine flour and 1/2 teaspoon salt in mixing bowl. Cut in shortening until consistency of coarse meal. Sprinkle water, 1 tablespoon at a time, over mixture, tossing quickly and lightly with fork until dough is just moist enough to hold together. Roll out pastry to fit 9-inch pie plate. Fit pastry gently into plate. Prick generously with fork. Bake in 450-degree oven for 12 minutes, until golden brown. Beat together egg whites, vinegar, cinnamon and remaining 1/4 teaspoon salt until stiff but not dry. Add sugar gradually; beat until very stiff. Spread meringue over bottom and sides of baked pastry shell. Bake in 325-degree oven for 15 to 18 minutes, until lightly browned. Cool.

Chocolate Cream Filling

1 6-oz. package semisweet chocolate morsels
2 egg yolks
1/4 c. water
1 c. heavy cream
1/4 c. sugar
1/4 tsp. cinnamon

CHOCOLATE ANGEL STRATA PIE

1 c. flour
3/4 tsp. salt
1/3 c. shortening
3 to 4 tbsp. cold water
2 eggs, separated
1/2 tsp. vinegar
1/2 tsp. cinnamon
3/4 c. sugar
1/4 c. water
1 pkg. chocolate chips, melted
1 c. whipping cream

Sift flour and 1/2 teaspoon salt together; cut in shortening. Blend in enough water to hold mixture together. Roll out; place in 9-inch pie pan. Bake in preheated 450-degree oven for 10 to 12 minutes. Beat egg whites with vinegar, remaining 1/4 teaspoon salt and 1/4 teaspoon cinnamon until soft peaks form; add 1/2 cup sugar gradually. Beat until meringue stand in peaks; spread over baked pastry shell. Bake at 325 degrees for 15 to 18 minutes. Cool. Combine egg yolks, water and chocolate; mix well. Spread 3 tablespoons chocolate mixture over meringue. Chill remaining chocolate mixture. Combine remaining 1/4 cup sugar and 1/4 teaspoon cinnamon; add whipping cream. Beat until thick. Spread half over chocolate in pie shell. Combine remaining with chocolate mixture; spread over top of pie. Chill for 4 hours.

Shirley Ann Krcmar, Pres.
Delta Gamma No. 2478
Broadview Heights, Ohio

Recipes on page 93.

CHOCOLATE MARBLE PIE

1 env. unflavored gelatin
1 c. sugar
1/8 tsp. salt
2 eggs, separated
1 c. milk
1/4 c. rum (opt.)
12 oz. semisweet chocolate morsels
1 tsp. vanilla extract
1   9-oz. carton whipped topping
1   9-in. baked pie crust, chilled

Mix gelatin, 1/4 cup sugar and salt in top part of double boiler. Beat in egg yolks, milk and rum. Cook over boiling water, stirring constantly, until slightly thickened. Remove from heat; stir in chocolate morsels until blended thoroughly. Chill until thickened but not set. Beat egg whites until foamy; add 1/2 cup sugar gradually and beat until very stiff. Fold into chocolate mixture. Add remaining sugar and vanilla to whipped topping; mix until blended. Alternate 2 mixtures in chilled pie shell. Swirl and peak with spoon. Chill until firm.

Doug Carter
Alpha Kappa No. 4604
Savannah, Georgia

EASY CHOCOLATE PIE

1 lg. chocolate bar with almonds
1 med. carton Cool Whip
1 graham cracker crust

Melt chocolate bar in double boiler; add Cool Whip, blending well. Pour into graham cracker crust. Refrigerate until completely cool.

Linda Parker, Pledge
Beta Epsilon
Taylorville, Illinois

CHOCOLATE SILK PIE

1 1/2 c. butter, softened
2 1/4 c. sugar
6 sq. unsweetened chocolate, melted
3 tsp. vanilla
6 eggs

Recipe on page 114.

2   9-in. baked pastry shells
Whipped cream

Cream butter and sugar; add melted chocolate and vanilla. Add 2 eggs at a time, beating for 5 minutes after each addition. Pour into pastry shells; chill for 2 hours. Top with whipped cream to serve.

Rosanna Kinney, Pres.
Gamma Delta No. 2208
Peru, Indiana

FUDGE PIE

2 sq. chocolate
1 stick margarine
2 eggs
1 c. sugar
1/4 c. flour
1/8 tsp. salt
1 tsp. vanilla

Melt chocolate and margarine together. Beat eggs until light; add sugar, beating until sugar is dissolved. Add chocolate mixture to egg mixture. Sift flour and salt together; add to chocolate mixture. Add vanilla. Pour into greased 9-inch pie pan. Bake in preheated 350-degree oven for about 25 minutes. Serve with ice cream, whipped cream or mint sauce. This freezes well.

Connie Frieze, Pres.
Alpha Rho No. 4350
Broken Arrow, Oklahoma

CHOCOLATE REVEL PIE

1 c. milk
24 marshmallows
1 1/2 sq. bitter chocolate, grated
1 c. whipping cream, whipped
1 tsp. vanilla
1 baked pie shell

Scald milk; add marshmallows. Stir over low heat until marshmallows are melted. Chill mixture just until cold. Add chocolate; fold in whipped cream and vanilla. Pour into pie shell. Chill until firm. Top with additional whipped cream.

SueAnn Simon, Pres.
Alpha Alpha No. 1657
Salt Lake City, Utah

GRASSHOPPER PIE

14 Oreo cookies, crushed
2 tbsp. melted butter
24 lg. marshmallows
1/2 c. milk
4 tbsp. green creme de menthe
2 tbsp. white creme de cacao
1 c. whipped cream
Shaved chocolate

Mix cookie crumbs and butter; press into 8-inch pie pan. Chill. Melt marshmallows and milk in top of double boiler; add creme de menthe, creme de cacao and whipped cream. Pour into pie shell; cover with foil. Freeze until firm. Remove from freezer 10 to 15 minutes before serving. Top with shaved chocolate.

Carmelita Cottle, Treas.
Beta Pi No. 2076
St. Petersburg, Florida

GERMAN CHOCOLATE PIE

4 oz. Baker's semisweet chocolate
1 stick butter or margarine
1 lg. can evaporated milk
2 eggs, beaten
2 c. sugar
3 tbsp. cornstarch
1 tsp. vanilla
1 sm. can angel flaked coconut
1/2 c. chopped pecans
2 frozen pie shells

Combine chocolate and butter in saucepan; melt over low heat. Add evaporated milk gradually, stirring constantly until well blended. Remove from heat. Stir in eggs gradually. Add sugar, cornstarch, vanilla, coconut and pecans. Pour into pie shells. Bake in preheated 350-degree oven for 30 minutes. Cool, then refrigerate.

Angie S. Ligon, Parliamentarian
Alpha Epsilon No. 1461
Greenville, South Carolina

COTTAGE CHEESE PIE

2 eggs, separated
1 sm. box sm. curd cottage cheese
2 tbsp. flour
1/4 tsp. salt
1/2 c. milk
Sugar
1 tbsp. lemon juice and grated rind
1 unbaked pie shell
1/2 tsp. cinnamon

Beat egg whites until stiff. Beat egg yolks until light. Combine cottage cheese, flour, salt, milk, 1/2 cup sugar and lemon juice and rind; mix well. Blend in egg yolks, then fold in egg whites. Pour into pie shell. Combine cinnamon and 2 tablespoons sugar; sprinkle over pie. Bake in preheated 400-degree oven for 5 minutes. Reduce oven temperature to 325 degrees; bake for 40 minutes longer.

Jean Marris, Philanthropic Chm.
Gamma Delta No. 2208
Peru, Indiana

AMISH CREAM PIE

1 c. milk
1 c. cream
1 c. sugar
1/4 c. cornstarch
1 stick butter
No-Roll Pie Dough

Combine milk, cream, sugar and cornstarch together. Cook until thick and pudding-like, stirring constantly. Remove from heat. Add butter. Pour into baked No-Roll Pie Dough. Bake for 15 minutes at 350 degrees.

No-Roll Pie Dough

1 1/2 c. flour
1 1/2 tsp. sugar
1 tsp. salt
1/2 c. oil
2 tbsp. cold milk

Place dry ingredients in pie pan. Mix oil and milk together. Pour over dry mix; mix well. Press into pan. Prick surface. Bake at 350 degrees for 10 to 15 minutes.

Cathy A. Constable, V.P.
Beta Omega No. 4263
Peru, Indiana

DELICIOUS CREAM PIE

1/3 c. flour
2/3 c. sugar
1/4 tsp. salt
2 c. milk, scalded
3 eggs, separated
2 tbsp. butter
1/2 tsp. vanilla
1 baked pie shell

Mix flour, sugar and salt. Add a small amount of hot milk to beaten egg yolks. Add with remaining milk to dry ingredients. Cook in double boiler until thick. Add butter and vanilla. Cool. Pour into baked pastry. Beat egg whites until stiff; add sugar to taste. Spread meringue over filling. Brown lightly in oven.

Lyna M. Abshier, Treas., Ed. Dir.
Alpha Sigma No. 3300
Eunice, New Mexico

AMAZING COCONUT PIE

2 c. milk
3/4 c. sugar
1/2 c. Bisquick mix
4 eggs
1/4 c. margarine, softened
1 1/2 tsp. vanilla
1 c. flaked coconut

Combine milk, sugar, Bisquick mix, eggs, margarine and vanilla in electric blender container. Cover; blend on low speed for 3 minutes. Pour into greased 9-inch pie pan. Let stand about 5 minutes; sprinkle with coconut. Bake at 350 degrees for 40 minutes. Serve warm or cool.

Marilyn Herren
Epsilon Pi No. 2559
Pratt, Kansas
Edith Collins
Alpha Mu No. 346
Muncie, Indiana

FRESH COCONUT CREAM PIE

1 3/4 c. milk
3/4 c. sugar
1/2 tsp. salt
3 1/2 tbsp. flour
2 tbsp. cornstarch
1 egg, slightly beaten
1 egg yolk, slightly beaten
1 tbsp. butter
1 1/2 teaspoons vanilla
1/4 tsp. almond extract
2 egg whites
1   9-in. baked pie shell
1 c. heavy whipping cream
1/2 c. grated fresh coconut

Heat 1 1/4 cups milk in a double boiler. Add 1/2 cup sugar and salt. Bring to a light rolling boil over direct heat. Mix flour and cornstarch; add gradually to slightly beaten egg and egg yolk. Beat until smooth. Stir remaining 1/2 cup milk into egg mixture; blend until smooth. Add small amount of hot milk to egg mixture; combine both mixtures. Return to double boiler, stirring constantly until thick. Beat vigorously to smooth lumps. Cook 30 minutes in double boiler. Remove from heat. Add butter, 1/2 teaspoon vanilla and almond extract; mix thoroughly. Beat egg whites until frothy; gradually add remaining 1/4 cup sugar. Beat until soft peaks form. Fold hot custard carefully into meringue. Pour into baked pie shell. Cool. Whip cream; add 1 teaspoon vanilla. Spread on pie. Top with fresh coconut. Fresh coconut may be folded into cream filling if desired.

Crust For Two 9-Inch Pie Shells

2 c. flour, sifted
1 tsp. salt
1 c. vegetable shortening
4 to 6 tbsp. cold water

Sift flour and salt together. Add shortening. Cut in with pastry blender until the size of small peas. Sprinkle water slowly over mixture; stir with a fork until flour and fat mixture is moist enough to hold together. Turn out on lightly floured board. Knead just enough to form a smooth compact ball. Wrap in waxed paper or plastic wrap. Chill until needed.

Arla Wagner, Pres.
Alpha Phi No. 1438
Winner, South Dakota

OLD-FASHIONED EGG CUSTARD PIE

3 eggs
1 tbsp. flour
1 c. sugar
2 c. milk
1 tsp. vanilla
Dash of nutmeg
1 unbaked pie shell

Beat eggs until creamy; add flour and sugar. Beat until light. Add milk, vanilla and nutmeg. Pour into pie shell. Bake in preheated 400-degree oven for 10 minutes. Reduce temperature to 325 degrees. Bake until pie is set and pastry is brown.

Karen Jones, Shoals City Coun. Pres.
Beta Alpha No. 3075
Florence, Alabama

DATE-NUT AND CHEESE PIE

1 1/4 c. fine graham cracker crumbs
5 tbsp. melted butter
2 c. creamed cottage cheese
2 eggs
1/2 c. sugar
1/4 c. milk
2 tbsp. flour
3/4 tsp. grated lemon rind
1 tbsp. lemon juice
1 c. chopped dates
2 tbsp. chopped pecans

Mix crumbs and butter together thoroughly. Turn mixture into a 9-inch pie pan; press down firmly on bottom and sides of pan with fingers or back of a spoon. Press cottage cheese through fine sieve or beat with electric mixer until smooth. Add eggs, one at a time, beating well after each addition. Add sugar, milk, flour, lemon rind and juice. Beat until smooth and thoroughly blended. Add dates; beat just enough to mix. Pour into crumb crust. Sprinkle with chopped pecans. Bake in preheated 300-degree oven for 1 hour or until set. Cool.

Marguerite H. Adams, W. and M. Com. Chm.
Alpha Lambda No. 3592
Arlington, Virginia

FRUIT SALAD PIE

1 can sour pie cherries
1 sm. can crushed pineapple
1 c. sugar
1/3 c. flour
1 pkg. orange gelatin
1 tsp. vanilla
1 c. chopped pecans
6 ripe bananas, diced
2 baked pie shells

Combine cherries, pineapple, sugar and flour in saucepan; cook until thick, stirring constantly. Remove from heat; add gelatin. Mix well; cool. Add vanilla, pecans and bananas; mix well. Pour into pie shells; chill thoroughly. Serve with whipped cream or Cool Whip.

Pearl L. Cole
Gamma Delta No. 702
Tulsa, Oklahoma

JAPANESE FRUIT PIE

1 stick butter or margarine, melted
1 c. sugar
2 eggs
1/2 c. raisins
1/2 c. coconut
1/2 c. chopped nuts
1 unbaked pie shell

Cool butter; add sugar, eggs, raisins, coconut and nuts. Mix well. Turn into pie shell. Bake in preheated 350-degree oven for 45 minutes until brown. Top with Cool Whip, if desired.

Gussie Luebke, W. and M. Chm.
Gamma Gamma No. 4030
Mount Prospect, Illinois

GRAPEFRUIT PIE

1 1/4 c. graham cracker crumbs
1/4 c. sugar
6 tbsp. butter or margarine, melted
2 lg. red grapefruit
1/4 c. orange juice
24 lg. marshmallows
1 c. whipped cream

Combine crumbs, sugar and butter; mix well. Press firmly into 9-inch pie plate. Bake in preheated 375-degree oven for 6 to 8 minutes. Cool. Peel grapefruit, removing white membrane. Cut each segment into 2 pieces. Place on paper towels to drain. Place orange juice and marshmallows in top of double boiler; melt, then cool. Fold in whipped cream. Fold grapefruit pieces carefully into marshmallow mixture. Pour into cooled crust. Refrigerate overnight.

Pauline McDonough, Pres.
Alpha Mu No. 763
Des Moines, Iowa

HUCKLEBERRY PIE

1 8-oz. package cream cheese, softened
1 c. sifted confectioners' sugar
1 tsp. vanilla
1 c. whipping cream, whipped
1/4 tsp. almond extract
1 baked 9-in. pastry shell
2 c. huckleberries
3 tbsp. flour
Dash of salt
Lemon juice to taste
3/4 c. sugar

Combine cream cheese, confectioners' sugar and vanilla; beat until smooth. Fold in whipped cream and almond extract. Pour into pastry shell. Combine remaining ingredients in saucepan; cook until thick. Cool. Pour over cheese filling.

Dee Booher
Beta Theta No. 1528
LaGrande, Oregon

MILLIONAIRE PIE

1 can sweetened condensed milk
1/2 c. chopped black walnuts or pecans
1 9-oz. carton Cool Whip
1 No. 2 can crushed pineapple, drained
1/2 c. lemon juice
2 9 or 10-in. graham cracker crusts

Combine milk, walnuts and Cool Whip; fold in pineapple. Add lemon juice. Turn into crusts. Refrigerate for 3 to 4 hours.

Mrs. Mary Ewing, Area Coun. Pres.
Alpha Gamma No. 4426
Stephens City, Virginia

LEMON CHIFFON PIE

1 1/2 c. graham cracker crumbs
1/3 c. powdered sugar
1/2 c. (scant) softened butter
1 tbsp. unflavored gelatin
4 eggs, separated
1 c. sugar
1/2 c. lemon juice
1/2 tsp. salt

Combine crumbs and sugar. Add butter; mix well. Press into 9-inch pie pan; chill thoroughly. Soften gelatin in 1/4 cup cold water. Place beaten egg yolks, 1/2 cup sugar, lemon juice and salt in double boiler; cook, stirring constantly, over boiling water until of custard consistency. Remove from heat; add gelatin. Mix thoroughly. Beat egg whites until stiff; add remaining 1/2 cup sugar. Fold in custard gently. Pour into crust. Additional crumbs may be sprinkled over top, if desired. Chill until firm.

Laretta Schmid, Chaplain
Gamma Omicron No. 1595
Omaha, Nebraska

DELICIOUS LEMON PIE

2 egg yolks
2/3 c. sugar
3 tbsp. flour
1 c. milk, heated
Grated rind and juice of 1 lemon
1 tbsp. butter
1 baked pie crust
1 recipe meringue

Beat egg yolks until light; add sugar and flour, beating until smooth. Add milk, stirring constantly. Blend in lemon juice and rind. Add butter. Cook over boiling water in double boiler until thick, stirring constantly. Turn into pie crust; cover with meringue. Bake in preheated 350-degree oven for 15 minutes.

Mildred Wages, Past Pres.
Alpha Chi No. 3171
Cocoa, Florida

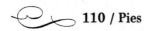

LEMON MERINGUE PIE

4 eggs, separated
Sugar
1/4 c. lemon juice
2 tsp. grated lemon rind
1 baked pie shell

Beat egg yolks in top of double boiler until thick and lemon colored. Add 2/3 cup sugar gradually, beating well after each addition. Cook over hot water until mixture begins to thicken or about 5 to 7 minutes. Blend in lemon juice and rind. Cool. Beat 2 egg whites until stiff; blend into lemon mixture. Turn into cooled pie shell. Beat remaining 2 egg whites and 4 tablespoons sugar until stiff peaks form. Spread over filling. Bake in preheated 350-degree oven until meringue is lightly browned.

Shirley Dreyer, Past State Coun. Pres.
Alpha Psi No. 3549
High Point, North Carolina

LEMON CLOUD PIE

1 c. sugar
3 tbsp. cornstarch
1 tsp. grated lemon peel
1/4 to 1/3 c. lemon juice
2 eggs, separated
1 3-oz. package cream cheese, softened
1 9-in. baked pie shell

Combine 3/4 cup sugar, cornstarch, 1 cup water, lemon peel, lemon juice and lightly beaten egg yolks. Beat with beater until well blended. Cook over medium heat, stirring constantly, until thick. Remove from heat; add cream cheese, stirring until well blended. Cool. Beat egg whites until foamy; add remaining 1/4 cup sugar. Beat until stiff peaks form. Fold into lemon mixture. Pour into pie shell. Chill for 2 hours before serving.

Janet Massagli, Corr. Sec.
Lambda Delta No. 4224
Redway, California

PINK VELVET PIE

2 tbsp. butter or margarine, melted
1 1/2 c. flaked coconut

1 6-oz. can frozen pink lemonade
1 can sweetened condensed milk
1 4 1/2-oz. carton Cool Whip
Red food coloring

Combine butter and coconut. Press firmly and evenly against sides and bottom of pie pan. Bake in preheated 350-degree oven for about 10 minutes or until lightly browned. Cool. Mix lemonade and sweetened condensed milk together until well blended. Stir in Cool Whip and desired amount of food coloring; mix well. Place in coconut crust. Chill thoroughly. Graham cracker crust may be used, if desired.

Edythe Wendt
Beta Gamma No. 6110
Newton, Kansas

LIME PIE

1 6-oz. can frozen limeade, thawed
1 can sweetened condensed milk, chilled
1 9-oz. carton Cool Whip, thawed
1 pie crust

Combine limeade and milk in a bowl; stir until thick. Fold in Cool Whip. Pour into crust; chill until served.

Jackie Duchaine, Past Pres.
Alpha Chi No. 3171
Cocoa, Florida

OPEN-FACED PEACH PIE

6 to 8 peaches, peeled, pitted and
halved
1 9 or 10-in. unbaked pie crust
1/2 stick butter
3/4 to 1 c. sugar
Heavy cream

Place peach halves, cut-side up, close together in pie shell. Cream butter and sugar together; fill peach cavities with butter mixture. Dribble several tablespoons cream over peaches. Bake in preheated 350-degree oven for 30 to 40 minutes.

Mary Nell McKinley
Alpha Nu No. 1596
Wilmington, North Carolina

ICE CREAM PIE

3/4 stick margarine
12 to 15 graham crackers, crushed
2 tbsp. sugar
1 3-oz. package lemon gelatin
2 c. vanilla ice cream
2 c. fresh peaches or strawberries

Melt margarine; add crackers and sugar. Press into 9-inch pie pan. Add 1 cup boiling water to gelatin; stir until dissolved. Add ice cream; stir until well mixed. Fold in peaches. Turn into crust. Refrigerate for at least 1 hour before serving.

> Cathy Blahauvietz, Sec.
> Alpha Beta No. 165
> Lincoln, Nebraska

PEACH ICE CREAM PIE

1 1/2 c. (about) cut-up canned, frozen
   or fresh peaches
1 3-oz. package lemon or peach gelatin
1 pt. vanilla ice cream
1 9-in. graham cracker crust

Drain peaches, measuring syrup; add enough water to syrup to make 1 cup liquid. Bring liquid to a boil; add gelatin. Stir until dissolved. Add ice cream by spoonfuls, stirring until melted. Chill until thickened. Fold in peaches. Turn into crust; chill until firm. Garnish with graham cracker crumbs.

> Lynette Wanasek, Soc. Chm.
> Beta Alpha No. 3329
> Brookfield, Wisconsin

FRESH PEACH PIE

1 1/2 c. flour
1/2 c. cooking oil
1/2 tsp. salt
Sugar
2 tbsp. milk
3 tbsp. cornstarch
2 tbsp. white corn syrup
1 c. water
2 tbsp. dry peach-flavored gelatin
6 fresh peaches, peeled and sliced

Combine flour, oil, salt, 2 tablespoons sugar and milk. Mix with electric beater. Press into pie pan. Bake in preheated 400-degree oven for 15 to 20 minutes or until browned. Cool. Combine 1/2 cup sugar, cornstarch, syrup and water in saucepan; boil until thick and clear, stirring constantly. Remove from heat; add gelatin. Cool slightly. Stir in peaches. Turn into pie shell; chill thoroughly. Garnish with whipped cream to serve.

> Mary A. Recker, Educational Dir.
> Beta Kappa No. 4484
> Arlington, Iowa

PEACHESSY PIE

1 1-lb. 13-oz. can peach slices
Sugar
2 tbsp. cornstarch
2 tbsp. corn syrup
2 tsp. pumpkin pie spice
2 tsp. vanilla
2 eggs, lightly beaten
1 3-oz. package cream cheese, softened
1/2 c. sour cream
1 tbsp. lemon juice
Pastry for 2-crust pie
Butter

Drain peaches, reserving syrup. Combine peaches, 1/2 cup sugar, cornstarch, corn syrup, spice and vanilla; set aside. Combine eggs, 1/3 cup sugar and 2 tablespoons reserved peach syrup in a saucepan. Cook over low heat, stirring constantly, until thickened. Combine cream cheese, sour cream and lemon juice; mix until well blended. Add hot mixture gradually, beating until cool. Place peach filling in pastry-lined pie pan; dot with butter. Spread cheese mixture over filling. Top with pastry; flute edges. Brush pastry with peach syrup. Bake in preheated 425-degree oven for 10 minutes; reduce temperature to 350 degrees. Bake for 30 to 35 minutes longer or until brown. It will be necessary to cover fluted pie edges with foil during last 20 minutes of baking time to prevent burning.

> Linda Fox, Pres.
> Alpha Delta No. 4265
> Dallas, Oregon

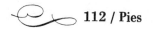

MACADAMIA NUT CREAM PIE

1 1/3 c. milk
Sugar
3/4 c. chopped macadamia nuts
1/2 tsp. salt
Drop of yellow food coloring
1/2 tsp. vanilla
1 egg
1 tbsp. cornstarch
1/3 c. egg whites
1   10-in. baked pie shell

Combine 1 cup milk, 1/2 cup sugar, nuts, salt, food coloring and vanilla in a double boiler. Heat to simmering over boiling water. Combine remaining 1/3 cup milk, egg and cornstarch. Blend into nut mixture, mixing thoroughly. Cook until thickened. Beat egg whites with 1/3 cup sugar until stiff peaks form. Fold into nut mixture. Spoon into pie shell. Chill. Garnish with whipped cream and additional chopped macadamia nuts.

Carol Roberta Straayer
Iota Zeta No. 4424
Plano, Texas

CHOCOLATE-PECAN PIE

3 eggs
1/2 c. sugar
3/4 c. dark corn syrup
2 sq. chocolate, melted
2 tbsp. melted butter
3/4 c. pecan halves
Dash of vanilla
1 unbaked 8-in. pie shell

Beat eggs well; add sugar and corn syrup. Blend in chocolate and butter. Add pecans and vanilla. Turn into pie shell. Bake in preheated 375-degree oven for 50 to 60 minutes or until set. Serve with dash of whipped cream or ice cream on top, if desired.

Alice R. Wagner, Arizona State Counselor
Alpha Sigma No. 354
Phoenix, Arizona

CHEWY PECAN PIE

1 box light brown sugar
4 eggs

1 tsp. vanilla
Pinch of salt
1 c. broken pecans
1 unbaked pie shell

Combine sugar, 4 eggs, vanilla and salt in bowl. Beat until eggs are frothy and mixed but not dry. Do not overbeat. Add pecans; stir. Pour into pie shell. Bake in preheated 350-degree oven for 40 to 45 minutes. Serve with real whipped cream, if desired.

Marie Fawcett, Pres.
Beta Iota No. 3690
Tacoma, Washington

MAPLEY NUT PIE

1 1/2 c. pancake and waffle syrup
3 eggs, lightly beaten
6 tbsp. sugar
2 c. coarsely chopped pecans
1   9-in. unbaked pie shell

Add syrup to eggs; stir in sugar and pecans. Pour into pie shell. Bake in preheated 350-degree oven for about 1 hour and 10 minutes or until knife inserted in center comes out clean. Cool.

Helen McSpadden
Colorado State Coun. Pres.
Epsilon Epsilon No. 1896
Littleton, Colorado

SOUTHERN PECAN PIE

3 eggs
2/3 c. sugar
1/3 tsp. salt
1/3 c. butter, melted
1 c. dark corn syrup
1 c. pecan halves
1   9-in. unbaked pie shell

Beat eggs, sugar, salt, butter and corn syrup together with rotary beater. Mix in pecans. Pour into pie shell. Bake in preheated 375-degree oven for 40 to 50 minutes or until set and nicely browned.

Jean Pagan, Corr. Sec.
Beta Rho No. 4135
Owensboro, Kentucky

DELUXE PECAN PIE

3 eggs
1 c. dark or light corn syrup
1 c. sugar
2 tbsp. margarine, melted
1 tsp. vanilla
1/8 tsp. salt
1 c. pecans
1 unbaked 9-inch pastry shell

Beat eggs slightly. Mix in corn syrup, sugar, margarine, vanilla and salt; add pecans. Pour into unbaked shell. Bake in 400-degree oven 15 minutes. Decrease temperature to 350 degrees; continue baking 30 to 35 minutes longer. Filling should be slightly less set in center than around edge.

Photograph for this recipe on page 97.

PINEAPPLE CHIFFON PIE

4 eggs, separated
1 c. sugar
1 sm. can crushed pineapple
1 env. unflavored gelatin
1 graham cracker crust

Beat egg whites until foamy; add 1/2 cup sugar gradually, beating until stiff peaks form. Chill. Combine egg yolks, pineapple and remaining 1/2 cup sugar in saucepan; cook over medium heat, stirring constantly, until thickened. Soften gelatin in 1/4 cup water; stir into pineapple mixture. Cool, then fold into egg whites. Turn into crust. Chill for 3 hours. Garnish top with graham cracker crumbs.

Theresa Bollig, Publicity Chm.
Epsilon Mu No. 1693
Victoria, Kansas

PINEAPPLE-CHEESE PIE

2 8-oz. packages cream cheese
6 tbsp. butter
1/2 c. sugar
1/8 tsp. salt
1 tbsp. vanilla
1/4 c. milk
2 eggs, beaten
1 can pineapple pie filling

1 9-in. unbaked pie shell
Chopped almonds

Combine cream cheese, butter and sugar; beat until creamy. Add salt; blend in vanilla, milk and eggs. Spread pineapple filling in pie shell; top with cheese mixture. Sprinkle with almonds. Bake in preheated 350-degree oven for 40 minutes.

Bea Casad
Zeta Mu No. 2412
Stockton, Kansas

PINEAPPLE CREAM PIE

3 eggs
1 1/2 c. sugar
1 stick butter or margarine, melted
1 sm. can crushed pineapple
1 tsp. vanilla
1 unbaked pie shell

Beat eggs until light; add sugar, beating until sugar is dissolved. Add butter; stir in pineapple and vanilla. Pour into pie shell. Bake in preheated 375-degree oven for 10 minutes. Reduce oven temperature to 350 degrees; bake until filling is set and crust is browned.

Betsy Fleitman, Sec.
Kappa Theta No. 4343
Gainesville, Texas

PINEAPPLE-SOUR CREAM PIE

1 5 1/2-oz. package vanilla instant
   pudding and pie filling mix
1 8-oz. can crushed pineapple
2 c. sour cream
1 tbsp. sugar
1 baked 9-in. pie shell, cooled

Combine pie filling mix, pineapple with juice, sour cream and sugar in deep narrow-bottomed bowl. Beat slowly with rotary beater or at lowest speed of electric mixer for 1 minute. Pour into pie shell. Chill for about 3 hours. Garnish with whipped topping, additional pineapple or maraschino cherries, if desired.

Ruthe Hollodick, Philantrophic Chm.
Alpha Nu No. 15960
Wilmington, North Carolina

FRESH ORCHARD-STYLE PLUM PIE

1 recipe pastry for 1-crust 10-in. pie
3 lb. fresh plums
1 3-oz. package cream cheese
2/3 c. sugar
2 tbsp. flour
1/2 c. plum jelly
2 tbsp. pistachios

Line 10-inch pie pan with pastry; set aside. Remove pits from plums. Cut cream cheese into 16 strips. Tuck strips into openings in plums. Arrange plums close together in pastry-lined pan. Mix sugar and flour. Sprinkle over plums. Bake in preheated 350-degree oven for 1 hour and 20 minutes, or until plums are tender but not mushy. Bring plum jelly to a boil. Pour over warm pie. Garnish with pistachios. Serve warm or cold. Yield: 8 to 10 servings.

Photograph for this recipe on page 104.

DOWNSIDE-UP PLUM PIE

1/4 c. butter or margarine, softened
1 c. sugar
3 tbsp. cornstarch
4 c. quartered fresh plums
2 c. sliced fresh peaches
1 recipe pastry for 1-crust 9-in. pie
Strawberries (opt.)

Spread butter on bottom of 9-inch layer cake pan. Blend sugar and cornstarch in small bowl. Toss plums and peaches in sugar-cornstarch mixture. Arrange plums closely around edge of pan. Fill center area with peaches. Prepare pastry; roll out to 9-inch circle. Place on top of fruit. Bake in 400-degree oven 45 to 50 minutes or until pastry is golden. Cool for 45 minutes. Invert onto serving plate. Garnish tart with strawberries. Cut into wedges. Serve warm. Yield: 6 servings.

Photograph for this recipe on page 2.

EASY PUMPKIN PIE

1 can pumpkin
1 can sweetened condensed milk
1 1/2 tsp. pumpkin pie spice
1 egg, beaten
1 unbaked pie shell

Combine pumpkin, milk, spice and egg; mix well. Pour into pie shell. Bake in preheated 375-degree oven for 50 minutes.

Nancy Eskridge, V.P.
Beta Rho No. 4135
Owensboro, Kentucky

EGGLESS PUMPKIN PIE

1 c. cooked pumpkin
30 marshmallows
1/4 tsp. ginger
1/4 tsp. nutmeg
1/2 tsp. salt
2 c. whipping cream, whipped
1 9-in. pie crust

Combine pumpkin, marshmallows, ginger, nutmeg and salt in top of double boiler; cook, stirring occasionally, until marshmallows melt. Cool for 1 hour. Fold 1/3 cup whipped cream into pumpkin mixture until smooth, then stir in remaining whipped cream. Turn into pie crust. Chill until set.

Ann Gray, Past Pres.
Alpha Chi No. 3171
Merritt Island, Florida

ORANGE SUPREME PIE

1 can sweetened condensed milk
1 9-oz. carton Cool Whip
1 6-oz. can frozen orange juice,
   thawed
1 graham cracker crust

Combine milk, Cool Whip and orange juice; mix well. Pour into crust; chill thoroughly.

Ruth Hay
Gamma Tau No. 811
Elk City, Oklahoma

PUMPKIN PIE

2 c. pumpkin
3/4 c. (firmly packed) light brown sugar
2 tsp. cinnamon

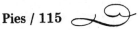

lemon juice. Beat until very stiff. Fold into orange mixture; spoon into crust. Chill for 1 hours.

Marian K. White
Alpha Chi
Deming, New Mexico

FRENCH RHUBARB PIE

2 eggs
1 c. sugar
Flour
Dash of salt
1 tsp. vanilla
2 c. diced rhubarb
1 unbaked pie shell
1/2 c. (packed) brown sugar
1/3 c. margarine

Beat eggs; add sugar, 2 tablespoons flour, salt and vanilla. Beat until well combined. Stir in rhubarb. Pour into pie shell. Combine 3/4 cup flour and brown sugar; cut in margarine. Sprinkle over pie. Bake in preheated 400-degree oven for 10 minutes. Reduce oven temperature to 350 degrees; bake for 30 minutes longer.

Betty Little, Educational Dir.
Eta Beta No. 2676
Liberal, Kansas

PINK LADY PIE

1 1/2 c. vanilla wafer crumbs
1/4 c. softened butter
1/4 c. sugar
3/4 c. orange juice
3/4 c. marshmallows
1 1/4 c. whipping cream, whipped
1 10-oz. package frozen strawberries

Blend crumbs with butter and sugar. Press into 9-inch pie pan. Bake in preheated 375-degree oven for 5 minutes; cool. Heat orange juice in double boiler; add marshmallows. Stir until melted. Cool, then chill. Fold in whipped cream and strawberries. Pour into pie shell. Chill. Top with additional whipped cream to serve.

Elizabeth Nelius
Alpha Omicron No. 1827
Burlington, Iowa

3/4 tsp. salt
3/4 tsp. ginger
1/2 tsp. nutmeg
1/4 tsp. mace
1/8 tsp. ground cloves
4 eggs, slightly beaten
1 1/2 c. light cream or half and half
1 9-in. unbaked pie shell
Sweetened whipped cream

Combine pumpkin and brown sugar in a large bowl. Blend in cinnamon, salt, ginger, nutmeg, mace and cloves. Add eggs; gradually stir in cream. Pour into pie shell. Bake in preheated 400-degree oven 40 to 45 minutes or until knife inserted off center comes out clean. Cool on wire rack. Top with whipped cream.

Photograph for this recipe above.

ORANGE-PINEAPPLE PIE

2/3 c. water
1/3 c. orange juice
1 3-oz. package orange gelatin
1/4 c. sugar
1/2 c. crushed pineapple
1 c. whipping cream
2 tbsp. lemon juice
1 graham cracker crust

Heat water and orange juice to boiling; pour over gelatin and sugar. Stir until gelatin is dissolved. Add pineapple; chill until syrupy. Whip cream until soft peaks form; add

FRESH STRAWBERRY PIE

1 1/2 c. sugar
3 tbsp. cornstarch
1 1/2 c. water
1 3-oz. package strawberry gelatin
1 qt. whole fresh strawberries
2 baked pie shells
Whipped cream

Combine sugar, cornstarch and water; cook, stirring constantly, until thick and clear. Add gelatin; cool to room temperature. Place whole fresh washed berries in pie shells; pour gelatin mixture over berries. Chill in refrigerator thoroughly. Serve with whipped cream over top.

Carolyn Smith, V.P.
Alpha Nu No. 1596
Wilmington, North Carolina

NEVER-FAIL PIE CRUST

3 c. flour
1 c. shortening
1 tsp. salt
1 egg
5 1/2 tbsp. water
1 tsp. vinegar

Work flour, shortening and salt together until very fine. Beat egg, water and vinegar together. Make a well in center of flour mixture; add liquid mixture. Stir until mixture holds together. Yield: 4 pie crusts.

Debby Oller
Gamma Omega No. 4408
Spivey, Kansas

PERFECT PIE CRUST

4 c. unsifted flour
2 tbsp. sugar
1 3/4 c. shortening
1 tbsp. vinegar
1 lg. egg
1/2 c. water

Combine flour and sugar in large bowl; mix well with fork. Add shortening; mix until crumbly. Combine vinegar, egg and water in small bowl; beat well. Combine the 2 mix-

tures. May be refrigerated for 3 days or may be frozen until ready to use. Yield: 5 pie crusts.

Mary Chase, W. and M. Chm.
Gamma Tau No. 4050
Springfield, Ohio

EASY CREAM PUFFS

1 c. water
1 stick butter
1 c. sifted flour
4 eggs
1 sm. box vanilla pudding, cooked and
   cooled
1 env. whipped topping, prepared

Bring water to a simmer; add butter. Bring to a boil. Add flour; stir until mixture leaves side of pan. Remove from heat; beat in eggs, one at a time, until satiny and breaks away from spoon. Spoon by heaping tablespoonfuls onto ungreased cookie sheet. Bake in preheated 350-degree oven for 40 to 45 minutes. Split while warm; remove soft centers. Cool. Combine pudding and topping; fill puffs. Refrigerate.

Pat Kuehn
Delta Epsilon No. 4507
Garden City, Kansas

SOPAIPILLAS

4 c. flour
1 tsp. salt
1 tbsp. soda
3 tbsp. shortening, melted

Combine dry ingredients; stir in shortening. Add enough cold water to make a soft dough. Roll as for pie crust. Cut into rectangles or squares. Fry in deep hot fat until done. Serve with butter and honey.

Jackie Mills, Pres.
Zeta Epsilon No. 4614
Seminole, Oklahoma

GREAT GRANDMA'S OVERNIGHT DOUGHNUTS

3 eggs
1 c. sugar

1/2 c. sour milk
1/2 c. sour cream
4 c. flour
1 tsp. soda
1 tsp. baking powder
1/2 tsp. salt
1/2 tsp. nutmeg
1 tsp. vanilla

Beat eggs; add sugar. Add milk and cream alternately with combined dry ingredients. Mix well; stir in vanilla. Let stand overnight. Roll 1/4 inch thick; cut with doughnut cutter. Fry in deep 350-degree fat until brown on both sides.

Jana Marsh, Historian
Alpha Alpha No. 1657
Bountiful, Utah

TEATIME TASSIES

1 stick margarine
1 3-oz. package cream cheese
1 c. flour
1 egg
3/4 c. (packed) brown sugar
Dash of salt
1/2 tsp. vanilla
1 tsp. melted margarine
3/4 c. chopped nuts

Blend margarine and cheese until creamy; add flour and mix. Shape 24 small balls; press into tassie pans. Combine remaining ingredients; mix thoroughly. Place about 1 teaspoon filling in each pastry. Bake in preheated 350-degree oven for 18 minutes. Yield: 24 tassies.

Jane Clarke
Alpha Phi No. 2051
Staunton, Virginia
Pat Ross
Beta Iota No. 3512
Belleville, Illinois

RUFFLED PEAR TART

1 1/2 c. all-purpose flour
3/4 tsp. salt
2 tsp. grated orange rind
1/2 c. shortening
6 tbsp. orange juice

4 or 5 fresh Bartlett pears
2/3 c. sugar
2 tbsp. cornstarch
1 tbsp. butter or margarine

Mix flour, 1/2 teaspoon salt and 1 teaspoon orange rind. Cut in shortening until mixture resembles coarse meal. Add 3 tablespoons orange juice; toss to moisten. Press 1/4 the mixture into ball; cover and set aside. Press remainder into ball. Roll on floured surface into 12-inch circle. Fit into 9-inch round layer cake pan with removable bottom, allowing pastry to extend about 1 inch up sides of pan. Flute edge. Pare, halve and core pears. Reserve 1 pear; dice remainder to make 4 cups. Combine in saucepan diced pears, sugar, cornstarch, butter, 1/4 teaspoon salt, 1 teaspoon orange rind and 3 tablespoons juice. Cook, stirring frequently until mixture comes to a boil; reduce heat and cook 5 minutes. Turn into pastry-lined pan. Slice reserved pear; arrange over fruit mixture. Roll reserved pastry into strip about 14 x 2 1/4 inches. Cut into 3/4-inch strips; twist strips. Arrange spiral fashion over fruit. Moisten ends; pinch together to make a continuous spiral. Bake on lowest shelf at 400 degrees for 35 to 40 minutes, or until pastry is golden. Cool. Place tart, still on bottom of cake pan, on serving plate. Cut into wedges. Serve with whipped cream if desired. Yield: 6 or 7 servings.

Photograph for this recipe below.

Meringues, Tortes and Cheesecakes

As unusual as it might sound, Meringues, Tortes, and Cheesecakes all have something in common: their elegance is simple and uncomplicated, yet they are considered to be among the fanciest of desserts. Meringues and tortes are rarely served or eaten alone, as they get their personalities from the addition of almost any desired filling, flavoring, or topping — fruit, chocolate, custard, nuts, hard candy, whipped cream. Even a basic cheesecake recipe quite often includes at least a light lemon, orange or pineapple flavoring, and most also call for a fruit topping, such as strawberry, cherry, blueberry or pineapple.

Meringue is created from sweetened egg whites, which are beaten until quite stiff, and then baked until delicately browned, light as air and crunchy when eaten. The meringue can be baked in individual serving-sized mounds, or after being spread into cake-sized layers. The topping most preferred for meringue seems to be mocha or chocolate flavored, whipped cream. Although, custard sauces, nutmeats, ice cream, and fresh fruit slices also complement meringues extremely well.

A torte is a cake (often angel food cake), that is sliced in thin layers and then filled, sprinkled, topped and frosted with whatever sweet icing or frosting suits the imagination of the cook. It can be chocolate custard and slivered, toasted almonds; apricot jam, meringue, walnuts and whipped cream; or pineapple sherbet and filberts. Imaginative tortes look absolutely elegant and festive, and yet are quite uncomplicated and easy for the homemaker to master.

Cheesecakes are probably one of the richest desserts ever created. The typical ingredients for a cheesecake may include liberal amounts of cream cheese, sour cream, sweetened condensed milk, cottage cheese, sugar and eggs. The simpler ones have only a slightly spiced cookie crumb crust and topping, while the fanciest ones go so far as to include a sweetened fruit topping, chocolate and even whipped cream. Cheesecake is considered a rich, heavy, filling dessert, and yet is characterized by a texture that is fluffy and light, and a flavor that is subtly sweet and satisfying.

When ESA members want to serve a dessert that is uncommonly elegant, they think first of their recipes for meringues, tortes, and cheesecakes. You too, will find any one of these recipes just right the next time that it's your turn to entertain for an important person or occasion.

CHERRY DESSERT

3 egg whites
1 c. sugar
1 tsp. vinegar
24 soda crackers, crushed
1 tsp. baking powder
1/2 c. chopped pecans
6 oz. cream cheese, softened
1 c. powdered sugar
2 tsp. vanilla
2 pkg. Dream Whip, prepared
1 can cherry pie filling

Beat egg whites until fluffy; add sugar and beat until stiff. Add vinegar. Combine crumbs, baking powder and pecans; fold into egg whites. Turn into buttered 9 x 13-inch baking dish. Bake in preheated 325-degree oven for 20 minutes. Cool. Blend cream cheese, powdered sugar and vanilla together. Add Dream Whip; mix until well blended. Spread over crust; top with cherry pie filling. Refrigerate for 24 hours.

Lenere Rouse, Scrapbook Chm.
Alpha Kappa No. 1005
Midwest City, Oklahoma

HEAVENLY ANGEL PIE

6 eggs, separated
1/2 tsp. cream of tartar
2 c. sugar
1 tsp. vinegar
1 tsp. vanilla
Dash of salt
5 tbsp. cold water
Juice of 1 1/2 lemons
1 pt. whipping cream, whipped
Chopped nuts to taste

Beat egg whites until soft peaks form. Combine cream of tartar and 1 1/4 cups sugar; add to egg whites gradually, beating constantly until stiff peaks form. Beat in vinegar and vanilla. Spread in well-buttered, large, oblong baking dish. Bake in preheated 250-degree oven for 1 hour. Cool completely. Combine egg yolks, remaining 3/4 cup sugar, salt, water and lemon juice in top of double boiler; cook, stirring constantly, until thick. Cool completely. Spread half the cream over shell, then spread sauce over cream. Cover with remaining cream. Sprinkle with nuts. Refrigerate for several hours or overnight. Yield: 12 servings.

Helen Scofield, I.C. Bike Ride Chm.
Omicron No. 374
Tacoma, Washington

NIGHTY-NIGHTS

2 egg whites
3/4 c. sugar
1 c. chocolate chips or crushed
    peppermint candy

Preheat oven for 15 minutes at 350 degrees. Beat egg whites until frothy; add sugar gradually, beating until egg whites are stiff. Fold in chocolate chips. Turn oven off. Drop mixture from spoon onto foil-lined cookie sheet. Place in oven; leave overnight. Food coloring may be added to egg whites, if desired.

Sally Moutardier, Sec.
Beta Psi No. 4062
Murphysboro, Illinois

STRAWBERRIES ROMANOFF IN MERINGUE SHELLS

2 qts. ripe strawberries
Sugar (opt.)
1 6-oz. can frozen orange juice
    concentrate
1 c. port
3 tbsp. orange liqueur
2 c. heavy cream
8 individual meringue shells

Hull the strawberries; add sugar if needed. Add orange juice concentrate and port; let stand for 2 hours. Toss carefully several times. Add orange liqueur. Whip cream just before serving. Fill meringue shells with strawberries; top with whipped cream. Garnish with chopped pistachio nuts.

Judith Benbow, Pres.
Lambda Delta No. 4224
Garberville, California

SPICY WALNUT MERINGUE SHELLS

3 egg whites
1/4 tsp. cream of tartar
1/8 tsp. salt
1 c. sugar
1/2 tsp. cinnamon
1/2 c. plain or toasted finely chopped
  walnuts

Beat egg whites with cream of tartar and salt in deep bowl to soft peaks. Beat in sugar gradually, about 2 tablespoons at a time, until meringue forms glossy peaks. Beat in cinnamon with last 1/4 cup sugar. Gently fold in walnuts. Pile meringue in lightly greased 9 or 10-inch pie plate. Spread over bottom and up sides to form crust. Bottom of shell should be about 1/4 inch thick, sides about one inch. Bake at 275 degrees 50 to 60 minutes or until golden. Turn oven off; leave meringue to cool with door closed. Meringue will crack and fall in center but this is normal. Press center lightly to level before filling. Spoon meringue into 8 mounds on lightly greased baking sheet for individual shells. Shape into shells with spoon, piling up sides. Bake as for pie shells allowing 45 minutes baking time.

Chiffon Cranberry Filling

1 1/2 env. unflavored gelatin
2 tbsp. water
1 c. canned or freshly made whole
  cranberry sauce
1 c. sugar
2 egg whites
1/4 tsp. cream of tartar
1/8 tsp. salt
1 c. whipping cream

Soften gelatin in water. Press cranberry sauce through sieve for velvety smooth filling. Add with 2/3 cup sugar to gelatin. Heat to boiling, stirring constantly. Remove and cool. Chill until mixture begins to thicken. Beat egg whites to soft peaks with cream of tartar and salt. Beat in remaining 1/3 cup sugar to form meringue. Beat cream stiff. Fold meringue and cream into cranberry filling. Deepen color with a few drops red food color, if desired. Turn into baked, cooled shell; chill until firm. Decorate with walnut halves and whole raw or cooked cranberries.

Chiffon Pumpkin Filling

1 env. unflavored gelatin
1/4 c. sherry or orange juice
2/3 c. (firmly packed) brown sugar
1/2 tsp. salt
1 tsp. cinnamon
1/2 tsp. nutmeg
1/2 tsp. ginger
3 eggs, separated
3/4 c. milk
1 c. canned pumpkin
1/3 c. sugar
1 c. plain or toasted finely chopped
  walnuts

Soften gelatin in sherry. Combine with brown sugar, salt, spices, beaten egg yolks and milk. Cook and stir until mixture thickens, about 5 to 10 minutes. Remove from heat; add pumpkin. Cool. Chill until mixture thickens. Beat egg whites to soft peaks; beat in sugar to form meringue. Fold into pumpkin mixture along with 2/3 cup walnuts. Spoon into baked meringue shells; sprinkle remaining walnuts over top. Chill until firm. Yield: 8 servings.

Photograph for this recipe below.

LEMON MERINGUE

3 egg whites
1/4 tsp. cream of tartar
1/4 tsp. salt
Sugar
4 egg yolks
1/4 c. lemon juice
1 tbsp. grated lemon peel
1 c. heavy cream
Powdered sugar to taste

Beat room temperature egg whites with cream of tartar and salt just to very soft peaks. Beat in 3/4 cup sugar, 2 tablespoons at a time, gradually until stiff peaks form. Meringue should be shiny and moist. Spread in buttered 9-inch pie pan. Bake in preheated 275-degree oven for 1 hour. Cool. Beat egg yolks with 1/2 cup sugar until thick and light in top of double boiler with rotary beater. Stir in lemon juice and peel. Cook over hot, not boiling water, stirring for about 10 minutes or until thickened and smooth. Remove from heat. Let cool completely, stirring occasionally. Whip 1/2 cup cream until stiff. Fold into cooled lemon mixture gently just until smooth. Turn into shell, spreading evenly. Refrigerate overnight. Whip remaining cream with powdered sugar just before serving; swirl over top.

Jackie Bonds
Zeta Gamma No. 4333
Denton, Texas

BLUEBERRY-CHEESE TORTE

2 1/2 c. graham cracker crumbs
1 1/4 c. sugar
1/4 c. flour
1 c. melted butter
2 8-oz. packages cream cheese, softened
3 eggs
1 tbsp. vanilla
2 cans blueberry pie filling
Whipped cream or Cool Whip

Combine crumbs, 1/4 cup sugar and flour; mix well. Shape into a mound in 9 x 12-inch baking dish; pour butter in center of crumbs. Mix and press to bottom and sides of pan. Bake in preheated 350-degree oven for 5 minutes. Combine cream cheese, eggs, re-

maining 1 cup sugar and vanilla; beat for about 5 minutes or until smooth. Pour into crust. Bake for 20 minutes. Let cool until set. Spread pie filling over top. Refrigerate. Top with whipped cream just before serving.

Nancy Gentz, Pres.
Beta Alpha No. 3329
Milwaukee, Wisconsin

CHERRY MERINGUE TORTE

3 egg whites
1/8 tsp. salt
1 c. sugar
1 tsp. vanilla
3/4 c. chopped walnuts
1/2 c. saltine cracker crumbs
1 tsp. baking powder
1 c. heavy cream, whipped
1 can cherry pie filling

Beat egg whites and salt together until foamy and slightly stiff; add sugar gradually, beating until stiff peaks form. Add vanilla. Combine walnuts, cracker crumbs and baking powder; fold into egg white mixture. Spread in well-greased 9-inch pie plate, building up sides. Bake in preheated 300-degree oven for about 40 minutes. Cool. Spread half the whipped cream over torte shell. Spoon cherry mixture over top; garnish with remaining whipped cream. Chill for several hours. Yield: 6-8 servings.

Connie Hall, Rec. Sec.
Alpha Rho No. 3539
Pleasant Hill, California

CREAMY CHERRY TORTE

1 1/2 c. flour
1 1/2 sticks margarine
2 tbsp. sugar
1 c. chopped pecans
1 8-oz. package cream cheese, softened
2 c. powdered sugar
1 tsp. vanilla
1 lg. carton Cool Whip, thawed
1 can cherry pie filling

Combine flour, margarine and sugar; mix until crumbly. Add pecans. Press into 9 x 13-inch pan. Bake in preheated 350-degree oven for 20 minutes. Cool. Combine cream cheese, powdered sugar and vanilla; mix until smooth. Fold in Cool Whip. Spread over crust. Top with pie filling; refrigerate until thoroughly chilled. Blueberry or strawberry pie filling may also be used.

Sandra Brown, Pres.
Beta Rho No 681
Independence, Kansas

CHOCOLATE-CREAM CHEESE DESSERT

1 c. flour
1 c. chopped pecans
1 stick margarine, melted
1 8-oz. package cream cheese, softened
1 c. powdered sugar
1 9-oz. carton Cool Whip
1 sm. package instant vanilla pudding
1 sm. package instant chocolate pudding
2 1/2 c. milk

Combine flour and pecans; add margarine and mix well. Spread in 9 x 13-inch pan. Bake in preheated 350-degree oven for 10 to 15 minutes. Blend cream cheese, powdered sugar and 3/4 cup Cool Whip together until smooth. Spread over crust. Combine puddings and milk; beat for 2 minutes. Spread over cream cheese mixture. Spread remaining Cool Whip over top and garnish with nuts. Chill.

Karen Shelton, Pres.
Gamma Lambda No. 4241
Tulsa, Oklahoma

FLORIDA ORANGE TORTE

1 pkg. yellow cake mix
1 6-oz. can frozen orange juice
*   concentrate, thawed, undiluted*
2 pkg. vanilla pudding and pie filling
*   mix*
1/2 c. semisweet chocolate pieces
1 tbsp. light corn syrup

Prepare cake mix according to package directions. Place in 2 greased and floured 8-inch square pans. Bake at 350 degrees for 25 to 30 minutes. Cool for 10 minutes. Remove from pan; continue cooling on racks. Mea-

sure out 2 tablespoons orange juice concentrate; set aside for glaze. Add water to remaining concentrate to make 3 cups reconstituted range juice. Place contents of pudding packages into saucepan. Add orange juice, stirring to blend. Cook over medium heat, stirring constantly, until mixture comes to a full boil. Place waxed paper directly on pudding while cooling. Refrigerate for several hours. Remove paper; stir briefly. Melt semisweet chocolate pieces over hot, not boiling water. Remove from water. Stir in light corn syrup and reserved orange concentrate until smooth. Cut each square layer in half horizontally. Place 1 layer on serving plate. Top with 1 cup orange pudding filling. Repeat with remaining 2 layers. Spread chocolate-orange glaze over top of cake. Store in refrigerator. Yield: 12 to 16 servings.

Photograph for this recipe on page 119.

HUNGARIAN NUT TORTE

9 eggs, separated
9 tbsp. sugar
9 tbsp. bread crumbs
9 tbsp. ground nuts
1 tsp. baking powder
1 tsp. vanilla

Beat egg whites until stiff, adding sugar gradually. Beat egg yolks until thick and light. Fold in meringue and remaining ingredients. Spread in 3 greased and floured 9-inch round cake pans. Bake in preheated 375-degree oven for 10 minutes. Cool.

Frosting

1/2 lb. margarine or butter, softened
3/4 lb. box powdered sugar
1 egg
1 tsp. vanilla
1 med.-sized chocolate bar, melted
2 pkg. redi-blend chocolate

Combine all ingredients in mixer bowl; beat until smooth. Frost between layers and over top of torte.

Nancy Keller, Sec.
Beta Pi No. 2076
St. Petersburg, Florida

LEMON TORTE

2 egg whites
1/8 tsp. cream of tartar
1/8 tsp. salt
1/2 c. sugar
1/2 c. chopped walnuts
1   3-oz. box lemon chiffon pie filling

Combine egg whites, cream of tartar and salt; beat until foamy. Add sugar gradually, beating until stiff. Fold in walnuts. Spread in 9 x 13-inch baking dish. Bake in preheated 300-degree oven for 45 minutes or until golden brown. Cool. Prepare pie filling according to package directions; spread over crust. Chill thoroughly. Garnish with Cool Whip before serving.

Betty Eusebio
Beta Alpha
Milwaukee, Wisconsin

MOKKA NUSSTORTE

5 eggs, separated
1 c. sugar
1 tbsp. instant coffee powder
1/2 c. sifted all-purpose flour
1/2 c. hazelnuts or walnuts, finely
    ground
Mokka Creme
Confectioners' sugar

Beat egg whites until soft peaks form; add sugar gradually, beating constantly until stiff peaks form. Beat egg yolks until thick and light; fold into egg white mixture. Combine coffee, flour and walnuts. Fold into egg mixture gently but thoroughly or until no white streaks remain. Spoon into a greased and floured 9-inch tube pan with removable bottom. Stir once to remove air bubbles. Bake in preheated 325-degree oven for 50 to 55 minutes. Cool on rack. Split cake into 4 layers. Spread layers with Mokka Creme; sprinkle top with confectioners' sugar.

Mokka Creme

2 c. whipping cream
2 tbsp. confectioners' sugar
1 tbsp. instant coffee powder
1 tbsp. rum or brandy

Beat cream until thick; blend in sugar. Dissolve coffee in rum; stir into cream until smooth. Do not use freeze-dried coffee.

Almut J. Austin, Awards Chm.
Beta Pi No. 2792
Huntsville, Alabama

PISTACHIO TORTE

1 c. flour
2 tbsp. sugar
1 stick margarine
1/4 c. chopped nuts
1   8-oz. package cream cheese, softened
2/3 c. powdered sugar
1 lg. carton Cool Whip
2 pkg. instant pistachio pudding
2 1/2 c. cold milk
Chopped nuts to taste
Maraschino cherry halves

Combine flour, sugar and margarine; mix until crumbly. Add nuts. Press into 9 x 13-inch pan. Bake in preheated 375-degree oven for 15 minutes. Cool completely. Combine cream cheese, powdered sugar and half the Cool Whip; beat until smooth. Spread over crust. Combine pudding mix and milk; mix until smooth. Spread over cream cheese mixture. Spread remaining Cool Whip over top. Sprinkle with nuts; garnish with cherry halves.

Corrine Johnson, Treas.
Alpha Sigma No. 637
Madison, Wisconsin

APPLE CHEESECAKE

1 2/3 c. graham cracker crumbs
1/3 c. (packed) light brown sugar
1/2 c. melted butter
1/4 tsp. cinnamon
3 med. cooking apples
1/4 c. butter
Sugar
1   8-oz. package cream cheese
Grated rind of 1 lemon
2 tsp. vanilla
4 eggs
1 c. whipping cream

Combine crumbs, brown sugar, melted butter and cinnamon; mix well. Press in bottom and 1 inch up side of springform pan. Peel and slice apples into 1/2-inch rings. Fry apples for about 4 minutes or until glazed in butter and 2 tablespoons sugar. Reserve 6 rings; arrange remaining rings on crust. Combine cream cheese, rind, vanilla, eggs and 3/4 cup sugar; blend for 1 minute. Add whipping cream; blend at low speed until mixed. Pour over apple rings. Arrange reserved rings over top. Bake in preheated 450-degree oven for 10 minutes. Reduce heat to 300 degrees; bake for 55 minutes longer. Cool for 30 minutes; remove pan side.

> Bertha Warner, Pres.
> Alpha Epsilon No. 1461
> Greenville, South Carolina

AUNT MARY'S CHEESECAKE

1 1/4 c. sugar
1/4 c. softened or melted butter
1 2/3 c. graham cracker crumbs
2 lg. packages cream cheese
1 pt. sour cream
2 tsp. lemon juice
1 tsp. vanilla
2 tbsp. flour
4 eggs, separated

Combine 1/4 cup sugar, butter and crumbs; mix thoroughly. Press into bottom and side of springform pan. Combine cream cheese, sour cream, lemon juice and vanilla; beat until creamy and smooth. Combine remaining 1 cup sugar, flour and egg yolks; beat until light. Add to cream cheese mixture, mixing until smooth. Beat egg whites until stiff; fold into cheese mixture. Turn into prepared pan. Bake in preheated 350-degree oven for 45 minutes. Turn off oven; let cheesecake stand in oven for 45 minutes. Remove from oven; chill thoroughly before serving.

> Roberta Minardi
> Alpha Beta No 4073
> Greensburg, Pennsylvania

BILL'S CHEESECAKE

2 tbsp. butter
3/4 box Zwieback, crushed
Sugar

Cinnamon to taste
24 oz. cream cheese, softened
5 eggs
24 oz. sour cream
1 tsp. vanilla

Grease 9-inch springform pan with butter; add remaining butter to crumbs. Add 1 tablespoon sugar and cinnamon; mix well. Sprinkle mixture in bottom of pan, reserving small amount for top. Beat cream cheese until smooth; add one egg at a time, beating until creamy. Add 1 1/2 cups sugar; continue beating. Add sour cream and vanilla; beat until very creamy. Pour into pan. Cover with reserved crumbs. Bake in preheated 350-degree oven for 30 minutes. Turn oven off; leave cake in for 2 to 3 hours longer. Chill.

> Florence Ellis, State Coun. Pres.
> Zeta Phi No. 2593
> Junction City, Kansas

BLUEBERRY CHEESECAKE

1/2 c. margarine, softened
1/2 c. sugar
1 1/2 c. powdered sugar
1/2 c. oil
1/2 tsp. vanilla
1/2 tsp. soda
1/2 tsp. cream of tartar
1/4 tsp. salt
2 c. flour
1 8-oz. package cream cheese, softened
2 env. Dream Whip, prepared
1 can blueberry pie filling

Combine margarine, sugar, 1/2 cup powdered sugar, oil and vanilla; beat until creamy. Combine soda, cream of tartar, salt and flour; blend into mixture. Spread evenly in 13 x 9 x 2-inch pan. Bake in preheated 350-degree oven for 20 minutes. Let cool. Combine cream cheese and remaining 1 cup powdered sugar; beat until creamy. Fold Dream Whip into cream cheese mixture. Pour over crust. Refrigerate for about 1 hour. Spread blueberries over top. Refrigerate overnight.

> Kathy Stoddard
> Beta Gamma No. 3413
> Metairie, Louisiana

CHEESECAKE CUPCAKES

18 to 20 vanilla wafers
1 lb. cream cheese, softened
1/2 c. sugar
3 eggs
1 tsp. vanilla
1 can cherry, blueberry or lemon
    pie filling
Whipped cream or prepared Dream Whip

Place 18 to 20 cupcake liners on tray. Place 1 vanilla wafer in bottom of each cup. Combine cream cheese, sugar, eggs and vanilla; mix until well blended. Fill cups 3/4 full. Bake in preheated 350-degree oven for 25 minutes. Top with pie filling; garnish with whipped cream.

Lida Snively, V.P.
Beta Zeta No. 3889
Waynesboro, Virginia

LOW-CALORIE REFRIGERATOR CHEESECAKE

16 graham crackers
3 tbsp. warm melted butter
1 tbsp. unflavored gelatin
2 eggs, separated
1/4 tsp. salt
1/2 c. skim milk
12 oz. cottage cheese
3 tsp. liquid artificial sweetener
1 tbsp. grated lemon rind
4 tbsp. lemon juice
1/2 tsp. vanilla
1/2 c. instant nonfat dry milk

Crush crackers very fine; add melted butter, reserving 1/4 cup crumbs for top. Press mixture in 9-inch square cake pan; bake in preheated 325-degree oven for 10 minutes. Chill before filling. Soften gelatin in 1/4 cup cold water for 5 minutes. Beat egg yolks; add salt and milk. Cook over boiling water until slightly thickened, stirring constantly. Add gelatin; stir until dissolved. Cool. Rub cottage cheese through a sieve; add to custard mixture. Add 2 teaspoons artificial sweetener, lemon rind, 3 tablespoons lemon juice and vanilla. Combine dry milk, 1 tablespoon lemon juice, 1/2 cup water and 1 teaspoon

sweetener in separate bowl; beat at high speed on electric mixer for about 10 minutes or until very thick. Beat egg whites until stiff but not dry; fold into whipped milk mixture, then fold into gelatin mixture. Turn into crumb-lined pan; sprinkle with reserved 1/4 cup crumbs. Chill for about 4 hours or until firm. Yield: 12 servings/137 calories per serving.

Mrs. Hazel Stout, Chap. Honorary Mother
Alpha Beta No. 165
Lincoln, Nebraska

STRAWBERRY CHEESECAKE

1 recipe graham cracker crust
21 oz. cream cheese, softened
4 eggs
Sugar
4 tsp. vanilla
1 pt. sour cream
Fresh or frozen strawberries

Press graham cracker crust mixture into 9 x 13-inch baking dish. Combine cream cheese, eggs, 1 cup sugar and 2 teaspoons vanilla; beat until smooth. Pour into graham cracker crust. Bake in preheated 350-degree oven for 25 minutes. Combine sour cream, 2 teaspoons sugar and remaining 2 teaspoons vanilla; mix until well blended. Spread over cake; return to oven for 10 to 12 minutes. Top with strawberries before serving.

Rose Roberts
Gamma Delta No. 3767
Atlanta, Georgia

PETITE CHERRY CHEESECAKES

24 vanilla wafers
2 8-oz. packages cream cheese,
    softened
2 eggs
1 tbsp. lemon juice
3/4 c. sugar
1 tsp. vanilla
1 1-lb. 5-oz. can cherry pie filling

Line small muffin pans with 24 paper liners. Place 1 vanilla wafer in the bottom of each.

Combine cream cheese, eggs, lemon juice, sugar and vanilla; beat until well blended. Fill cups 2/3 full with cream cheese mixture. Bake in preheated 375-degree oven for 15 to 20 minutes or until just set. Top each with 1 tablespoon cherry pie filling. Chill.

> *Janice Edene Riggs, 2nd V.P.*
> *Zeta Gamma No. 4333*
> *Denton, Texas*
> *Bonnie Schirmer, Philanthropic Chm.*
> *Alpha Kappa No. 2242*
> *Baltimore, Maryland*

CHEESECAKE PIE WITH HOT RASPBERRY SAUCE

3   3-oz. or 1   8-oz. package cream
   cheese
2 tbsp. butter
1/2 c. sugar
1 egg
2 tbsp. flour
2/3 c. milk
1/4 c. lemon juice
1   8-in. graham cracker crust
1 sm. jar raspberry jelly
Cornstarch
Kirsch to taste

Combine cream cheese and butter; beat until creamy. Add sugar and egg; mix well. Add flour, then milk and lemon juice, blending well. Pour into graham cracker crust; sprinkle with additional crumbs. Bake in preheated 350-degree oven for 35 minutes or until knife inserted in center comes out clean. Chill. Melt raspberry jelly over low heat; add small amount cornstarch to thicken slightly. Stir in kirsch. Serve over cold cheesecake.

> *Margret Atwood, Educational Dir.*
> *Gamma Pi No. 1155*
> *Yreka, California*

PINEAPPLE CHEESECAKE

3/4 c. graham cracker crumbs
Sugar
2 tbsp. butter, melted
1   1-lb. 4 1/2-oz. can crushed
   pineapple

2 tbsp. unflavored gelatin
2 tbsp. cornstarch
Dash of salt
1 1/2 c. milk
2 egg yolks, slightly beaten
1 tsp. vanilla
2 c. cottage cheese, sieved
2 egg whites
1 c. whipping cream
Whipped cream
Candied ginger, chopped

Combine crumbs, 2 tablespoons sugar and butter; press on bottom and 1 inch up side of 8-inch springform pan. Chill. Drain pineapple; reserve syrup. Soften gelatin in 3/4 cup syrup. Combine 1/4 cup sugar, cornstarch and salt in saucepan; gradually add milk. Cook over medium heat, stirring constantly, until mixture boils and thickens. Add small amount of hot mixture to egg yolks; return to pan. Cook 1 additional minute. Do not boil. Add softened gelatin and vanilla. Pour into bowl; cool to lukewarm. Stir in drained pineapple and cottage cheese. Beat together egg whites and 1/4 cup sugar in small mixing bowl until soft peaks form. Beat whipping cream until stiff. Fold egg whites and whipped cream into pineapple mixture; mound into pan. Chill until firm. Serve with additional whipped cream and ginger. Yield: 8-10 servings.

Photograph for this recipe below.

Cakes

Only too often homemakers reserve cake baking for a special occasion, when a cake is really one of the most easily prepared, versatile and economical desserts of all. How well a beautiful cake serves to brighten the finish of a Sunday dinner, with plenty left over to pack in lunch boxes during the week. Moreover, a cake can be flavored, shaped, and decorated to fit most any occasion, and is the perfect partner to any number of ice creams, toppings, and party beverages. Cake also freezes well, and travels almost anywhere — the beach, on a picnic, to a neighbor's house or a scout meeting — and there is always plenty for everyone.

The many kinds of packaged cake mixes on supermarket shelves is evidence of their variety and popularity. But, even a greater diversity is available with cakes that are baked right at home, the best place for a cook's creativity to surface. A home-baked cake usually tastes superior to commercial cake mixes. Packaged cake mixes must contain ingredients that cannot spoil, and the homemaker has no way of knowing how long the mix has been on the shelf. The better flavor of a cake made "from scratch" is partly the result of personal attention, but probably more the result of its fresh ingredients — whole eggs, fresh milk and butter or margarine, as well as fresh flavorings, such as vanilla, chocolate, coconut, lemon or orange.

The ingredients used to make a home-baked cake should be of the best quality, so that diligent cooking methods will assure a successful cake every time. Follow the recipe closely, then be sure to use properly prepared, shiny cake pans of the recommended size, which should be filled only 1/2 to 2/3 full for proper baking. Preheat the oven as specified in the recipe, place the pans uniformly spaced inside the oven, then close the oven door and do not peek until at least the minimum baking time has passed. Then, *voila*, a perfectly delicious cake will appear from the oven! Cool the cake fully before frosting. Frosting is another source of cake creativity, because it can be plain or fancy, light or rich, and flavored to taste like almost anything delicious under the sun.

ESA members are happy to report that their cake recipe collection assures you of a new idea for a cake every time you turn around — because everytime you turn around, the one you just baked will be gone!

BANANA CRUNCH CAKE

5 tbsp. butter or margarine
1 pkg. coconut-pecan frosting mix
1 c. rolled oats
1 c. sour cream
4 eggs
2 lg. bananas, mashed
1 pkg. yellow cake mix

Melt butter in saucepan; stir in frosting mix and rolled oats. Mix together until crumbly; set aside. Blend sour cream, eggs and bananas together in large bowl until smooth. Blend in cake mix; beat for 2 minutes at medium speed. Pour 1/3 of the batter into greased and floured 10-inch tube pan. Sprinkle with 1/3 of the crumb mixture. Repeat layers twice, ending with crumb mixture. Bake in preheated 350-degree oven for 50 to 60 minutes or until toothpick comes out clean. Let stand for several minutes, then turn out of pan.

Mrs. Ted McClure
Gamma Omega No. 4408
Kingman, Kansas

EASY DUMP CAKE

1 lg. can cherry pie filling
1 can pineapple tidbits
1 pkg. yellow cake mix
1 c. melted margarine
1 c. chopped pecans
1 c. flaked coconut

Place ingredients in 9 x 13-inch cake pan in order listed, spreading evenly but do not mix. Use juice and all. Bake in preheated 350-degree oven for 40 minutes or until brown.

Ruthann Thompson, Pres.
Delta Beta No. 3935
Naperville, Illinois

BOSTON CREAM LOAF

1 15 1/2-oz. package chocolate cake
    mix
1 pkg. vanilla pudding mix
1 tsp. unflavored gelatin
1 pkg. chocolate malt frosting mix

Prepare cake mix accoring to package directions. Spread in jelly roll pan. Bake according to package directions for 22 to 28 minutes. Cool. Cut cake into 3 layers. Cook vanilla pudding mix according to package directions for thick pudding, adding gelatin. Cool for at least 30 to 45 minutes. Prepare frosting mix according to package directions. Spread pudding mixture between layers and on top cake. Frost sides and top with frosting.

Maudie Grace, Rec. Sec.
Alpha Zeta No. 1779
Tuscaloosa, Alabama

HEAVENLY CHERRY CAKE

1 box yellow cake mix
1 8-oz. package cream cheese, softened
1 c. powdered sugar
1 lg. container Cool Whip
1 can cherry pie filling
1/2 c. chopped pecans

Prepare and bake cake mix according to package directions for 2 layers. Cool. Combine cream cheese and powdered sugar; beat until smooth. Blend in Cool Whip. Frost bottom layer of cake and side; cover with half the pie filling. Add top layer; spread with remaining cheese mixture. Spoon remaining cherry pie filling over top, letting juice drizzle down sides. Sprinkle with pecans.

Helen Steele, Pres.
Rho Theta No. 4093
Irving, Texas

MILLION DOLLAR CAKE

1 box Jiffy devil's food cake mix
1 sm. package instant vanilla pudding
1 8-oz. package cream cheese, softened
2 c. milk
1 21-oz. can cherry pie filling
Whipped cream or Cool Whip

Prepare cake mix according to package directions; spread in 9 x 13-inch pan. Bake in preheated 350-degree oven for 12 minutes. Cool. This makes a thin base. Combine pudding and cream cheese with milk; mix until smooth. Spread over cooled cake. Top with pie filling; spread with whipped cream.

Bonnie Bohse, Pres.
Delta Phi No. 4658
Oregon, Wisconsin

SPECIAL DUMP CAKE

1 No. 2 can crushed pineapple
1 can cherry pie filling
1 box yellow or white cake mix
1 1/2 sticks butter or margarine
1/2 c. chopped nuts

Dump pineapple in greased 9 x 13-inch pan; spread evenly. Spread pie filling evenly over pineapple. Sprinkle cake mix over cherries. Cut butter into thin slices; cover top of mix. Sprinkle nuts over all. Bake in preheated 350-degree oven for 45 minutes to 1 hour.

Doris Balabon
Alpha Epsilon No. 414
Vancouver, Washington

DAISY CAKE

1 box Duncan Hines yellow cake mix
2 tbsp vanilla-butternut flavoring
1 box powdered sugar, sifted
1 8-oz. package cream cheese, softened
1 c. chopped nuts

Prepare cake mix according to package directions, adding 1 tablespoon flavoring. Turn into two 8-inch round cake pans. Bake according to package directions. Cool. Divide layers in half, making 4 layers. Combine sugar, cream cheese and remaining 1 tablespoon flavoring; beat until smooth. Stir in nuts. Spread between layers and over top.

Wanda Walton, W. and M. Chm.
Alpha Kappa No. 1005
Midwest City, Oklahoma

EASY COCONUT CAKE

1 box white cake mix
2 eggs
1/4 c. sugar
1 1/2 c. water
1 tsp. vanilla

Combine all ingredients; mix well. Pour into oblong sheet cake pan or baking dish. Bake in preheated 350-degree oven for 25 to 30 minutes or until cake tests done.

Topping

2 c. sugar
1 c. milk
2 6-oz. packages frozen coconut
1 lg. carton Cool Whip

Combine sugar, milk and 1 package of coconut in saucepan; simmer over low heat until mixture is slightly thick. Pour over hot cake. Cool. Spread Cool Whip over cake; top with remaining coconut. Slice and serve. Cake keeps well in refrigerator.

Penny Floyd
Alpha Theta No. 3511
Anderson, South Carolina

MINCEMEAT CAKE ROLL

1 pkg. yellow cake mix
Confectioners' sugar
1 9-oz. package mincemeat
3/4 c. water
1 8-oz. package cream cheese, softened
1/2 c. chopped walnuts
2 tbsp. milk

Prepare half the cake mix according to package directions. Bake in greased 15 1/2 x 10 1/2 x 1-inch pan as directed on package. Turn out of pan onto clean towel lightly sprinkled with confectioners' sugar. Starting at one of the narrow ends, gently roll towel and cake together jelly roll fashion. Place on cake rack; cool about 10 minutes. Crumble mincemeat in medium saucepan; add water. Boil 1 minute over medium heat, stirring constantly. Remove from heat; cool slightly. Cream 1/2 package cream cheese until fluffy. Stir in walnuts and cooled mincemeat. Gently unroll towel and cake. Spread filling evenly on top of cake to within 1/2 inch of edges. Reroll cake. Cream remaining 1/2 package cream cheese; stir in milk, blending well. Frost cake. Garnish with walnut halves and cherries. Yield: 8-10 servings.

Photograph for this recipe on page 199.

HARVEY WALLBANGER CAKE

1 pkg. Duncan Hines orange cake mix
1 pkg. instant vanilla pudding mix
1/2 c. cooking oil
4 eggs
1/4 c. vodka
1/4 c. Galiano
1/2 c. orange juice

Combine all ingredients; beat for 3 minutes. Turn into bundt pan. Bake in preheated 350-degree oven for 45 minutes or until cake tests done.

Icing

1 c. powdered sugar
1 tbsp. orange juice
1 tbsp. Galiano
1 tbsp. vodka

Combine all ingredients; pour over cake.

Jane Jeffcoat, Treas.
Alpha Sigma No. 3887
Columbia, South Carolina

LEMON-ORANGE CAKE

1   11-oz. can mandarin oranges
1 pkg. white cake mix
2 egg whites
1 tsp. almond extract (opt.)
1 pkg. lemon frosting mix
1/4 c. margarine or butter, softened

Drain oranges; reserve juice. Add enough water to juice to make 1 1/3 cups liquid. Combine half the oranges, liquid, cake mix, egg whites and extract in mixer bowl; beat at low speed until well combined, then beat at medium speed for 2 minutes. Pour into greased and floured 9 x 13-inch pan. Bake in preheated 350-degree oven for 30 to 35 minutes or until toothpick inserted in center comes out clean. Cool completely. Combine frosting mix, margarine and remaining oranges; mix according to package directions, adding several drops of water, if needed. Spread over cake.

Susan Pender
Zeta Alpha No. 2624
Dallas, Texas

GLAZED LEMON CAKE

1 pkg. lemon cake mix
4 eggs
1/2 c. sugar
1/2 c. Mazola oil
1 c. apricot nectar
1 c. powdered sugar
Juice of 1 lemon

Combine first 5 ingredients in large bowl; blend until just combined. Beat at medium speed for 2 minutes. Turn into greased and floured 10-inch tube pan or bundt pan. Bake at 350-degree oven for 45 to 55 minutes. Cool for 15 minutes, then remove from pan. Combine powdered sugar and lemon juice; stir until well blended. Pour glaze over warm cake.

Mrs. William H. Passick, Educational Dir.
Beta Upsilon No. 1831
Fremont, Nebraska

DOROTHY'S PINK SQUIRREL

1 pkg. Duncan Hines supreme white cake
  mix
2/3 c. oil
1 pkg. instant vanilla pudding mix
5 egg whites, at room temperature
1 c. pineapple juice
6 tbsp. white creme de cacao
6 tbsp. creme de noyau

Combine all ingredients; mix until well blended. Beat for about 4 minutes or until smooth. Turn into a greased bundt pan. Bake according to package directions.

Topping

1 c. powdered sugar
5 tbsp. fruit juice
3 tbsp. white creme de cacao
3 tbsp. creme de almond

Combine all ingredients in saucepan; bring to a boil. Punch cake with cake tester; pour hot glaze over hot cake.

Dorothy Roy, Pres.
Alpha Phi No. 674
Cedar Rapids, Iowa

PEANUT BUTTER CAKE

1 yellow cake mix
1 c. creamy peanut butter

Prepare cake mix according to package directions, adding peanut butter. Bake in layer pans according to package directions.

Peanut Butter Icing

2 c. sugar
1 c. water
2 egg whites
1/8 tsp. salt
*1/8 tsp. cream of tartar or several
   drops of lemon juice*
1 tsp. vanilla
*3/4 to 1 c. creamy or crunchy peanut
   butter*

Combine sugar and water in saucepan; stir until sugar is dissolved. Bring to a boil. Cover; cook for about 3 minutes or until steam has washed down any crystals which may have formed on side of pan. Uncover; cook to 238 degrees to 240 degrees on candy thermometer or until syrup will spin a very thin thread on the end of a coarser thread. This final thread will almost disappear, like a self-consuming spider web. Whip egg whites and salt until frothy; add syrup in a thin stream, whipping eggs constantly until well combined. Add cream of tartar and vanilla. Stir in desired amount of peanut butter. Frost between layers, top and side of cake.

Gayle Traywick, Educational Dir.
Zeta Eta No. 4009
Midwest City, Oklahoma

SEVEN-UP CAKE

1 box lemon supreme cake mix
1 box instant lemon pudding mix
1   10-oz. bottle 7-Up
4 eggs
3/4 c. Crisco oil

Prepare cake mix according to package directions, adding pudding mix, 7-Up, eggs and oil. Place in desired sized pans. Bake in preheated 325-degree oven for 45 to 50 minutes or until cake tests done. Let cool.

Frosting

1 1/2 c. sugar
1 stick margarine
1 sm. can crushed pineapple, undrained
2 eggs
2 tsp. flour

Combine all ingredients; cook until mixture begins to thicken. Remove from heat, then frost cake. Coconut may be added when removed from heat, if desired.

Patricia L. Miller, Awards Chm.
Gamma Epsilon No. 2570
Spokane, Washington

PISTACHIO-ALMOND MARBLE CAKE

1 pkg. yellow cake mix
1 pkg. instant pistachio pudding mix
4 eggs
1/2 tsp. almond extract
1/2 c. oil
1 c. water
1/2 c. chocolate syrup

Combine all ingredients except chocolate syrup. Beat for at least 2 minutes at medium speed. Set aside 1 1/2 cups batter; pour the remaining batter into tube or bundt pan. Combine chocolate syrup with reserved batter; mix well. Pour over yellow batter, then zigzag a spatula through to marble. Bake in preheated 350-degree oven for 50 minutes. Cool 15 minutes; remove from pan.

Icing

2 tbsp. creme de menthe
1 carton Cool Whip
1 pkg. instant pistachio pudding mix

Combine all ingredients; mix until well blended. Spread over cake. May frost with canned chocolate frosting, if desired, or frost with chocolate frosting, then cover with Cool Whip mixture.

Shirley P. Eldridge, Treas.
Kappa Tau No. 4642
Brevard, North Carolina

PISTACHIO SHEET CAKE

1 pkg. yellow cake mix
1 pkg. pistachio instant pudding mix
3/4 c. oil
4 eggs
2 tbsp. margarine
2 c. powdered sugar
1 tsp. vanilla

Blend first 4 ingredients and 3/4 cup water together in large bowl; beat at medium speed for 5 minutes. Turn into 10 x 14-inch cake pan. Bake in preheated 350-degree oven for 35 to 40 minutes or until done. Combine remaining ingredients and 1/2 cup water in saucepan; bring to a boil, stirring constantly. Prick holes evenly all over cake; pour boiled mixture over cake. Return to oven for 2 minutes.

Martha Fausett
Alpha Gamma No 3457
Omaha, Nebraska

WATERGATE CAKE

1 box white cake mix
1 c. cooking oil
1 c. club soda
2 boxes instant pistachio pudding mix
4 eggs, beaten
1/2 to 1 c. ground nutmeats
1 tsp. vanilla
1/2 tsp. almond flavoring

Combine all ingredients; beat for at least 2 minutes. Turn into greased bundt pan. Bake in preheated 350-degree oven for 45 to 55 minutes. Refrigerate before frosting.

Frosting

1 box pistachio pudding mix
1 env. Dream Whip or 2 c. Cool Whip
1 c. sour cream
1 c. cold milk

Combine all ingredients; beat well. Frost cake; refrigerate until serving time.

Sharie Michael
Alpha Phi No. 1438
Winner, South Dakota

POPPY SEED CAKE WITH CARAMEL TOPPING

4 eggs, beaten
1 pkg. yellow cake mix
1 pkg. instant butterscotch pudding
1/3 c. poppy seed, soaked in 1 c. cold
   water
3/4 c. oil

Combine all ingredients; mix thoroughly. Beat for 4 minutes. Pour into greased 9 x 13-inch pan. Bake in preheated 350-degree oven for 45 minutes.

Caramel Topping

1 c. butter
2 c. (packed) brown sugar
2 tbsp. flour
1 c. milk
2 tsp. vanilla

Melt butter; add brown sugar and flour. Add milk gradually. Bring to a full boil. Add vanilla. Serve hot over cake.

Marcia Knutson, V.P.
Beta Eta No. 3055
Elk Point, South Dakota

SHERRY AND POPPY SEED CAKE

1 pkg. Duncan Hines golden butter cake
   mix
4 eggs
1 sm. package instant vanilla pudding
   mix
3/4 c. dry cooking sherry
1 tsp. almond extract
2 tbsp. poppy seed
1 tsp. nutmeg

Combine all ingredients; beat at slow speed for 10 minutes. Turn into bundt pan. Bake in preheated 350-degree oven for 40 to 50 minutes or until cake tests done.

Becky Franz, Treas.
Alpha Rho No. 3735
Biloxi, Mississippi

RUM CAKE

1/2 to 1 c. pecans, chopped
1 box yellow cake mix
1 sm. box instant vanilla pudding mix
4 eggs
1/2 c. cold water
1/2 c. Wesson oil
1/2 c. dark rum

Sprinkle pecans over bottom of floured 10-inch tube or 12-inch bundt pan. Combine remaining ingredients; beat for 2 minutes. Pour batter over pecans. Bake in preheated 325-degree oven for 1 hour. Cool. Invert on serving plate. Prick top.

Glaze

1/4 lb. butter or margarine
1/4 c. water
1 c. sugar
1/2 c. dark rum

Melt butter in saucepan; stir in water and sugar. Boil for 5 minutes, stirring constantly. Remove from heat. Stir in rum. Drizzle and smooth glaze evenly over top and side of cake, repeating until all of glaze is used.

Janice Eubank
Delta Delta
San Angelo, Texas
Trisha Cook
Beta Gamma No. 3413
New Orleans, Louisiana

SHERRY-PECAN CAKE

1 pkg. yellow cake mix
1 pkg. instant vanilla pudding
4 eggs
3/4 c. sherry
3/4 c. finely chopped pecans
3/4 c. cooking oil
3/4 tsp. cinnamon

Combine all ingredients; beat for 4 minutes. Turn into lightly greased and floured tube pan. Bake in preheated 325-degree oven for 1 hour and 10 minutes. Cool for 10 minutes; remove from pan. Place on rack to cool com-

pletely. May dust top with powdered sugar or add glaze.

Carol Pelzer
Delta Delta
San Angelo, Texas

SOCK-IT-TO-ME CAKE

1 pkg. butter-type yellow cake mix
1 c. sour cream
3/4 c. oil
1/2 c. chopped nuts
4 eggs
2 tbsp. brown sugar
2 tsp. cinnamon

Combine first 5 ingredients; mix well. Pour into greased tube pan. Mix brown sugar and cinnamon; sprinkle over batter. Cut into batter with knife. Bake in preheated 350-degree oven for 45 to 50 minutes or until cake tests done.

Dawn Walton, Philanthropic Chm.
Delta Epsilon No. 2566
La Grande, Oregon

SOUR CREAM CAKE

1/2 c. sugar
1/2 c. chopped pecans
1 tsp. cinnamon
4 eggs
1 pkg. instant vanilla pudding mix
1 pkg. yellow cake mix
1/2 c. oil
1 c. sour cream

Combine first 3 ingredients; set aside. Combine remaining ingredients; beat for 4 minutes. Spoon 1/2 of the batter into well-greased and floured bundt or springform pan. Sprinkle half the pecan mixture over batter, then add remaining batter. Sprinkle remaining pecan mixture over top. Bake in preheated 350-degree oven for 1 hour. May be glazed with thin icing or dusted with powdered sugar, if desired.

Louise Owen, Treas.
Alpha Mu No. 346
Muncie, Indiana

PINK CHAMPAGNE CAKE

1 pkg. white cake mix
1 1/2 c. strawberry pop
3 eggs
1/2 pt. whipping cream, whipped

Prepare cake mix according to package directions, using pop for liquid and 3 eggs. Turn into 2 greased and floured 9-inch cake pans. Bake in preheated 350-degree oven for 25 to 30 minutes. Cool; cut each layer in half. Spread whipped cream between layers. Chill in refrigerator until ready to serve.

Linda Haberstock, Soc. Dir.
Lambda Delta No. 4224
Redway, California

SPECIAL STRAWBERRY CAKE

1   18 1/2-oz. package white cake mix
1   3-oz. package strawberry gelatin
3/4 c. vegetable oil
1 c. chopped nuts
4 eggs
4 tbsp. flour
1   10-oz. package frozen sliced
*   strawberries, thawed*

Combine cake mix, gelatin, vegetable oil, nuts, eggs, flour and strawberries in large bowl; beat with electric mixer at medium-high speed for 3 minutes or until well blended. Pour batter into greased angel food or bundt pan. Bake in preheated 350-degree oven for 55 to 65 minutes or until cake tester comes out clean. Cool for 10 minutes on rack. Turn out of pan to cool completely. Serve plain or with sweetened whipped cream.

H. Terry Minchey, Pres.
Beta Sigma No. 2904
Savannah, Georgia

STRAWBERRY-COCONUT CAKE

1 pkg. white cake mix
1 c. frozen strawberries, thawed
1/2 c. chopped pecans
1 box strawberry gelatin
1 c. cooking oil
1 c. coconut
4 eggs

Combine all ingredients in bowl; beat with mixer at medium speed until fluffy. Spread in 3 layer pans or loaf pan. Bake in preheated 350-degree oven for about 30 minutes, or until cake tests done. Cool completely.

Frosting

4 1/2 c. confectioners' sugar
1/2 c. drained strawberries
1 stick margarine, softened
1/2 c. chopped pecans
1/2 c. coconut

Combine sugar, strawberries and margarine; beat until smooth. Stir in pecans and coconut. Spread between layers and over top of cake. Pecans may be used either in frosting or as garnish.

Joyce Stefanoff, Educational Dir.
Gamma Epsilon No. 2570
Spokane, Washington

STRAWBERRY-RUM CAKE

1 box yellow cake mix
1 pkg. Dream Whip
4 eggs
1 c. tap water
1 sm. package instant vanilla pudding mix
1/3 c. (about) rum
1   18-oz. jar strawberry preserves
1 lg. tub Cool Whip

Prepare cake mix according to package directions, adding Dream Whip, eggs and water. Turn into 2 layer cake pans. Bake in preheated 350-degree oven for 30 to 35 minutes or until cake tests done. Cool; cut into 4 layers. Prepare pudding mix according to package directions. Poke holes in each layer; spoon rum over layers. Spread preserves and pudding between layers; top with Cool Whip.

Pam Grubb, Sec.
Delta Omicron No. 1391
Ness, Kansas

WINE CAKE

1 pkg. yellow cake mix
1 pkg. instant vanilla pudding mix

1 tsp. nutmeg
4 eggs
3/4 c. Vino Bianco da Pranzo or red wine
3/4 c. (scant) oil
Powdered sugar

Combine all ingredients except powdered sugar in bowl; beat for 5 minutes or until smooth. Place in greased angel food cake pan. Bake in preheated 350-degree oven for 45 minutes or until cake tests done. Place upright on rack for 5 minutes to cool. Turn out; dust with powdered sugar.

Helen M. Grabiec
Ohio State Coun. Past Pres.
Delta Gamma No. 2478
Brecksville, Ohio

ALMOND TOFFEE CAKE

1/2 c. butter or margarine
1 c. sugar
2 eggs
2 c. sifted cake flour
1/2 tsp. salt
3 tsp. baking powder
2/3 c. milk
1 tsp. vanilla
Almond Toffee Frosting

Cream butter. Add sugar gradually; cream together until light and fluffy. Add eggs, one at a time, beating well after each addition. Sift together dry ingredients. Combine milk and vanilla. Add to creamed mixture alternately with dry ingredients, beginning and ending with dry ingredients. Beat until smooth after each addition. Pour batter into 2 greased and floured 8-inch layer pans. Bake at 350 degrees for about 25 minutes, until cake begins to draw away from sides of pan. Cool cake. Frost with Almond Toffee Frosting.

Almond Toffee Frosting

1/2 c. butter or margarine
4 1/2 c. sifted confectioners' sugar
1 tsp. vanilla
1/4 c. cream
2 to 3 tbsp. warm water
Toasted almond halves

Melt butter; heat, stirring constantly, until butter is deep golden brown. Remove from heat. Beat in sifted confectioners' sugar, vanilla and cream. Add warm water. Continue beating until frosting is cool and of spreading consistency. Wreathe top of cake with toasted halved almonds.

Photograph for this recipe below.

FRESH APPLE-DATE CAKE

2 c. sugar
1 1/2 c. salad oil
3 eggs
2 tsp. vanilla
2 1/2 c. sifted flour
1 tsp. soda
1/2 tsp. salt
1 tsp. cinnamon
3 c. peeled chopped apples
1 c. chopped dates
1 c. chopped pecans

Combine sugar, oil, eggs and vanilla; mix well. Sift flour, soda, salt and cinnamon together. Blend dry ingredients into sugar mixture. Add apples, dates and pecans. Turn into greased and floured tube pan. Bake in preheated 300-degree oven for 1 hour and 30 minutes. Cool for 15 minutes in pan before removing.

Thelma Waggoner, State Coun. Pres.
Alpha Delta No. 1138
Hopkinsville, Kentucky

APPLESAUCE LOAF

2 c. applesauce
1 c. raisins, washed and scalded
1 c. (packed) brown sugar
1/2 c. shortening
2 c. flour
1 tsp. soda
2 tsp. baking powder
1/2 tsp. salt
1 tsp. cinnamon or nutmeg
1/4 tsp. ginger
1/4 tsp. allspice
1 egg, beaten
1 tsp. vanilla or lemon extract

Combine applesauce and raisins. Cream sugar and shortening together; stir in applesauce mixture. Sift flour, soda, baking powder, salt and spices; blend into applesauce mixture. Add egg and vanilla; mix well. Turn into greased and floured loaf pan. Bake in preheated 350-degree oven until cake tests done. May be frosted, if desired.

Libby Knight
Beta Theta No. 1528
La Grande, Oregon

APPLESAUCE-BLACKBERRY CAKE

2 sticks margarine
2 c. sugar
2 1/2 c. applesauce
1 c. blackberry jam
5 c. all-purpose flour
4 tsp. soda
1 tsp. cinnamon
1 tsp. cloves
1 tsp. allspice
1 tsp. nutmeg
1 box seedless raisins
1 16-oz. package dates, chopped
2 c. chopped nuts

Cream margarine and sugar until light; add applesauce and jam. Mix well. Sift flour, soda and spices together; add to creamed mixture, a small amount at a time. Sprinkle a small amount additional flour over raisins and dates to keep from sticking together; add to batter, mixing well. Stir in nuts last. Turn into large tube pan or 2 medium-sized tube pans. Bake in preheated 325-degree oven until cake springs back when touched. Cool; wrap in cloth and keep in cake tin. Cake may be soaked in blackberry wine for about 2 weeks before eating, if desired. Cake will keep for 2 to 3 months.

Margaret Davis, W. and M. Chm.
Alpha Iota No. 1098
Jackson, Tennessee

APPLE-NUT SHEET CAKE

3 eggs
1 tsp. vanilla
1 c. (packed) brown sugar
3/4 c. unsifted flour
1 tsp. baking powder
1/2 tsp. salt
2 c. chopped apples
1/2 c. chopped nuts

Combine eggs and vanilla in large mixing bowl; beat until light. Add brown sugar gradually, beating well after each addition. Add flour, baking powder and salt; blend until dry ingredients are moistened. Stir in apples and nuts. Pour into greased and floured 13 x 9-inch pan. Bake in preheated 350-degree oven for 25 to 30 minutes. Serve with whipped cream or ice cream.

Patricia Donica, Treas.
Gamma Delta No. 702
Tulsa, Oklahoma

FRESH APPLE-WALNUT CAKE

1 c. sugar
1 c. (packed) brown sugar
1/2 c. margarine
2 eggs
1 c. buttermilk
1 tsp. vanilla
2 c. sifted flour
1 tsp. soda
1/2 tsp. salt
1/2 tsp. cloves
1 c. chopped apples
1/2 c. chopped walnuts

Cream sugars with margarine thoroughly. Add eggs; beat well. Stir in buttermilk; add vanilla. Sift flour, soda, salt and cloves together 3 times. Add apples and walnuts. Add to sugar mixture; mix well. Pour into greased 9 x 13-inch pan. Bake in preheated 350-degree oven for 35 minutes.

Jennetta Horchem, Pres.
Beta Eta No. 4378
Ransom, Kansas

APPLESAUCE-STRAWBERRY CAKE

1 c. margarine
1 1/2 c. sugar
2 eggs
1 No. 303 can applesauce
1/4 c. strawberry preserves
2 1/2 c. flour
2 tsp. soda
1/2 tsp. salt
1/2 tsp. cinnamon
1/4 tsp. cloves
1 c. raisins
3/4 c. chopped nuts
1/2 c. boiling water

Cream margarine and sugar; add eggs, applesauce and preserves. Mix well. Sift dry ingredients together; add to creamed mixture. Add raisins and nuts. Stir in boiling water. Pour into greased and floured oblong cake pan. Bake in preheated 350-degree oven for 1 hour.

Nancy Young, Sec.-Treas.
Kappa Nu No. 4415
Newton, Kansas

APPLESAUCE-CHERRY CAKE

2 c. sugar
1 c. butter
2 1/2 c. unsweetened applesauce
4 c. flour
1 tbsp. soda
2 c. raisins
1 tsp. cinnamon
1 tsp. allspice
1 tsp. nutmeg
1 c. halved cherries
1 c. chopped walnuts

Combine sugar and butter; beat until creamy. Add applesauce; beat well. Stir in sifted flour and soda. Add raisins, cinnamon, allspice, nutmeg, cherries and walnuts; mix well. Turn into bundt pan. Bake in preheated 350-degree oven for 1 hour.

Mrs. Jane Ray, W. and M. Chm.
Alpha Gamma No. 4426
Winchester, Virginia

CALIFORNIA BUNDT CAKE

3 c. all-purpose flour, sifted
1 tsp. cinnamon
1 tsp. salt
1 tsp. soda
2 c. sugar
2 c. diced bananas
1 1/2 c. oil
1 1/2 tsp. vanilla
3 eggs, beaten
1 8-oz. can crushed pineapple, undrained

Combine first 5 ingredients in mixing bowl; stir until blended. Add bananas, oil, vanilla, eggs and pineapple; stir until well blended. Place in greased and floured bundt pan. Bake in preheated 350-degree oven for about 1 hour. Leave in pan until completely cool.

Ernestine DeJarnatt, Treas.
Beta Rho No. 4135
Owensboro, Kentucky

BANANA-HONEY CAKE

1 c. honey
1 tsp. soda
1 c. rolled oats
3/4 c. butter or margarine, softened
1/2 c. sugar
2 eggs
1 c. mashed bananas
1 1/2 c. sifted all-purpose flour
3/4 tsp. salt
3/4 tsp. baking powder
2   3-oz. packages cream cheese,
   softened
2 1/2 c. sifted confectioners' sugar

Bring honey to a boil in medium saucepan. Add 1/2 teaspoon soda. Pour over oats. Stir and cover. Let stand for 10 minutes. Beat butter until creamy; gradually add sugar, beating until fluffy. Blend in eggs. Add oats mixture and bananas; beat until blended. Sift together flour, remaining 1/2 teaspoon soda, salt and baking powder. Add to creamed mixture, mixing well. Pour batter into 2 greased and waxed paper-lined 8-inch round cake pans. Bake in preheated 350-degree oven 30 to 35 minutes. Cool on wire rack about 10 minutes. Remove from pans; cool. Beat cream cheese until fluffy. Add confectioners' sugar gradually, beating until frosting is of spreading consistency. Spread between layers and over top of cake. Refrigerate. Garnish with banana slices.

Photograph for this recipe above.

BANANA BAKED IN DOUGH CAKE

1/2 c. butter
1 1/2 c. sugar
1 tsp. vanilla
2 eggs, well beaten
1/2 c. sour milk
1 tsp. soda
2 c. flour
3 or 4 overripe bananas, mashed

Cream butter and sugar; add vanilla, eggs and milk. Mix well. Blend in soda and flour. Stir in bananas. Turn into cake pan. Bake in preheated 350-degree oven for 30 minutes.

Icing

1/4 c. butter, melted until brown
2 1/2 c. powdered sugar
1 tsp. vanilla

Combine all ingredients; mix until thick. Spread over cake.

Paralee Johnson, Sec.
Gamma Delta No. 702
Tulsa, Oklahoma

BANANA-NUT CAKE

2/3 c. butter
1 2/3 c. sugar
3 eggs
1 1/4 c. mashed bananas
2 1/4 c. flour
1 1/4 tsp. baking powder
1 1/4 tsp. soda
1 tsp. salt
2/3 c. buttermilk
2/3 c. chopped nuts
Caramel frosting
Pecan halves

Cream butter with sugar; blend in eggs. Add bananas; mix well. Combine flour, baking powder, soda and salt; add to creamed mixture alternately with buttermilk. Stir in nuts. Pour into greased and floured 13 x 9-inch pan. Bake in preheated 350-degree oven for 45 to 50 minutes. Cool; frost with caramel frosting. Cut into squares; top each with pecan half.

Ruth Bohlen, Pres.
Alpha Chi
Cocoa, Florida

BREAD PUDDING CAKE

2 loaves French bread
1/2 gal. milk
2 1/2 c. sugar
1/2 tsp. salt
1 tbsp. vanilla
4 eggs
1 3-oz. package instant vanilla
    pudding mix

Remove crust from bread; break into pieces. Soak in milk. Run mixture through blender. Add sugar, salt, vanilla and eggs; mix well. Pour into well-greased tube pan. Bake in preheated 375-degree oven for 1 hour and 30 minutes. Cool in pan for 2 hours. Invert on plate. Cool for 3 hours at room temperature. Refrigerate overnight. Prepare pudding mix according to package directions, using 1 1/2 cups cold milk. Frost cake.

Wyoma Jackson, Publ. Chm.
Alpha Zeta No. 1779
Tuscaloosa, Alabama

BABY FOOD CARROT CAKE

2 c. flour
2 c. sugar
2 tsp. soda
2 tsp. cinnamon
1 tsp. salt
1 c. oil
4 eggs
3 sm. jars baby food carrots

Sift dry ingredients together; add oil, mixing well. Add eggs, one at a time, mixing well after each addition. Add carrots; blend thoroughly. Pour into greased and floured bundt pan. Bake in preheated 350-degree oven for 40 to 45 minutes.

Icing

1 stick butter
1 8-oz. package cream cheese
1 1-lb. box of confectioners' sugar
2 tsp. vanilla extract
1 c. chopped pecans

Cream butter and cream cheese thoroughly; blend in sugar. Add vanilla extract and pecans. Add a small amount of milk if mixture is too dry to make of spreading consistency. Spread on cake.

Linda D. Young, Pres.
Delta Alpha No. 2664
St. Cloud, Florida

CARROT-COCONUT CAKE

1 1/2 c. cooking oil
2 c. sugar
3 eggs
2 1/4 c. flour
2 tsp. cinnamon
2 tsp. soda
1 tsp. salt
2 c. shredded carrots
2 c. flaked coconut
1 c. chopped nuts
1 c. crushed pineapple
2 tsp. vanilla

Cream oil, sugar and eggs together. Sift next 4 ingredients together; add to oil mixture. Blend thoroughly. Add remaining ingredients; mix well. Pour into well-greased 13 x 9-inch pan. Bake in preheated 350-degree oven for about 40 minutes.

Frosting

1 3-oz. package cream cheese, softened
1/4 c. melted butter
2 c. powdered sugar
2 tsp. milk
1 tsp. vanilla

Blend all ingredients together; beat thoroughly until of spreading consistency, adding either milk or powdered sugar as required. Spread on cake.

Edna Jacob, Educational Dir.
Alpha Beta No. 165
Lincoln, Nebraska

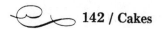

CARROT-PECAN CAKE

2 c. sugar
1 1/2 c. salad oil
4 eggs, well beaten
2 tsp. soda
2 c. all-purpose flour
2 tsp. baking powder
2 tsp. cinnamon
1 tsp. salt
1 c. chopped pecans or walnuts
3 c. grated carrots

Combine sugar and oil; add eggs, mixing well. Combine dry ingredients; stir into oil mixture. Mix until smooth. Add chopped pecans and carrots. Turn into 3 greased 9-inch cake pans. Bake in preheated 325-degree oven about 30 minutes or in 9 x 13-inch loaf pan for about 45 minutes. Cool.

Icing

1 1-lb. box powdered sugar
1 8-oz. package cream cheese,
    softened
1/2 stick margarine, softened
1 tsp. lemon extract

Combine all ingredients; mix until smooth. Spread on cooled cake. Top with nuts, if desired.

Jeanne Haase, Pres.
Beta Omicron No. 1881
Seattle, Washington

CARROT-PINEAPPLE CAKE

1 c. sugar
1 1/2 c. Mazola oil
4 eggs
1 sm. can crushed pineapple, drained
1 tsp. vanilla
2 c. sifted flour
2 tsp. soda
1/2 tsp. salt
1 tsp. cinnamon
2 c. grated carrots

Cream sugar and oil together; add eggs, one at a time, beating well after each addition. Add pineapple and vanilla. Sift dry ingredi-

ents together; blend into creamed mixture. Stir in carrots. Turn into well greased and floured 9 x 13-inch pan. Bake in preheated 350-degree oven for 30 to 35 minutes.

Frosting

1/2 stick margarine, softened
1 8-oz. package cream cheese, softened
2 c. powdered sugar

Combine all ingredients; mix until smooth. Spread over cake.

Shirley Perkins
Zeta Lambda No. 2395
Salina, Kansas

GLAZED CARROT CAKE

2 c. sifted flour
2 tsp. baking powder
2 tsp. soda
1 tsp. salt
2 tsp. cinnamon
2 c. sugar
1 c. corn oil
4 lg. eggs
2 c. (lightly packed) grated carrots
1/2 c. chopped pecans
1/2 c. chopped walnuts
2 c. sifted confectioners' sugar
4 to 4 1/2 tbsp. water
1/4 tsp. almond extract

Sift flour, baking powder, soda, salt and cinnamon together. Beat sugar and oil for 2 minutes in a large mixing bowl with electric beater at medium speed. Add sifted dry ingredients alternately with eggs, beginning and ending with dry ingredients and beating after each addition. Stir in carrots and nuts. Turn into greased angel food pan. Bake in preheated 350-degree oven for 1 hour or until cake tests done. Don't open oven during baking. Cool in pan for 5 minutes; loosen around pan. Turn out and cool. Mix confectioners' sugar, water and extract, adding more water to make a thick pouring consistency. Pour over cake; let drizzle down sides of cake.

Jan Stumpo, Sec.
Gamma Delta No. 3767
Tucker, Georgia

CARROT SHEET CAKE

4 eggs
2 c. sugar
1 1/2 c. salad oil
2 c. flour
2 tsp. soda
1 tsp. salt
1 tsp. cinnamon
3 sm. jars strained baby food carrots
1 c. chopped nuts

Beat eggs until thick; add sugar and oil. Sift flour, soda, salt and cinnamon together. Blend into egg mixture. Add carrots, then nuts; blend well. Pour into 15 x 11-inch jelly roll pan. Bake in preheated 350-degree oven for 40 minutes.

Frosting

1 8-oz. package cream cheese, softened
1 1-lb. box powdered sugar
4 tsp. margarine
1/2 tsp. vanilla

Combine all ingredients; mix well. Spread on cake.

Kay Thompson, Soc. Chm.
Epsilon Iota No. 1572
Garden City, Kansas

CHERRY COFFEE CAKE

2 c. flour
1 c. sugar
2 tsp. baking powder
1/2 c. butter
1 egg
Milk
1 can cherry pie filling
Topping Mixture

Sift flour, sugar, and baking powder together; cut in butter. Break egg into a 1-cup measuring cup, add enough milk to make 1 cup liquid. Beat the egg into the milk; add to flour mixture. Pour into a greased and floured jelly roll pan. Cover with pie filling. Sprinkle with the Topping Mixture. Bake in preheated 400-degree oven for 30 to 35 minutes.

Topping Mixture

1 c. flour
1/2 c. butter
1 c. sugar

Combine all ingredients; mix until crumbly.

Karen S. Ford, Pres.
Alpha Theta No. 4472
Columbia, Missouri

CHERRY UPSIDE-DOWN CAKE

3 tbsp. butter
1/2 c. (packed) light brown sugar
1 1-lb. can water-packed sour cherries
1 1/4 c. flour
1 1/2 tsp. baking powder
1/2 tsp. salt
3/4 c. sugar
1 egg
1/4 c. shortening
1/2 c. milk
1/2 tsp. vanilla

Melt butter in 8-inch pan in 350-degree oven. Stir in brown sugar, spreading over bottom of pan. Drain cherries and reserve juice; distribute cherries evenly in pan. Combine flour, baking powder, salt and sugar; mix in egg, shortening, milk and vanilla until smooth. Pour over cherries. Bake for 45 minutes. Let stand in pan, then loosen and turn out.

Cherry Sauce

Reserved cherry juice
1/4 c. water
1 tbsp. lemon juice
2 tbsp. sugar
1 tbsp. cornstarch

Combine cherry juice, water and lemon juice in saucepan; blend in combined sugar and cornstarch. Cook, stirring, over medium heat until thickened. Pour over cake or individual servings.

Marsha Kendall
Alpha Phi No. 1438
Winner, South Dakota

CHERRY-WALNUT CAKE

1 can sour cherries
1 c. flour
1 c. sugar
1 tsp. soda
1/4 tsp. salt
1 egg, beaten
1 tbsp. melted butter
3/4 c. chopped walnuts

Drain cherries; reserve juice for glaze. Combine flour, sugar, soda and salt; add cherries. Combine egg, melted butter and walnuts; add to batter. Mix well. Turn into greased and floured 9 x 13-inch glass baking dish. Bake in preheated 350-degree oven for 35 minutes.

Glaze

Reserved juice
1 tbsp. cornstarch
1/2 c. sugar
1 tbsp. butter
Pinch of salt
1/2 pt. whipping cream, whipped

Combine reserved juice with enough water to make 1 cup liquid; place in saucepan. Add cornstarch, sugar, butter and salt. Bring to a boil, stirring constantly. Cool. Frost cake with whipped cream; pour glaze over top. Refrigerate until serving time.

Esther Bonzelet, Pres.
Beta Lambda No. 2679
West Allis, Wisconsin

DELICIOUS CHERRY-NUT CAKE

1 1/2 c. sugar
1 c. butter
5 egg yolks
2 egg whites, beaten
3 c. flour
2 1/2 tsp. baking powder
1/2 tsp. salt
3/4 c. milk
1 tsp. vanilla
1 bottle cherries, drained and diced
1 c. chopped nuts

Cream sugar and butter until fluffy; add egg yolks. Beat until light. Add egg whites; beat

for 1 minute on slow speed. Add flour, baking powder and salt alternately with milk and vanilla. Dust cherries and nuts with small amount additional flour; fold into batter. Turn into greased and floured angel food pan. Bake in preheated 325-degree oven for 1 hour. Cool; remove from pan. Top with powdered sugar and milk glaze, if desired.

Dawn Gould
Delta Nu No. 4528
Tempe, Arizona

EASY CHERRY CAKE

1 can cherries
2 c. flour
1 c. sugar
2/3 c. Wesson oil
2 eggs
1 1/2 tsp. soda
1/2 c. chopped nuts
6 oz. cream cheese, softened
2 c. powdered sugar
1 tsp. vanilla
4 tbsp. softened butter

Drain cherries; reserve juice. Combine cherries, flour, sugar, oil, eggs and soda; add half the reserved juice. Mix well; stir in nuts. Pour into 9 x 13-inch pan. Pour remaining juice over top. Bake in preheated 350-degree oven until done. Combine remaining ingredients for icing; blend well. Spread over warm cake.

Ruth Livingston, Parliamentarian
Gamma Mu No. 749
Garden City, Kansas

SPECIAL CHERRY-NUT CAKE

2 c. sugar
1 lb. butter
12 eggs
4 c. flour, sifted
2 oz. lemon flavoring
1/2 lb. red candied cherries, cut up
1/2 lb. green candied cherries, cut up
1 lb. white raisins
1 qt. pecans, chopped

Cream sugar and butter until light; beat in 6 eggs, one at a time. Add 2 cups flour. Add remaining eggs, flavoring and 1 cup flour; mix well. Add remaining flour to cherries, raisins and pecans. Stir into batter. Turn into greased and floured tube pan. Bake in preheated 350-degree oven for 1 hour and 30 minutes.

Louise Raby, W. and M. Chm.
Alpha Epsilon No. 1461
Greenville, South Carolina

CHESS CAKE

1 1-lb. box light brown sugar
1 c. sugar
4 eggs
2 sticks margarine
2 c. self-rising flour
1/2 c. chopped nuts
1 tsp. vanilla

Combine sugars, eggs and margarine; beat until light. Add flour; mix well. Blend in nuts and vanilla. Pour into greased and floured 13 1/2 x 9 1/2-inch pan. Bake in preheated 325-degree oven for 45 minutes.

Jessie G. Morris, Pres.
Beta Rho No. 4135
Owensboro, Kentucky

CHOCOLATE CHIP-OATMEAL CAKE

1 3/4 c. boiling water
1 c. oatmeal
1 c. (lightly packed) brown sugar
1 c. sugar
1/2 c. margarine
2 lg. eggs
1 3/4 c. flour
1 tsp. soda
1/2 tsp. salt
1 tbsp. cocoa
1 12-oz. package chocolate chips
3/4 c. chopped walnuts

Pour water over oatmeal. Let stand for 10 minutes. Add sugars and margarine; stir until melted. Add eggs; mix well. Sift flour, soda, salt and cocoa together; add to sugar mixture. Mix well. Add 1/2 of the chocolate chips to dough. Pour batter into greased and floured 9 x 13-inch pan. Sprinkle walnuts

and remaining chocolate chips over top. Bake in preheated 350-degree oven for 40 minutes.

Georgia Stephen
Beta Tau No. 472
Grand Junction, Colorado

CHOCOLATE CHIFFON CAKE

2 1/4 c. sifted cake flour
1 c. sugar
3 tsp. baking powder
1 tsp. salt
1/2 c. corn oil
6 eggs, separated
3/4 c. chocolate-flavored syrup
1/4 c. water
1 tsp. vanilla
1/2 tsp. cream of tartar

Sift cake flour, sugar, baking powder and salt together into mixing bowl. Make well in center; add corn oil, egg yolks, chocolate syrup, water and vanilla in order listed. Beat with spoon until smooth. Beat cream of tartar with egg whites until stiff peaks form. Fold in first mixture gently, blending well. Do not stir. Turn batter into ungreased 10-inch tube pan. Bake in 325-degree oven until cake springs back when lightly touched with finger, about 1 hour and 10 to 15 minutes. Invert over bottle or funnel immediately. Let cool. Loosen sides of cake with spatula; remove from pan.

Photograph for this recipe below.

CHOCOLATE BUNDT CAKE

1/2 lb. butter or margarine
2 c. sugar
4 eggs
8 sm. plain chocolate candy bars,
    melted
1/4 tsp. salt
2 1/2 c. flour, sifted
1/4 tsp. soda
1 c. buttermilk
1 5 1/2-oz. can chocolate syrup
2 tsp. vanilla
1 c. chopped pecans
Powdered sugar

Cream butter and sugar. Add eggs, one at a time, beating well after each addition. Add candy bars. Sift dry ingredients together; add alternately with buttermilk, beating well after each addition. Add chocolate syrup and vanilla; fold in pecans. Turn into a large, greased tube or bundt pan. Bake in preheated 315-degree oven for 1 hour and 30 minutes to 1 hour and 45 minutes. Cool; remove from pan. Sprinkle with powdered sugar.

> Janet Shaw, Sec.
> Rho Zeta No. 4625
> Austin, Texas

CHOCOLATE DELIGHT CAKE

3/4 c. butter or margarine
2 1/4 c. sugar
1 1/2 tsp. vanilla
3 eggs
3 1-oz. squares unsweetened
    chocolate, melted
3 c. sifted cake flour
1 1/2 tsp. soda
3/4 tsp. salt
1 1/2 c. ice water
Date Cream Filling
Fudge Frosting

Cream butter and sugar together with mixer at medium speed until light and fluffy; beat in vanilla. Add eggs, one at a time, beating well after each addition. Blend in chocolate. Sift flour, soda and salt together; add alternately with water to creamed mixture, beating well after each addition. Pour batter into 3 greased and waxed paper-lined 8-inch round cake pans. Bake in preheated 350-degree oven 30 to 35 minutes or until cake tests done. Cool in pans on rack for 10 minutes; remove from pans. Cool on racks. Spread filling between layers; cover with frosting.

Date Cream Filling

1 c. milk
1/2 c. chopped dates
1 tbsp. flour
1/4 c. sugar
1 egg, beaten
1/2 c. chopped walnuts
1 tsp. vanilla

Combine milk and dates in top of double boiler; heat mixture over low heat. Combine flour and sugar in small bowl. Add egg; beat until smooth. Stir into hot milk mixture. Place over simmering water. Cook, stirring constantly, until thick. Cool. Stir in walnuts and vanilla.

Fudge Frosting

2 c. sugar
1/4 tsp. salt
1 c. light cream
2 tbsp. light corn syrup
2 1-oz. squares unsweetened
    chocolate

Combine all ingredients in 2-quart saucepan. Cook over low heat, stirring constantly, until sugar dissolves. Cover saucepan; cook for 2 minutes. Remove cover; cook to 234 degrees on candy thermometer or to soft-ball stage. Remove from heat. Beat with wooden spoon to spreading consistency. Add a small amount hot water if frosting becomes too stiff or confectioners' sugar if too thin.

> Sondra Davis, Corr. Sec.
> Gamma Lambda No. 2937
> Weslaco, Texas

CHOCOLATE DUMP CAKE

2 c. all-purpose flour
2 c. sugar
1 tsp. salt

1 stick butter or margarine
4 tbsp. cocoa
1/2 c. vegetable oil
1 c. water
2 eggs
1 tsp. vanilla
1/2 c. buttermilk
1 tsp. soda

Sift flour, sugar and salt together in large bowl. Combine butter, cocoa, vegetable oil and water in skillet; bring to a boil. Pour over flour mixture; beat well. Add eggs, vanilla and buttermilk with soda added; beat well. Pour into greased 13 x 9 x 2-inch baking pan. Bake in preheated 350-degree oven for 35 minutes or until done.

Topping

1 stick butter
4 tbsp. cocoa
6 tbsp. milk
1   1-lb. box powdered sugar
1 c. chopped pecans
1 tsp. salt

Combine butter, cocoa and milk in skillet; bring to a boil. Stir in powdered sugar; fold in pecans and salt. Pour over cake as soon as cake is removed from oven.

Gretchen Schranty, Pres.
Beta Theta No. 3956
Louisville, Kentucky

CHOCOLATE FRUITCAKE

1 c. sugar
1/2 c. salad oil
1 1/2 c. applesauce
2 c. flour, sifted
3 tbsp. cocoa
1 tbsp. cornstarch
1 tsp. cinnamon
1/2 tsp. cloves
1/2 tsp. nutmeg
1/2 tsp. soda
1 c. chopped nuts
1 c. raisins
1 c. chopped mixed candied fruit

Combine sugar, oil and applesauce; mix well. Sift dry ingredients together; stir into applesauce mixture. Blend in nuts, raisins and candied fruit. Pour into loaf pan or angel food pan. Bake in preheated 350-degree oven until cake tests done.

Sharon K. Riggert
ESA Headquarters No. 9006
Loveland, Colorado

CHOCOLATE POTATO CAKE

2 c. sugar
1 c. (scant) butter or margarine
1/2 c. milk
1/4 c. cocoa
1 c. mashed potatoes
1 c. nuts, chopped (opt.)
3 eggs, separated
2 c. (scant) flour
2 tsp. (heaping) baking powder
1 tsp. vanilla

Cream sugar and butter; add milk and cocoa. Add mashed potatoes, nuts and beaten egg yolks. Sift flour and baking powder together, then add to batter, mixing well. Fold in beaten egg whites and vanilla. Spread into 5 medium-sized round cake pans. Bake in preheated 350-degree oven until cake tests done. Frost with favorite icing.

Mary E. Kay
Beta Eta Chap.
Fairfield, Illinois

DATE-CHOCOLATE CHIP CAKE

1 c. cut-up dates
1 1/2 c. boiling water
1 tsp. soda
1 c. sugar
1/2 c. shortening
2 eggs
1 1/2 c. flour
1/2 tsp. salt
1/2 c. (or more) chocolate chips

Combine dates, boiling water and soda; set aside. Cream sugar and shortening together; add eggs, mixing well. Add flour and salt; mix well. Mix in date mixture. Pour into greased cake pan; sprinkle chocolate chips over top. Bake in preheated 350-degree oven for 30 minutes.

Susan H. Duckworth, W. and M. Com.
Alpha Alpha No. 1657
Salt Lake City, Utah

CHOCOLATE SHEET CAKE

2 c. sugar
2 c. flour
1 tsp. soda
1 tsp. cinnamon
2 sticks margarine
4 tbsp. cocoa
1 c. water
1/2 c. buttermilk
2 eggs, slightly beaten
1 tsp. vanilla

Sift first 4 ingredients together. Combine margarine, cocoa and water in saucepan; bring to a rapid boil. Pour over flour mixture; stir until well blended. Add remaining ingredients; mix well. Pour into greased 11 x 16-inch jelly roll pan. Bake in preheated 400-degree oven for 20 minutes. Begin making frosting about 5 minutes before cake is done.

Frosting

1 stick margarine
4 tbsp. cocoa
6 tbsp. milk
1   1-lb. box (scant) powdered sugar
1 tsp. vanilla
1 c. chopped walnuts or pecans

Combine first 3 ingredients; bring to a boil. Remove from heat; add remaining ingredients. Beat well. Spread on hot cake. Cut into squares to serve.

Paula Pendergrass, W. and M. Com.
Epsilon Epsilon No. 3475
Gresham, Oregon

COCA-COLA CAKE

2 c. all-purpose flour
2 c. sugar
1/4 tsp. salt
2 sticks margarine
1 c. Coca-Cola
2 tbsp. cocoa
1/2 c. buttermilk
1 tsp. soda
2 eggs
1 tsp. vanilla
1 1/2 c. miniature marshmallows

Sift flour, sugar and salt together in bowl. Combine margarine, Coca-Cola and cocoa in saucepan; bring to a boil. Pour over flour mixture. Add buttermilk, soda, eggs and vanilla; mix well. Stir in marshmallows. Batter will be thin. Pour in 13 x 9 x 2-inch pan. Bake in preheated 325-degree oven for 30 to 35 minutes.

Icing

1 stick margarine
1 tbsp. cocoa
1/3 c. Coca-Cola
1   1-lb. box powdered sugar
1 tsp. vanilla
1 c. chopped pecans

Combine margarine, cocoa and Coca-Cola in saucepan; bring to a boil. Pour over sugar. Add vanilla and pecans; mix well. Pour over cake while hot.

Margaret True Johnson, Treas.
Beta Sigma No. 2853
Florence, Alabama

DEVIL'S FOOD CAKE

1/2 c. cocoa
2 tsp. soda
1 c. hot water
2 c. sugar
1/2 c. shortening
Dash of salt
2 eggs
2 1/2 c. flour
1 tsp. cinnamon
1 c. sour milk or buttermilk

Dissolve cocoa and soda in hot water; cool. Combine sugar, shortening, salt and eggs in mixing bowl, mix thoroughly. Add cocoa mixture alternately with flour and cinnamon mixture; beat well. Stir in sour milk. Spread in greased and floured oblong baking dish. Bake in preheated 350-degree oven until cake tests done.

Fudge Frosting

3 tbsp. cocoa
1/3 c. milk
1 c. sugar

1/4 c. margarine
1/4 tsp. salt
1 tsp. vanilla

Place cocoa, milk, sugar, margarine and salt in saucepan; bring to a full boil. Boil for 3 minutes, stirring constantly. Remove from heat; beat until lukewarm. Add vanilla; beat until thick enough to spread. Add 1 table-spoon cream if too thick. Spread over cake. May be doubled for 2-layer cake.

Theresa Clark, Pres.
Alpha Omicron No. 577
Enid, Oklahoma

HEATH BAR CAKE

2 c. sifted flour
1/4 tsp. salt
2 c. (packed) light brown sugar
1/3 c. margarine
1 egg, slightly beaten
1 1/2 tsp. vanilla
1 c. milk
1 tsp. soda
6 Heath bars, chilled and broken up
1/2 c. chopped pecans

Combine flour, salt, brown sugar and margarine; mix until crumbly. Reserve 1 cup crumb mixture. Combine egg, vanilla, milk and soda; stir into remaining crumb mixture. Pour into greased 9 x 13-inch pan. Combine reserved crumb mixture, candy and pecans; sprinkle over batter. Bake in preheated 350-degree oven for 30 to 35 minutes.

Hilda Holston, Ed. Dir.
Gamma Beta No. 4513
Poway, California

MAYONNAISE CAKE

2 c. flour
1 c. sugar
1 1/2 tsp. baking powder
1 1/2 tsp. soda
4 tbsp. cocoa
1 c. cold water
1 c. mayonnaise
2 tsp. vanilla

Sift dry ingredients together. Add remaining ingredients. Mix until smooth. Place in greased and floured baking pan Bake in pre-heated 350-degree oven until cake tests done.

Frosting

1 c. sugar
1/4 c. cocoa
1/4 c. milk
1/2 c. butter or margarine

Combine all ingredients in saucepan; bring to a boil. Boil for 1 minute. Poke holes in hot cake with a fork. Pour hot Frosting over cake.

Sharon Ellenburg, Jr. Past Pres.
Gamma Kappa No. 3265
Thornton, Colorado

MILKY WAY CAKE

8 Milky Way bars
2 sticks margarine
2 cups sugar
4 eggs, well beaten
1/2 tsp. soda
1 1/4 c. buttermilk
2 1/2 c. flour
1 c. chopped pecans

Melt Milky Way bars and 1 stick margarine together in top of double boiler; set aside to cool. Cream sugar and remaining margarine; add eggs. Dissolve soda in buttermilk; add to egg mixture alternately with flour, beating well after each addition. Add candy mixture and pecans. Turn into tube pan. Bake in pre-heated 325-degree oven for 1 hour and 10 minutes or until cake tests done.

Chocolate Icing

2 1/2 c. sugar
1 c. milk
1   6-oz. package semisweet
    chocolate chips
1 c. marshmallow creme
1 stick margarine

Cook sugar and milk to soft-ball stage; add chocolate chips, marshmallow creme and margarine. Stir until melted and smooth. Beat until of spreading consistency; spread on cake.

Evette Miller, Treas.
Alpha Kappa No. 4604
Savannah, Georgia

ONE-BOWL
BUTTERMILK-CHOCOLATE CAKE

1 3/4 c. sifted cake flour
1 1/2 c. sugar
1 tsp. soda
1 tsp. salt
1/2 c. cocoa
1/2 c. soft shortening
1 c. buttermilk
2 eggs, unbeaten

Sift cake flour, sugar, soda, salt and cocoa together. Add shortening and 2/3 cup buttermilk. Beat vigorously by hand, 300 strokes, or beat with electric mixer at medium speed, 2 minutes. Add remaining 1/3 cup buttermilk and eggs. Beat 2 minutes. Pour batter into two 8-inch greased layer cake pans, lined with waxed paper and greased again. Bake in 350-degree oven until cake shrinks from edge of pan and springs back when lightly touched with finger in center of cake, about 30 minutes. Remove from oven. Cool at room temperature in pans for 10 minutes; remove from pans. Frost with your favorite frosting.

Photograph for this recipe above.

MISSISSIPPI MUD CAKE

2 sticks butter or margarine
2 tbsp. cocoa
4 eggs
1 1/2 c. coconut
2 c. sugar
1 tsp. vanilla
1 1/2 c. flour
1 1/2 c. nuts

Combine all ingredients; mix well. Spread in greased and floured 13 x 9-inch pan. Bake in preheated 350-degree oven for 30 to 40 minutes.

Icing

1   7 1/2-oz. jar marshmallow creme
1   1-lb. box powdered sugar

1 stick butter or margarine, softened
1/2 c. cocoa
1/2 c. milk
1 tsp. vanilla

Remove cake from oven; spread marshmallow creme over top. Cool cake. Combine powdered sugar, butter, cocoa, milk and vanilla; mix until smooth. Spread over cake.

Linda Northum, Treas.
Sigma Chi No. 4375
Richardson, Texas

NEVER-FAIL CHOCOLATE CAKE

1 1/2 c. sifted flour
1 1/2 c. sugar
1/2 c. cocoa
3/4 tsp. salt
1 1/4 tsp. soda
2/3 c. shortening
1 c. sour cream or buttermilk
1 tsp. vanilla
2 eggs

Combine first 5 ingredients; add shortening, 2/3 cup sour cream and vanilla. Beat for 2 minutes. Add remaining 1/3 cup sour cream and eggs; beat for 1 minute longer. Pour batter into 2 greased and floured 8-inch round cake pans. Bake in preheated 350-degree oven for 25 minutes or until cake tests done.

Dorothy Boyd
Zeta Lambda No. 2395
Salina, Kansas

EASY DUMP CAKE

1 c. sugar
1 egg
1 stick butter, melted
1/4 c. cocoa
1 1/2 c. flour
1/2 c. sour milk
1/2 c. hot water
1 tsp. soda
1 tsp. vanilla
Pinch of salt

Combine all ingredients; mix until well blended with mixer. Pour into greased and floured 8-inch square pan. Bake in preheated 350-degree oven for about 30 minutes or until done.

Icing

1 stick margarine
4 tbsp. cocoa
6 1/2 tbsp. milk
1 1-lb. box confectioners' sugar
1 tbsp. vanilla
1/2 c. chopped nuts

Combine margarine, cocoa and milk in saucepan; bring to a boil. Add sugar and vanilla; beat with mixer until smooth. Stir in nuts. Pour over hot cake; spread evenly.

Peggy Diehl
Alpha Iota No. 3365
Waynesboro, Virginia

SAUERKRAUT CHOCOLATE CAKE

2/3 c. butter or margarine
1 1/2 c. less 2 tbsp. sugar
3 eggs
1 tsp. vanilla
1/2 c. cocoa
2 1/4 c. sifted flour
1 tsp. baking powder
3/4 tsp. soda
1/4 tsp. salt
1 1/4 c. water
2/3 c. rinsed sauerkraut, drained
    and coarsely chopped

Cream together butter and sugar thoroughly. Beat in eggs and vanilla. Sift dry ingredients together. Add dry ingredients alternately with water to egg mixture. Stir in sauerkraut. Turn batter into 2 greased and floured 8-inch square or round baking pans. Bake in preheated 350-degree oven for about 30 minutes or until a wooden pick inserted in center comes out clean. Frost with favorite icing.

Esther Johnston, Pres.
Beta Nu No. 510
Pueblo, Colorado

NO-FROST CHOCOLATE CHIP CAKE

1 tsp. soda
1 c. chopped dates
1 c. shortening
1 c. sugar
2 eggs
2 c. flour
1/2 tsp. salt
1 tbsp. cocoa
1 tsp. vanilla
1 c. chocolate chips
1/2 c. chopped nuts

Add soda to dates; pour 1 cup and 3 tablespoons hot water over dates. Cream shortening and sugar; add date mixture, eggs, flour, salt, cocoa and vanilla. Beat well. Add 1/2 cup chocolate chips. Pour into greased and floured 9 x 13-inch baking pan. Sprinkle remaining chocolate chips and nuts over top. Bake in preheated 350-degree oven for 40 minutes.

Madonna York, Awards Chm.
Alpha Omega
Kirkwood, Missouri

WACKY CAKE

1 c. sugar
1 1/2 c. flour
3 tbsp. cocoa
1 tsp. soda
1/2 tsp. salt
1 tbsp. vinegar
1 tsp. vanilla
6 tbsp. vegetable oil
1 c. cold water
1/3 c. soft butter
1/4 c. cream or evaporated milk
2/3 c. (packed) brown sugar
1/2 c. Angel Flake coconut

Sift sugar, flour, cocoa, soda and salt together in an ungreased 8-inch cake pan. Make 3 holes in flour mixture; pour vinegar in first hole, vanilla in second hole and oil in third hole. Cover with cold water. Stir mixture with fork until lumps are gone. Bake in preheated 350-degree oven for 30 minutes. Combine remaining ingredients, mixing well.

Spread over hot cake. Place under broiler until lightly browned.

Mary Haines
Alpha Chi No. 871
Deming, New Mexico

BLACK BOTTOM CUPCAKES

1/8 tsp. salt
2 eggs
2 8-oz. packages cream cheese
1 2/3 c. sugar
1 tsp. soda
1/4 c. cocoa
1 1/2 c. flour
1 tsp vanilla
1 tbsp. vinegar
1/3 c. cooking oil
1 c. water
1 6-oz. package chocolate chips
Finely chopped pecans to taste

Combine salt, eggs, cream cheese and 2/3 cup sugar in mixer bowl; beat until creamy and smooth. Set aside. Combine soda, cocoa, flour, vanilla, vinegar, oil, water and remaining 1 cup sugar; mix until well blended. Stir in chocolate chips. Line muffin tins with liners; fill 1/3 full with chocolate mixture. Add heaping spoonful of cream cheese mixture. Sprinkle with pecans. Bake in preheated 350-degree oven for 20 to 25 minutes or until done. Yield: About 36 cupcakes.

Gladys Jenkins, Pres.
Delta Delta No. 3602
San Angelo, Texas

FUDGE CUPCAKES

1/2 lb. margarine
4 sq. semisweet chocolate
1 1/2 c. broken pecans
1 c. flour
1 3/4 c. sugar
4 lg. eggs
1 tsp. vanilla

Melt margarine and chocolate together; add pecans. Combine flour, sugar, eggs and vanilla; mix lightly but do not beat. Add chocolate mixture, stirring until well blended.

Fill muffin tins almost full. Bake in pre-heated 350-degree oven for 35 minutes.

Virginia Smith, Pres.
Zeta Epsilon No. 2399
Merriam, Kansas

CLINGCAKE

1   1-lb. 13-oz. can cling peach slices
2 c. sifted flour
2 tsp. soda
1 tsp. salt
2 eggs
1 1/2 c. sugar
1 c. (packed) brown sugar
3/4 c. chopped nuts

Drain peaches; reserve syrup. Chop peaches coarsely. Sift flour with soda and salt. Cream eggs and sugar together; blend in flour mixture and reserved peach syrup. Stir in peaches. Turn batter into greased and floured 13 x 9-inch baking pan or bundt pan. Mix brown sugar and nuts; sprinkle evenly over batter. Bake in preheated 300-degree oven for 1 hour or until toothpick inserted comes out dry.

Mabel Wells, Sec.
Gamma Tau No. 811
Elk City, Oklahoma

AUNT MAY'S OLD-FASHIONED COCONUT CAKE

1 c. butter
2 c. sugar
3 c. cake flour
3 tsp. baking powder
1/4 tsp. salt
5 egg yolks
1 c. milk
3 egg whites
1 tsp. vanilla

Cream butter; add sugar gradually, beating well. Sift flour and measure, then sift again with baking powder and salt. Beat egg yolks until lemony in color; add milk and beat well. Beat egg whites until stiff but not dry. Add flour mixture and milk mixture alternately to creamed mixture, beginning and ending with flour mixture. Beat well after each addition. Add vanilla; beat well. Fold in egg whites. Pour into three 9-inch cake pans. Bake in preheated 350-degree oven for 30 to 35 minutes or until cake tests done.

Icing

14 lg. marshmallows
2 c. sugar
3/4 c. hot water
2 egg whites, stiffly beaten
1 or 2 cans coconut or 1 lg.
    coconut, grated

Cut marshmallows into small pieces; set aside. Combine sugar and water in top of double boiler; cook, stirring, until sugar is dissolved. Cook until mixture spins thread when dropped from spoon. Pour slowly into beaten egg whites, beating constantly until well combined. Add marshmallows; beat until thick. Spread between layers, over top and side of cake, sprinkling all with coconut.

Kay Woodbury, Pres.
Kappa Tau No. 4642
Brevard, North Carolina

COCONUT-VANILLA WAFER CAKE

2 sticks margarine
2 c. sugar
6 eggs
1   12-oz. box vanilla wafers, crushed
1/2 c. milk
1   7-oz. can Angel Flake coconut
1 c. chopped pecans

Combine margarine and sugar; cream until very fluffy. Add eggs, one at a time, beating well after each addition. Add crushed wafers and milk alternately. Blend in coconut and pecans. Turn into well-greased and floured tube pan. Bake in preheated 350-degree oven for 1 hour and 10 minutes or until done. Serve plain, with whipped cream or German chocolate icing.

Norma L. Chittenden, State Hist.
Epsilon Mu No. 1693
Hays, Kansas

ITALIAN COCONUT CAKE

2 c. sugar
5 eggs, separated
1 stick margarine
1/2 c. Crisco
1 tsp. soda
1 c. buttermilk
2 c. coconut
1/2 to 1 c. chopped pecans
2 c. flour
1 tsp. vanilla

Cream sugar, egg yolks, margarine and Crisco together. Add soda to buttermilk; blend into creamed mixture. Add coconut, pecans and flour; mix well. Fold in stiffly-beaten egg whites and vanilla. Divide batter into 3 layer pans. Bake in preheated 350-degree oven for 25 to 30 minutes.

Frosting

1 8-oz. package cream cheese
1/2 to 1 stick margarine
1 1-lb. box powdered sugar
1 tsp. vanilla
Pinch of salt

Combine softened cream cheese and margarine; beat until creamy. Add powdered sugar, vanilla and salt; mix until smooth. Spread between layers, over top and side of cake. May sprinkle layers with additional coconut, if desired.

Mrs. Betty W. Allen, Welfare Chm.
Alpha Chi No. 2055
Stuarts Draft, Virginia
Lois Ross, W. and M. Chm.
Delta Alpha
Columbia, Missouri

QUEEN ELIZABETH CAKE

1 c. boiling water
1 c. chopped dates
1 tsp. soda
1/4 c. butter
1 c. sugar
1 egg
1 tsp. vanilla
1 1/2 c. flour
1 tsp. baking powder

1/2 tsp. salt
1/2 c. chopped nuts

Pour boiling water over dates and soda; let stand while mixing cake. Cream butter and sugar; add egg and vanilla. Add sifted dry ingredients; fold in nuts and date mixture. Spread in greased 9 x 12-inch pan. Bake in preheated 350-degree oven for 35 minutes.

Topping

1/3 c. butter
1/2 c. (packed) brown sugar
3 tbsp. cream or milk
1/2 c. chopped nuts
1/2 c. flaked coconut

Heat butter and sugar until melted; add cream, nuts and coconut. Spread on warm cake immediately. Place under broiler for about 3 minutes or until brown.

Kathy Miller, Pres.
Beta Beta No. 4142
Longwood, Florida

DOUBLE CARAMEL CAKE

1/3 c. (firmly packed) brown sugar
1/4 c. boiling water
3/4 c. butter or margarine
1 1/4 c. sugar
3 eggs, unbeaten
3 c. sifted cake flour
3 1/2 tsp. baking powder
1 tsp. salt
1 c. milk
1 tsp. vanilla
Caramel Frosting

Melt brown sugar in heavy skillet, stirring constantly, until brown syrup is formed. Remove from heat. Stir in boiling water slowly. Set syrup aside to cool. Cream butter. Add sugar; cream together until light and fluffy. Add eggs, one at a time, beating well after each addition. Stir in 3 tablespoons cooled syrup. Sift dry ingredients together. Combine milk and vanilla. Add to egg mixture alternately with dry ingredients, beginning and ending with dry ingredients. Beat until batter is smooth. Prepare two

9-inch layer pans by lightly oiling the bottoms and line with plain paper. Pour batter into pans. Bake in 375-degree oven for about 25 minutes, until cake begins to draw away from sides of pans. Cool cake. Frost with Caramel Frosting.

Caramel Frosting

3 c. (firmly packed) brown sugar
1 1/8 c. light cream
1/4 c. butter or margarine
Vanilla to taste

Combine brown sugar and light cream. Cook over low heat to soft-ball stage. Remove from heat; add butter. Cool to 110 degrees. Add vanilla. Beat until frosting is of spreading consistency. A little cream may be added should frosting become too thick.

Photograph for this recipe above.

VANILLA WAFER CAKE AND ICING

1 stick butter
1 c. sugar

3 eggs
1   1-lb. box vanilla wafers, rolled
*   into crumbs*
1/2 tsp. baking powder
2/3 c. milk
1 c. coconut
1 c. chopped pecans

Cream butter and sugar; add eggs and remaining ingredients, mixing well. Place in large baking pan. Bake in preheated 350-degree oven for 30 to 40 minutes.

Icing

1 c. (packed) brown sugar
1/4 c. milk
1 stick butter
Powdered sugar

Combine brown sugar, milk and butter in saucepan; cook until butter melts. Cool. Add enough powdered sugar to make thick enough to spread. Spread on the cake.

Ellen Marie Harder, Treas.
Kappa Theta No. 4343
Gainesville, Texas

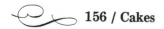

CRANBERRY-NUT CAKE

2 c. flour
3 tsp. baking powder
1/2 tsp. salt
1 c. sugar
1 c. chopped fresh cranberries
1 c. chopped walnuts
1 egg
3/4 c. milk
1/4 c. butter, melted
1 tsp. vanilla

Line bottom of loaf pan with brown paper; grease paper. Combine flour, baking powder and salt in large mixing bowl; stir in sugar, then cranberries and walnuts. Beat egg in small bowl; add milk, butter and vanilla. Mix just until combined. Add to flour mixture; stir just until dry ingredients are moistened. Turn into prepared pan. Bake in preheated 350-degree oven for about 50 to 60 minutes until toothpick inserted in center comes out clean. Turn out to cool on wire rack; frost when cool.

Mary TenEyck, Pres.
Zeta Omicron No. 2496
Dodge City, Kansas

CRANBERRY PUFFS

1 c. cranberry-orange relish
1 c. Bisquick
1/4 c. sugar
1 egg
1/3 c. milk

Spoon about 2 tablespoons cranberry relish into each of 8 large greased muffin cups. Combine Bisquick, sugar, egg and milk; mix with spoon, beating vigorously for 30 seconds. Fill muffin cups 2/3 full. Bake in preheated 400-degree oven for about 15 minutes or until tops are golden. Invert onto wire rack. Serve warm with Butter Sauce.

Butter Sauce

1/2 c. sugar
1/4 c. light cream
1/4 c. butter
1/2 tsp. vanilla

Combine sugar and cream; bring to a boil, stirring constantly. Remove from heat. Beat in butter and vanilla with rotary beater. Keep warm in fondue pot.

Julia McCullough
Beta Eta No. 3696
Fairfield, Illinois

DATE AND NUT PARTY CAKE

1 1/4 c. boiling water
1 c. quartered pitted dates
1 c. chopped walnuts
2 c. sifted flour
1 tsp. soda
1 tsp. cinnamon
1/2 tsp. salt
1 c. real mayonnaise
1 c. sugar
1/2 oz. unsweetened chocolate, melted
1 tsp. vanilla

Grease two 8-inch layer cake pans. Line bottoms with waxed paper and grease again. Pour boiling water over dates and walnuts in bowl; set aside. Sift flour, soda, cinnamon and salt together. Blend mayonnaise and sugar in mixing bowl. Stir in chocolate and vanilla. Drain water from dates and walnuts; reserve. Add sifted dry ingredients to mayonnaise mixture alternately with reserved water. Mix in dates and walnuts. Pour into prepared pans. Bake in 350-degree oven until cake tests done, about 35 minutes. Cool. Frost with white frosting, if desired.

Photograph for this recipe on opposite page.

CHRISTMAS CAKE

1 box muscat raisins
2 tsp. soda
1 1/2 c. sugar
1 1/2 sticks margarine
2 eggs, beaten
1 tsp. nutmeg
2 tsp. cinnamon
1/4 tsp. cloves
1 tsp. baking powder
1 tsp. salt

4 c. flour
1 c. chopped nuts

Cook raisins in 3 cups water until 1 cup water remains. Set aside; cool for 10 to 15 minutes. Add soda. Let stand. Cream sugar and margarine; add eggs, mixing well. Stir in raisins. Sift spices, baking powder, salt and flour together; stir into raisin mixture. Blend in nuts. Turn into tube pan. Bake in preheated 350-degree oven for 1 hour and 15 minutes to 1 hour and 30 minutes or until cake tests done. May drizzle with icing and garnish with cherries, if desired.

Mary Lou Hartman, State Pres.
Rho Chi No. 2988
O'Fallon, Missouri

WHISKY FRUITCAKE

1/2 lb. candied cherries
1/2 c. seedless raisins
1 c. 100-proof whisky
1 c. butter, softened
1/2 c. (firmly packed) brown sugar
1 c. sugar

3 eggs, separated
Flour
1 tsp. baking powder
1 tsp. nutmeg
1/4 tsp. salt
1/2 lb. coarsely chopped pecans

Combine cherries, raisins and whisky in medium-sized bowl; soak overnight. Beat butter until creamy in large bowl; add sugars gradually, beating until light and fluffy. Add egg yolks; beat well. Sift 2 1/2 cups sifted flour with baking powder, nutmeg and salt. Drain fruit mixture; add the liquid gradually to the egg mixture, alternating with flour mixture. Stir in fruit. Beat egg whites until stiff; fold into batter gently. Combine pecans and 1 teaspoon flour; toss well. Stir into batter. Pour into greased and floured 9-inch tube pan. Bake in preheated 275-degree oven for 1 hour and 45 minutes. Cool; remove from pan. Stuff center of cake with cheesecloth soaked in whisky; store tightly in covered container. May be frozen.

Mrs. Vauda Gaye Emmart
Alpha Omega No. 2060
Winchester, Virginia

A FRUIT BOWL CAKE

1   3-oz. package strawberry gelatin
1   11 1/2-oz. pound cake
1 fresh peach, peeled and quartered
3 fresh plums, halved
6 strawberries
1 fresh pear, peeled and quartered
1 c. seedless grapes
1   8-oz. package cream cheese, softened
1/4 c. sour cream
1/2   10-oz. jar apple jelly, melted

Prepare gelatin according to package directions. Pour into 8-inch square cake pan. Cool to lukewarm. Cut cake in half, lengthwise. Place layers into gelatin, side by side. Refrigerate at least 2 hours. Cake will absorb some of the gelatin. The rest will congeal around edges of cake. Unmold cake by setting pan in warm water for 5 seconds. Invert onto serving platter. Arrange fruits except grapes on cake. Beat together cream cheese and sour cream. Force all the cheese mixture through decorating tube onto fruit arrangement to simulate large grape cluster. Stud with grapes. Brush entire surface with melted jelly. Refrigerate 1 hour. Spoon cake and fruit onto serving plates to serve. Yield: 8 servings.

Photograph for this recipe on page 2.

EASY FRUITCAKE

1   1/2 c. blanched almonds
1 1/2 c. walnut halves
1 c. chopped dates
1 c. quartered candied cherries
1/2 c. raisins
3/4 c. sugar
3/4 c. flour
1/2 tsp. baking powder
1/2 tsp. salt
3 eggs
1 tbsp. brandy

Combine first 6 ingredients in bowl; sift flour, baking powder and salt over mixture. Mix well. Beat eggs until light; add brandy. Pour over fruit mixture; stir to mix until well combined. Line greased loaf pan with waxed paper, then grease the paper. Turn mixture into pan; press firmly. Bake in preheated 300-degree oven for 1 hour and 35 minutes.

Helen Linn, V.P.
Gamma Kappa No. 3265
Denver, Colorado

EVERY HOLIDAY FRUITCAKE

3/4 c. sugar
3/4 c. flour
Dash of salt
1 lb. chopped dates
1 c. drained maraschino cherries
3 c. chopped pecans
3 eggs, beaten

Mix sugar and flour with salt; add dates, cherries and pecans. Add eggs; mix well. Pour mixture into foil-lined, deep oblong or round pan. Bake in preheated 300-degree oven for 1 hour. May bake this early for holidays, then wrap in a wine or brandy soaked cloth.

Carol Allen, Scrapbook
Delta Omega No. 4414
Prescott, Arizona

CHRISTMAS CANDY CAKE

1 can sweetened condensed milk
1   7-oz. can coconut
1 box candied red cherries, chopped
1 box candied green cherries, chopped
1 box dates, cut up
1 1/2 c. chopped pecans

Combine all ingredients; mix well. Pour into waxed paper-lined pan. Bake in preheated 300 or 325-degree oven for 30 to 45 minutes or until a light brown color. Do not overcook. Remove from oven; let set until slightly cool. Turn out; peel off waxed paper, then turn back over. Cut into squares and store. May be stored in freezer or refrigerator but bring to room temperature before serving.

Joyce Mitchell, W. and M. Chm.
Kappa Theta No. 4343
Gainesville, Texas

AUSTRIAN FRUITCAKE

1 c. flour
1 c. sugar
2 tsp. baking powder
1 lb. whole pecans
1/2 lb. candied cherries
1/2 lb. red candied pineapple, diced
1 lb. whole dates
1 tsp. vanilla
4 eggs, well beaten

Combine flour, sugar and baking powder. Combine pecans, cherries, pineapple and dates. Add flour mixture. Toss to mix well. Add vanilla to eggs; pour over fruit mixture. Mix well. Turn into 2 large greased and waxed paper-lined loaf pans. Bake in preheated 275-degree oven for about 1 hour and 30 minutes.

Joan Johnson, Educational Dir.
Alpha Alpha No. 1657
Salt Lake City, Utah

GRANDMA'S EASY FRUITCAKE

2 c. flour
1 c. sugar
2 tsp. soda
2 tsp. baking powder
1/2 tsp. allspice
1/2 tsp. cinnamon
1/2 tsp. nutmeg
3 tbsp. cocoa
3 tbsp. cornstarch
2 c. applesauce
1/2 c. melted butter or margarine
1 pkg. citron or mixed fruit (opt.)
1 c. raisins
1 c. nuts
2 eggs, beaten
1 tsp. vanilla
Dash of salt

Combine all ingredients; mix until thoroughly blended. Place in loaf pan or tube pan. Place pan of water on lower shelf of oven. Bake cake in preheated 325-degree oven for 1 hour or until cake tests done.

Nancy Vandegrift, Publicity
Alpha Alpha No. 1657
Bountiful, Utah

TENNESSEE CHRISTMAS CAKE

2 tsp. nutmeg
1/4 c. whiskey
1 lb. pecans, chopped
1/2 lb. raisins
1 1/2 c. flour
1 c. butter, softened
1 1/2 c. sugar
5 eggs
1 tsp. cream of tartar
1/4 tsp. salt
1/4 tsp. soda

Soak nutmeg in whiskey for 10 minutes. Combine pecans, raisins and 1/4 cup flour; set aside. Cream butter and sugar in large mixer bowl until fluffy. Add eggs, one at a time, beating well after each addition; fold in remaining 1 1/4 cup flour, cream of tartar, salt, soda and nutmeg mixture. Fold in pecan mixture until well combined. Spoon into greased and floured 10-inch tube pan. Bake in preheated 325-degree oven for 1 hour and 15 minutes or until cake pulls away from side of pan. Let stand in pan for 30 minutes. Remove from pan; cool completely on rack. Store in airtight container. Keeps well.

Ruth Tuttle, Pres.
Alpha Nu No. 3245
Tempe, Arizona

POWDERED SUGAR WHITE CAKE

2 1/4 c. cake flour
2 1/4 tsp. baking powder
1/2 c. Crisco
1 c. sugar
1 c. powdered sugar
4 lg. egg whites
1 1/2 tsp. vanilla

Sift flour and baking powder together. Cream Crisco and sugars together. Add flour mixture alternately with 1 cup water, beginning and ending with flour. Beat egg whites until stiff peaks form; fold egg whites and vanilla into batter. Spread batter in 2 greased and waxed paper-lined 9-inch layer pans. Bake in preheated 350-degree oven for about 25 minutes.

Betty Bertogh, Parliamentarian
Alpha Lambda No. 231
Greeley, Colorado

DIFFERENT FRUIT COCKTAIL CAKE

2 1/4 c. flour
2 tsp. soda
1 tsp. salt
1 c. (packed) brown sugar
2 eggs
1/4 c. butter
1 1-lb. can fruit cocktail
1/2 c. semisweet chocolate chips
1/2 c. chopped nuts

Combine all ingredients except chocolate chips and nuts in large mixer bowl; blend at low speed. Beat for 2 minutes at medium speed. Pour batter into greased and floured 13 x 9-inch pan. Sprinkle with chocolate chips and nuts. Bake in preheated 350-degree oven for 35 to 40 minutes.

Dorothy Howard
Zeta Chi No. 3878
Fort Collins, Colorado

EASY FRUIT COCKTAIL CAKE

2 eggs
1 1/2 c. (packed) brown sugar
2 c. flour
2 tsp. soda
Pinch of salt
1 lg. can fruit cocktail
1 c. nuts (opt.)

Combine all ingredients except nuts; mix well. Pour into 13 x 9-inch pan. Top with nuts. Bake in preheated 350-degree oven for 40 minutes. Top with whipped cream before serving, if desired.

Arlene D. Wedebrook
Past Ohio State Coun. Pres.
Gamma Beta No. 3939
Dayton, Ohio

FRUIT PUDDING CAKE

2 c. flour
1 1/2 c. sugar
2 tsp. soda
1/4 tsp. salt
2 eggs, beaten

1 1-lb. can fruit cocktail
1/2 c. maraschino cherry halves (opt.)

Sift dry ingredients together; add eggs and fruit cocktail with juice, mixing well. Pour into greased 8 or 9-inch tube pan. Bake in preheated 300-degree oven for 1 hour. Cool for 10 minutes; remove from pan. Place on wire rack to cool completely.

Joyce Ahlstrom, Pres.
Gamma Zeta No. 4534
Boise, Idaho

HOT MILK SPONGE CAKE DELIGHT

4 eggs
2 c. sugar
2 c. sifted cake flour
2 tsp. baking powder
1 tsp. salt
2 tsp. vanilla
1 c. milk
2 tbsp. butter

Beat eggs; add sugar gradually, beating until fluffy and light colored. Add flour sifted with baking powder and salt; beat well. Add vanilla. Heat milk with butter until almost boiling; stir quickly into batter. Beat slightly. Pour at once into ungreased 9 or 10-inch tube pan. Bake in preheated 350-degree oven for 40 to 45 minutes or until done. Remove from oven; invert pan until cool, then remove from pan.

Garnet A. Hampton, Pres.
Gamma Chi No. 834
Comanche, Oklahoma

HOT MILK SPONGE SUPREME

4 eggs
2 c. sugar
2 c. flour
2 tsp. baking powder
1 tsp. vanilla
1 c. milk
1 tbsp. butter

Beat eggs; add sugar and beat until light. Sift flour and baking powder together; add to egg mixture. Add vanilla. Bring milk and butter to boil; blend into egg mixture. Lightly grease and flour bottom of round 9-inch cake pan; spread batter in pan. Bake in preheated 350-degree oven for 30 minutes.

Carol Sneed, V.P.
Beta Iota No. 3512
Belleville, Illinois

GREEK WALNUT CAKE

1 c. Wesson oil
1 1/2 c. sugar
3 eggs
1 c. buttermilk or sour milk
3 tsp. baking powder
1/2 tsp. soda
1 tsp. cinnamon
1 tsp. cloves
2 c. sifted flour
1 c. chopped nuts

Place oil in mixing bowl. Gradually add sugar, beating constantly. Add eggs, one at a time, beating well after each addition. Add buttermilk slowly, beating constantly. Sift dry ingredients together; add slowly to egg mixture, blending well. Stir in nuts. Place in oblong baking dish. Bake in preheated 350-degree oven for 35 minutes. Cool. Cut into squares.

Syrup

1 c. sugar
1 c. water
1 whole cinnamon stick
1 thinly sliced lemon slice

Combine all ingredients; bring to a boil. Boil until thread spins. Remove cinnamon and lemon. Pour over cake squares.

Angeline S. Pappas
Alpha Epsilon No. 4460
Albert Lea, Minnesota

BLACKBERRY JAM CAKE

1/2 c. butter or margarine
1 c. sugar
4 eggs, well beaten
1 tsp. soda
1/2 tsp. baking powder
1/2 c. buttermilk
2 c. flour
2 tsp. cinnamon
1/2 tsp. cloves
1/2 tsp. allspice
1 c. blackberry jam or jelly
1 c. chopped pecans or walnuts

Cream butter and sugar together; add eggs. Mix soda and baking powder with buttermilk, then add to batter. Blend in the remaining ingredients. Turn batter into layer pans or loaf pan. Bake in preheated 350-degree oven until cake tests done.

Frosting

2 2/3 c. (packed) brown sugar
2/3 c. milk
2/3 c. margarine
1/3 tsp. salt

Combine all ingredients in saucepan; bring to a full boil, stirring constantly. Boil for 8 minutes. Remove from heat. Beat until lukewarm and of spreading consistency. Frost cake.

Elizabeth Griffin, Pres.
Alpha Chi No. 871
Deming, New Mexico

MINCEMEAT CAKE

2 c. water
2 c. sugar
1 1/2 sticks margarine
1 9-oz. package mincemeat
1/2 apple, diced
3 c. flour
2 tsp. soda
1 c. chopped nuts

Combine first 5 ingredients in saucepan. Bring to a boil; boil for 2 to 3 minutes. Cool for 5 to 10 minutes. Add flour, soda and nuts; mix well. Turn into angel food cake pan or 2 loaf pans. Bake in preheated 350-degree oven for 35 to 40 minutes or until cake tests done.

Marge Davidson, Pres.
Beta Epsilon No. 4533
Lawton, Oklahoma

SPECIAL JAM CAKE

1/4 c. butter
1 c. sugar
3 eggs
2 c. flour
1 tsp. cloves
1 tsp. cocoa
1 tsp. allspice
1 tsp. cinnamon
1/2 c. buttermilk
1 tsp. soda
1 c. jam
1 c. pear preserves
1 c. chopped nuts
1/2 c. chopped figs or dates

Cream butter and sugar; add eggs, one at a time, beating well after addition. Sift flour and spices together; add to butter mixture alternately with combined buttermilk and soda. Stir in jam and preserves until well blended. Add nuts and figs, mixing well. Turn into oblong baking dish. Bake in preheated 350-degree oven until cake tests done.

Icing

1 c. sugar
1/4 c. butter
1/2 c. milk

Combine all ingredients in saucepan; bring to a rolling boil. Pour over hot cake.

Elizabeth B. Cochran, V.P.
Alpha Zeta No. 806
Lewisburg, Tennessee

RED BEET CAKE

2 sq. unsweetened chocolate
1 1/2 c. sugar
2 c. sifted flour
1/2 tsp. salt
1 c. cooking oil
1/2 tsp. vanilla
2   4 1/2-oz. jars baby food strained
    beets
3 eggs, lightly beaten

Melt chocolate; cool and transfer to large bowl. Add remaining ingredients; beat thor-

oughly to blend. Pour into two 8-inch pans or a 13 x 9-inch pan. Bake in preheated 350-degree oven for about 25 minutes.

Ceil Brace
Beta Pi
Benton, Arkansas

KANSAS CAKE

1 1/2 c. boiling water
1 c. quick-cooking oatmeal
1 c. (packed) brown sugar
1 c. sugar
1 stick margarine, softened
2 eggs
1 1/2 c. sifted flour
1 tsp. soda
1/2 tsp. cinnamon
1/2 tsp. cloves
1/2 tsp. salt

Pour boiling water over oatmeal; let stand. Combine sugars, margarine and eggs; beat until creamy. Add oatmeal, flour, soda, cinnamon, cloves and salt; mix well. Turn into greased and floured 9 x 13-inch pan. Bake in preheated 350-degree oven for 35 minutes.

Topping

1 stick margarine, softened
1/4 c. evaporated milk
1 c. chopped nuts
1 c. (packed) brown sugar
1 c. coconut
1 tsp. vanilla

Combine all ingredients; mix well. Spread on hot cake. Place under broiler until brown and bubbly.

Pam Atteberry
Sigma Kappa
Claflin, Kansas

ONE-EGG CAKE

2 c. flour
1 c. sugar
2 1/2 tsp. baking powder
1 tsp. salt
1/3 c. shortening
1 c. milk

1 egg
1 tsp. vanilla

Sift flour into bowl with sugar baking powder and salt; add shortening and milk. Beat at medium speed for 2 minutes. Add egg and vanilla; beat for 2 minutes longer. Pour into 2 greased and floured layer cake pans. Bake in preheated 350-degree oven for 25 to 30 minutes. Cool for 10 minutes; remove from pans.

Cathy Martin
Alpha Gamma No. 3457
Omaha, Nebraska

ORANGE KISS ME CAKE

1 lg. orange
1 c. raisins
1/3 c. chopped walnuts
2 c. sifted flour
1 tsp. soda
1 tsp. salt
1 c. sugar
1/2 c. plus 2 tsp. shortening
1 cup milk
2 eggs

Remove seeds from orange, then grind in food chopper. Add raisins and walnuts; set aside. Sift flour, soda, salt and sugar together; set aside. Blend shortening and 3/4 cup milk together in large bowl; beat for 2 minutes. Add eggs and remaining 1/4 cup milk. Add orange mixture, then dry ingredients. Pour into 9 x 12-inch pan. Bake in preheated 350-degree oven until cake tests done. Frost with a brown sugar frosting, if desired.

Audrey M. Petz, Pres.
Alpha Omega No. 4110
Bismarck, North Dakota

WILLIAMSBURG ORANGE CAKE

1 c. raisins
Rind from 1 orange
1/2 c. chopped walnuts
1/2 c. margarine
2 c. sugar
2 eggs
1 tsp. vanilla

2 c. flour
1 tsp. soda
1/2 tsp. salt
1 c. sour milk
1 tbsp. sherry
1/3 c. orange juice

Grind raisins and orange rind together; add walnuts. Set aside. Cream margarine and 1 cup sugar together; add eggs and vanilla. Sift flour, soda and salt together; add flour mixture alternately with sour milk; mix well. Add orange mixture. Spread batter in greased oblong baking pan. Bake in preheated 370-degree oven for 30 to 49 minutes or until cake tests done. Combine remaining 1 cup sugar, sherry and orange juice; pour over warm cake. Return to oven for 3 to 5 minutes or until sugar melts.

Bonnie M. Campbell
Alpha Tau No. 4182
Columbia, South Carolina

GRANDMOTHER'S ORANGE CAKE

1 1/2 c. raisins
1 c. sour milk
1 tsp. soda
1 c. sugar
1/2 c. Crisco
1 egg
Grated rind of 2 oranges
Dash of salt
2 c. flour

Soak raisins in hot water, then grind in food chopper. Combine milk and soda. Combine all ingredients; mix well. Turn into greased and floured tube pan. Bake in preheated 375-degree oven for 45 to 50 minutes.

Glaze

Juice of 2 oranges
1/2 c. sugar

Combine juice and sugar; bring to a boil, stirring until sugar is dissolved. Spoon over cake.

Jean Eslick
Zeta Alpha No. 2624
Dallas, Texas

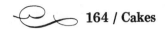

ORANGE SLICE CAKE

1 c. butter or margarine
2 c. sugar
4 eggs
4 c. flour
1 tsp. soda
1/4 tsp. salt
1/2 c. buttermilk
1 sm. package coconut
2 c. chopped pecans
1 8-oz. box chopped dates or raisins
1 1-lb. bag orange slice candy,
    chopped
2 c. powdered sugar
1 c. orange juice

Cream butter and sugar; add eggs, one at a time, beating well after each addition. Combine 3 1/2 cups flour, soda and salt; add to creamed mixture alternately with buttermilk. Dust coconut, pecans, dates and candy with remaining 1/2 cup flour; add to batter. Mix well. Turn into greased and floured tube pan. Bake in preheated 250-degree oven for 2 hours and 30 minutes to 3 hours. Combine powdered sugar and orange juice; beat until smooth. Pour over cake while still warm. Leave in pan overnight.

Susan Evans, Publ. Chm.
Beta Delta No. 4271
Tucson, Arizona

PEACH-TOPPED CHIFFON CAKE IN PEANUT CRUMB CRUST

1 1/2 c. crushed graham crackers
1/2 c. finely crushed salted peanuts
1 c. sugar
1/4 c. soft butter or margarine
Peanut halves
1 1/4 c. sifted flour
1 1/2 tsp. baking powder
1/2 tsp. salt
1/4 c. peanut oil
1/3 c. water or orange juice
2 egg yolks
1/2 c. egg whites
1/4 tsp. cream of tartar
1 c. peach or other fruit pie filling
Whipped cream

Combine graham cracker crumbs, peanuts and 1/4 cup sugar. Blend in butter until all crumbs are moistened. Press into 9-inch pie pan. Press peanut halves into edge as decoration. Sift together flour, 3/4 cup sugar, baking powder and salt into bowl. Form a well in center of dry ingredients; pour in oil, water and egg yolks. Beat with spoon until smooth. Beat egg whites until frothy. Add cream of tartar; continue beating until very stiff peaks form. Pour flour mixture slowly over egg whites; fold in carefully. Turn into prepared crumb crust. Bake in 325-degree oven for 40 to 45 minutes or until cake springs back when touched with finger. Cool. Spread with peach filling. Top with sweetened whipped cream. Yield: 6 servings.

Photograph for this recipe on cover.

PECAN-BUTTER CAKE

3/4 c. butter
1 1/4 c. sugar
2 eggs
2 3/4 c. sifted cake flour
3 tsp. baking powder
1/4 tsp. nutmeg
1 tsp. salt
1 1/2 c. eggnog
2 tsp. rum flavoring
1 c. finely chopped pecans

Cream butter. Add sugar gradually; beat until light and fluffy. Beat in eggs, one at a time. Add sifted dry ingredients alternately with eggnog and rum flavoring, mixing well after each addition. Brush 10-inch tube pan with salad oil. Sprinkle pecans in bottom of pan. Spoon in batter. Bake at 325 degrees for 1 hour and 20 minutes or until cake tests done. Cool about 1 hour without inverting cake. Remove from pan.

Eggnog Frosting

1/4 c. eggnog
2 tbsp. butter
2 1/2 c. sifted confectioners' sugar
1 tsp. rum flavoring

Heat eggnog and butter together until butter melts. Beat into confectioners' sugar. Add rum flavoring. Beat until smooth and right

consistency to spread. Frost sides of cake with frosting. Decorate with pecan halves.

Photograph for this recipe above.

DOUBLE PINEAPPLE CAKE

3/4 c. butter
1 1/2 c. sugar
3 eggs
1 1/2 tsp. vanilla
3/8 tsp. soda
1 1/2 c. undrained crushed pineapple
1 7/8 c. flour
2 1/4 tsp. baking powder

Cream butter, sugar, eggs and vanilla until light; stir soda into pineapple, Mix pineapple with creamed mixture. Add flour and baking powder; mix well. Spread in greased and floured 9 x 13-inch pan. Bake in preheated 350-degree oven for 40 minutes.

Pineapple-Cheese Icing

1 3-oz. package cream cheese,
     softened
2 tbsp. butter
2 1/2 c. powdered sugar
1/4 c. drained crushed pineapple

Combine all ingredients; beat until fluffy. Spread over cake.

Norma Thomas, Pres.
Gamma Tau No. 4050
Springfield, Ohio

PINEAPPLE-NUT CAKE

2 c. sugar
2 c. flour
2 eggs
2 tsp. soda
2 tsp. vanilla
1 1/2 c. chopped nuts
1 No. 2 can crushed pineapple
1 sm. package cream cheese, softened
1/4 c. margarine
1 3/4 c. powdered sugar

Combine sugar, flour, eggs, soda, 1 teaspoon vanilla, 3/4 cup nuts and undrained pineapple; beat until well combined. Pour into a 13 x 9-inch pan. Bake in preheated 350-degree oven for about 35 minutes. Combine cream cheese, margarine, powdered sugar, remaining 1 teaspoon vanilla and 3/4 cup nuts; mix well. Spread on warm cake. Garnish with maraschino cherry halves if desired.

Billie Gunsalus, Treas.
Epsilon Nu No. 2020
Hermosa Beach, California

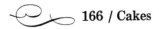

SPECIAL UPSIDE-DOWN PINEAPPLE CAKE

1   1-lb. 4-oz. can crushed pineapple
1   8 1/4-oz. can crushed pineapple
1/2 c. butter
1 c. (firmly packed) brown sugar
1 1/2 c. sifted all-purpose flour
1 tsp. baking powder
Salt
3 eggs, separated
1 c. sugar
1 c. whipping cream
2 tbsp. powdered sugar
1/2 tsp. vanilla

Drain both cans pineapple, reserving 1/2 cup syrup. Place 1/4 cup butter in each of two 9-inch layer cake pans. Place in 350-degree oven to melt, then add 1/2 cup brown sugar and half the well-drained pineapple to each pan, spreading evenly. Set aside. Sift flour with baking powder and 1/2 teaspoon salt; set aside. Beat egg whites just until stiff; Beat in 1/2 cup sugar gradually, beating until stiff peaks form. Beat egg yolks with remaining 1/2 cup sugar until thick and light. Pour over egg whites gradually, folding in carefully. Fold in sifted dry ingredients alternately with the reserved 1/2 cup pineapple syrup. Pour half the batter over pineapple in each pan. Bake at 350 degrees for 25 to 30 minutes or until cake tests done. Let stand 5 minutes, then loosen edges of cakes with spatula. Invert onto wire racks; cool. Combine cream, powdered sugar, dash of salt and vanilla; beat until stiff. Spread 3/4 of the cream over 1 layer. Place second layer, pineapple side up, over cream; press gently. Decorate top with remaining whipped cream. Garnish with sweet pitted cherries.

Jo Ann Fuciley
Beta Xi No. 1804
Canton, Illinois

PEANUT BUTTER-PINEAPPLE UPSIDE-DOWN CAKE

1/4 c. butter or margarine
1 c. (firmly packed) brown sugar
6 to 8 pineapple slices
Salted peanuts
Candied cherries
2 c. sifted enriched flour
1 1/4 c. sugar
1 tbsp. baking powder
1 tsp. salt
6 tbsp. shortening
1/4 c. peanut butter
1 c. milk
1 tsp. vanilla
2 eggs

Melt butter in bottom of 10-inch greased tube cake pan by placing in warm oven a few minutes. Add brown sugar; stir lightly. Spread to cover bottom of pan. Arrange pineapple slices in butter-sugar mixture. Decorate with peanut halves and cherries. Sift together flour, sugar, baking powder and salt into bowl. Add shortening, peanut butter and 2/3 cup milk. Beat 2 minutes at medium speed with electric mixer or 300 strokes by hand. Add remaining milk, vanilla and eggs; repeat beating instructions. Pour into prepared tube pan. Bake in 350-degree oven for 50 to 60 minutes or until cake tester comes out clean. Turn out immediately onto serving plate. Serve warm or cool, plain or topped with whipped cream.

Photograph for this recipe on cover.

EASY PINEAPPLE CAKE

2 c. flour
2 1/4 c. sugar
1 tsp. soda
2 eggs
1 No. 2 can crushed pineapple
1/2 c. (packed) brown sugar
1/2 c. chopped nuts
1 tsp. vanilla
3/4 c. evaporated milk
1/4 c. margarine

Combine flour, 1 1/2 cups sugar, soda, eggs and pineapple in bowl; blend well. Pour into rectangular pan. Mix brown sugar and nuts; pour over batter. Bake in preheated 350-degree oven for 30 minutes. Combine vanilla, milk, margarine and remaining 3/4 cup sugar in saucepan; cook for 5 minutes. Remove cake from oven; pour hot milk mixture over top.

Moraleen Dice, V.P.
Alpha Phi No. 2245
Nampa, Idaho

PINEAPPLE-ZUCCHINI CAKE

3 eggs
1 c. sugar
1 c. (packed) brown sugar
2 tsp. vanilla
1 c. oil
2 c. zucchini, peeled, grated and drained
3 c. flour
1 tsp. baking powder
1 tsp. soda
1 tsp. salt
1 c. crushed pineapple, drained
1/2 c. raisins
1 c. chopped nuts

Combine eggs, sugars, vanilla and oil; beat until fluffy. Blend in zucchini, then add flour, baking powder, soda, salt, pineapple, raisins and nuts. Mix well. Turn into 2 greased and floured loaf pans. Bake in preheated 325-degree oven for 1 hour.

Debbie Wilper
Beta Delta No. 4339
Boise, Idaho

TOP-ME-TWICE CAKE

1 1/2 c. sugar
2 eggs
1 tsp. vanilla
2 c. flour
1/2 tsp. salt
1/2 tsp. soda
1 13 1/2-oz. can crushed pineapple
1/2 c. (packed) brown sugar
1/2 c. coconut
1/2 c. chopped nuts
1/2 c. butter, melted
1/2 c. evaporated milk

Combine 1 cup sugar, eggs and vanilla; blend together for 1 minute. Add flour, salt, soda and undrained pineapple to sugar mixture; blend for 2 minutes. Pour into greased 8 x 12-inch pan. Combine brown sugar, coconut and nuts; sprinkle over top. Bake in preheated 350-degree oven for 45 to 50 minutes. Combine butter, milk and remaining 1/2 cup sugar in saucepan; heat until sugar is dissolved. Pour over hot cake.

Dora Dill, Nebraska State Pres.
Gamma Delta No. 2302
Pleasant Dale, Nebraska

PLUM BUNDT CAKE

1 c. Crisco oil
2 c. sugar
3 eggs
2 c. flour
1 tsp. baking powder
1/2 tsp. soda
3/4 tsp. cloves
1 tsp. cinnamon
1 tsp. vanilla
2 sm. jars baby food plums
1 c. chopped nuts

Combine oil, sugar and eggs; mix well. Add dry ingredients, vanilla and plums; mix until well blended. Stir in nuts. Turn into greased and floured bundt pan. Bake in preheated 350-degree oven for 1 hour. Remove from pan immediately.

Zella Thomas, Treas.
Alpha Omicron No. 77
Enid, Oklahoma

PLUM NUTTY CAKE

2 c. sugar
3 eggs
1 c. chopped pecans
1 c. oil
1 jar Jr. plum pudding with tapioca
    baby food
1 tsp. red food coloring
2 c. flour
1 tsp. cinnamon
Pinch of salt
1/2 tsp. soda

Combine sugar, eggs, pecans, oil, plums and food coloring; mix until well blended. Sift dry ingredients together; stir into oil mixture. Turn into bundt pan. Bake in preheated 350-degree oven for 1 hour. Remove from pan; cool completely.

Glaze

1 c. powdered sugar
2 1/2 tbsp. bottled lemon juice
1/2 tsp. red food coloring

Combine all ingredients in saucepan; bring to a boil. Brush on cake with pastry brush.

Sue Hunning
Gamma Omega No. 4408
Kingman, Kansas

POPPY SEED CAKE WITH FILLING

2 c. flour
Pinch of salt
1 c. sugar
2 tsp. baking powder
1/2 c. shortening
1 c. milk
1 tsp. vanilla
1/4 to 1/3 c. poppy seed
3 egg whites

Sift flour, salt, sugar and baking powder together. Cream shortening; add milk, vanilla and flour mixture; Beat well. Add poppy seed. Fold in softly beaten egg whites. Turn in 2 layer cake pans. Bake in preheated 370-degree oven for 25 to 30 minutes.

Filling

2 c. milk
3 tbsp. cornstarch
1 c. sugar
3 egg yolks
Vanilla to taste
Whipped cream

Combine milk, cornstarch, sugar, egg yolks and vanilla in top of double boiler; cook, stirring, until thickened. Cool; spread over cooled cake. Cover with whipped cream before serving.

Catherine Harre
Gamma Iota No. 3936
Carbondale, Illinois

POPPY SEED TEA CAKE

1/3 c. poppy seed
1 c. buttermilk
1 c. butter or margarine
1 1/2 c. plus 2 tbsp. sugar
4 eggs
2 1/2 c. sifted all-purpose flour
2 tsp. baking powder
1 tsp. soda
1/2 tsp. salt
1 tsp. orange extract
1 tsp. cinnamon

Combine poppy seed and buttermilk; refrigerate overnight for full flavor. Cream butter with 1 1/2 cups sugar until light and fluffy. Add eggs, one at a time, beating well after each addition. Sift together flour, baking powder, soda and salt. Add orange extract to creamed mixture. Blend in sifted ingredients alternately with seed mixture, beginning and ending with dry ingredients. Turn half the batter into greased and floured 10-inch tube pan or bundt pan. Mix 2 tablespoons sugar with cinnamon. Sprinkle cinnamon-sugar over batter in tube pan. Add remaining batter. Bake in 350-degree oven 1 hour or until cake tests done. Cool 10 minutes; remove from pan to finish cooling.

Photograph for this recipe above.

WISCONSIN POPPY SEED CAKE

1/2 c. sugar
1/2 c. butter
1/2 c. poppy seed soaked in 3/4 c. milk
2 c. flour
2 tsp. baking powder
4 egg whites, stiffly beaten

Combine all ingredients except egg whites; mix well. Fold in egg whites. Spread batter into two 8-inch round cake pans. Bake in preheated 350-degree oven for 25 to 30 minutes or until cake tests done.

Filling

2 c. milk
3/4 c. sugar
1 tsp. cornstarch
4 egg yolks, well beaten

Combine milk, sugar and cornstarch in saucepan; cook until thick. Blend in egg yolks. Spread between layers.

Frosting

1/2 pt. sour cream
1 1/2 c. (packed) brown sugar
4 egg yolks

Combine sour cream, brown sugar and 4 egg yolks in double boiler. Cook until thick enough to spread on cake.

Pearl Stock, Ed. Chm.
Beta Theta No. 2655
Manitowoc, Wisconsin

APPLE POUND CAKE

2 c. sugar
1 1/2 c. cooking oil
4 eggs
1 tsp. soda
1 tsp. salt
3 c. flour
3 c. diced apples
1 c. chopped pecans
3/4 c. coconut
1 1/4 tsp. vanilla

Blend sugar and oil together; add eggs, one at a time, beating well after each addition. Sift soda, salt and flour together. Add to egg mixture; beat well. Blend in apples, pecans, coconut, and vanilla. Pour into greased and floured tube or bundt pan. Bake in preheated 325-degree oven for 1 hour and 20 minutes. Do not open oven while cake is baking

Topping

1 1/2 c. (packed) brown sugar
1 stick butter
1/2 c. chopped pecans
3 tsp. milk

Place all ingredients in saucepan; bring to a boil. Cook for 3 minutes or to soft-ball stage. Pour over warm cake.

Barbara S. Clark, W. and M. Chm.
Alpha Alpha No. 599
Columbia, South Carolina

COCONUT POUND CAKE

3 c. sugar
2 sticks margarine
5 eggs
3 c. flour
1/2 tsp. salt
1 tsp. baking powder
1 c. milk
1/2 c. Crisco oil
1 tsp. coconut flavoring
1 tall can coconut

Cream sugar and margarine; add eggs, one at a time, beating well after each addition. Combine flour, salt and baking powder; add to creamed alternately with milk and oil. Blend in flavoring and coconut. Pour into greased and floured tube pan. Bake in preheated 325-degree oven for 1 hour.

Gerry Carroll, Treas.
Gamma Delta No. 3767
Marietta, Georgia

OLD-FASHIONED POUND CAKE

2 c. cake flour
1 c. shortening
1 3/4 c. sugar
1/4 tsp. salt
1 tsp. vanilla
5 eggs

Sift flour 3 times; set aside. Cream shortening until consistency of whipped cream. Add sugar, salt and vanilla. Cream or beat 300 strokes, if by hand. Add flour and eggs alternately, beating well after each addition. Turn into greased and floured tube or bundt pan. Bake in preheated 325-degree oven for 1 hour. Cool on rack for 15 to 20 minutes; invert pan to remove.

Rae McConathy, Treas.
Alpha Alpha No. 911
Victoria, Texas

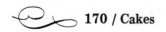

WISHING WELL CAKE

1 c. soft-type margarine, with liquid
    safflower oil
2 c. sugar
5 eggs
3 to 4 tsp. almond extract
1/2 tsp. salt
2 c. sifted all-purpose flour
Confectioners' Sugar Glaze

Blend together margarine and sugar. Add eggs, one at a time, beating well after each addition until light and fluffy. Stir in almond extract and salt. Blend flour gradually into creamed mixture. Turn into ungreased 10-inch tube pan. Bake in 325-degree oven for 1 hour and 20 minutes, until cake tester inserted in cake comes out clean. Allow cake to cool a few minutes. Turn out; cool completely. Invert cake. Spread top with Confectioners' Sugar Glaze. Serve plain or with ice cream, fruit, or whipped cream. Yield: 12 servings.

Confectioners' Sugar Glaze

1 c. sifted confectioners' sugar
4 tsp. water

Blend together sugar and water; spread over cake while warm.

Photograph for this recipe on page 129.

CHOCOLATE POUND CAKE

2 sticks margarine
1/2 c. shortening
3 c. sugar
5 eggs
3 c. flour
1/2 tsp. salt
1/2 tsp. baking powder
1/2 c. cocoa
1 c. milk
2 tsp. vanilla
1 c. pecan halves

Cream margarine, shortening and sugar together; add eggs, one at a time, beating well after each addition. Sift dry ingredients together; add to creamed mixture alternately with milk, beginning and ending with dry ingredients. Add vanilla; beat well. Pour into greased and floured 10-inch tube pan. Press pecans onto top of cake. Cover top with foil. Bake in preheated 325-degree oven for 45 minutes; remove foil. Bake for 45 minutes longer.

Barbara Cash, Pres.
Beta Delta No. 349
Nederland, Texas

LEMON POUND CAKE

1 c. butter
1/2 c. Crisco
3 c. sugar
5 eggs
3 c. flour
1/2 tsp. baking powder
Pinch of salt
1 c. milk
2 tsp. lemon extract

Cream butter and Crisco until light; add sugar. Beat until smooth. Add eggs, one at a time, beating well after each addition. Combine flour, baking powder and salt. Add to egg mixture alternately with milk, beating well after each addition. Blend in lemon extract. Turn into large greased and floured tube pan. Bake in preheated 325-degree oven for 1 hour and 30 minutes or until cake tests done.

Ann Kennedy
Alpha Chi No. 2055
Waynesboro, Virginia

STARDUST POUND CAKE

2/3 c. soft shortening
1 1/3 c. sugar
3 eggs
2 1/3 c. sifted flour
1 tsp. baking powder
1/2 tsp. soda
1/2 tsp. salt
3/4 c. milk
Grated rind of 1 lemon
Juice of 1/2 lemon
Confectioners' sugar

Combine shortening, sugar and eggs; beat until light and fluffy at high speed of mixer.

Sift dry ingredients together; add alternately with milk, lemon rind and juice to creamed mixture at low speed, scraping bowl frequently. Pour into greased and floured tube pan. Bake in preheated 350-degree oven for 55 to 60 minutes or until tester comes out clean. Cool on wire rack for 10 minutes; remove from pan. Cool thoroughly. Dust with confectioners' sugar.

Irmgard Hattery, Treas.
Alpha Beta No. 219
Rock Island, Illinois

NUT POUND CAKE

1 lb. butter
2 c. sugar
6 eggs, separated
3 c. sifted self-rising flour
2 tsp. vanilla
1/2 tsp. salt
2 c. chopped pecans, floured

Cream butter and sugar until fluffy. Add yolks; continue to cream for 5 minutes. Add flour gradually, beating for 5 minutes. Add egg whites, vanilla and salt; beat at high speed for 15 minutes. Fold in pecans. Pour into greased and floured 10-inch tube pan. Place in cold oven. Bake at 325 degrees for 1 hour and 30 minutes. Yield: 20 servings.

Vera Gattmann, Rec. Sec.
Alpha Pi No. 2036
Savannah, Georgia

POOR MAN'S POUND CAKE

2 c. all-purpose flour
1 1/2 c. sugar
4 eggs
2 sticks margarine
1/2 c. milk
1 tbsp. baking powder
1 tbsp. lemon or vanilla flavoring

Combine all ingredients in mixing bowl; beat at high speed of electric mixer for 10 minutes. Pour into tube pan or 13 x 9-inch pan. Bake at 350-degrees for 1 hour.

Mrs. Charlotte C. Ralston
Beta Theta No. 4270
Staunton, Virginia

PRUNE CAKE

1 c. salad oil
1 1/2 c. sugar
3 eggs
2 c. sifted flour
1 tsp. soda
1 tsp. allspice
1 tsp. nutmeg
1 tsp. cinnamon
1 c. sour milk
1 c. cooked chopped prunes
1 tsp. vanilla
1/2 c. chopped nuts

Combine oil, sugar and eggs; beat well. Combine dry ingredients; add to egg mixture alternately with milk, mixing well after each addition. Add prunes, vanilla and nuts; mix well. Turn into 3 greased and floured layer cake pans or 9 x 13-inch pan. Bake in preheated 350-degree oven until cake tests done.

Vi Snyder
Alpha Kappa
Schuyler, Nebraska

EASY PUMPKIN CAKE

2 c. sugar
1 1/2 c. Wesson oil
1 tsp. salt
3 tsp. cinnamon
4 eggs
2 c. flour
2 tsp. soda
1 c. pumpkin pie filling

Combine all ingredients; mix well. Pour into greased and floured bundt pan. Bake in preheated 350-degree oven for 1 hour.

Frosting

6 oz. cream cheese, softened
1/2 c. butter, softened
1/2 1-lb. box powdered sugar
1 tsp. vanilla

Combine all ingredients; beat until creamy. Spread on warm cake.

Terry Brinlee, Rec. Sec.
Beta Omega No. 4210
Midland, Texas

PUMPKIN CAKE ROLL

3 eggs
1 c. sugar
2/3 c. canned pumpkin
1 tsp. lemon juice
1/2 tsp. salt
3/4 c. flour
1 tsp. baking powder
2 tsp. cinnamon
1 tsp. ginger
1/2 tsp. nutmeg
1 c. chopped nuts
Powdered sugar
2 3-oz. packages cream cheese,
    softened
4 tbsp. butter or margarine
1/2 tsp. vanilla

Beat eggs at high speed for 5 minutes; beat in sugar gradually. Stir in pumpkin and lemon juice. Combine salt, flour, baking powder and spices; stir into egg mixture. Spread in greased and floured 15 x 10 x 1-inch jelly roll pan. Top with nuts. Bake in preheated 375-degree oven for 15 minutes. Turn out on towel sprinkled with powdered sugar; Roll cake and towel together, starting at narrow end; let cool. Combine 1 cup powdered sugar with remaining ingredients; beat until smooth. Unroll cake; spread with filling. Reroll; chill.

Lavergne Reale
Alpha Lambda No. 231
Greeley, Colorado
Shareen Price
Beta Theta No. 1528
LaGrande, Oregon

RHUBARB COFFEE CAKE

1/2 c. shortening or margarine
2 c. sugar
1 egg
2 c. flour
1 tsp. soda
1 tsp. vanilla
1 c. buttermilk
1 1/2 c. chopped rhubarb
2 tsp. cinnamon

Blend shortening, 1 1/2 cups sugar, egg and flour together; add soda, vanilla and butter-

milk. Mix well. Fold in rhubarb. Spread in greased and floured 9 x 13-inch pan. Combine remaining 1/2 cup sugar and cinnamon; sprinkle over batter. Bake in preheated 350-degree oven for 45 minutes.

Joyce Zimmer, V.P.
Alpha Lambda No. 618
Vermillion, South Dakota

BAVARIAN SPICE CAKE

2 c. (packed) brown sugar
1 c. shortening
2 eggs
2 c. chopped dates
1 c. chopped nuts
1 tsp. cinnamon
1/2 tsp. cloves
1/2 tsp. allspice
3 c. sifted flour
1/2 tsp. salt
2 tsp. soda
2 c. beer or ale

Cream sugar and shortening; stir in eggs, dates, nuts and spices. Sift flour, salt and soda together; stir in beer. Combine beer mixture and creamed mixture; mix until well blended. Pour in a tube pan or 2 loaf pans. Bake in preheated 350-degree oven for 1 hour and 15 minutes or until cake tests done.

Lorene Johnstone, V.P.
Alpha Beta No. 165
Lincoln, Nebraska

BEER SPICE CAKE

1/2 c. shortening
1/2 c. (packed) brown sugar
1/2 c. sugar
2 eggs
2 c. flour
2 tsp. baking powder
1/2 tsp. soda
1 tsp. cinnamon
1/4 tsp. salt
1/4 tsp. nutmeg
1/2 tsp. allspice
1/2 tsp. cloves
1 c. beer

Cream shortening; add sugars gradually, blending thoroughly. Add eggs; beat well. Mix and sift dry ingredients; add to creamed mixture alternately with beer, beginning and ending with dry ingredients. Turn into greased loaf pan. Bake in preheated 350-degree oven for 40 to 45 minutes.

Frosting

1 c. butter
2/3 c. sugar
1/3 c. light molasses
2 c. powdered sugar
2 tbsp. evaporated milk

Melt butter in saucepan; add sugar and molasses. Bring to a boil on low heat; boil for 2 minutes, stirring constantly. Remove from heat; cool. Stir in powdered sugar and milk. Beat until thick enough to spread.

Shirley Petersen, Treas.
Beta Upsilon No. 2127
Myrtle Creek, Oregon

GRANDMA SECKERSON'S MOLASSES CAKE

1 c. sugar
2 eggs
1 c. sour cream
2/3 c. molasses
1 tsp. soda
1/2 tsp. ginger
1/2 tsp. cloves
1/2 tsp. cinnamon
1/2 tsp. salt
2 1/2 c. flour

Combine sugar, eggs, sour cream and molasses; mix well. Combine soda and 1/2 cup hot water. Sift dry ingredients together. Add flour mixture and water mixture alternately to sugar mixture, mixing well after each addition. Pour into 9 x 13-inch pan. Bake in preheated 350-degree oven until cake tests done. Cut into squares. Serve plain or with whipped cream.

Joyce Rosene, Scrapbook Chm.
Alpha Omega No. 4110
Bismarck, North Dakota

GRANDMA'S BUTTERMILK CAKE

2 c. sugar
1 c. (scant) butter or margarine
2 c. buttermilk
4 c. (scant) flour
1 tsp. (heaping) soda
1 tsp. cinnamon
1/2 tsp. nutmeg
1/4 tsp. cloves
1/4 tsp. salt
1 tsp. vanilla
2 c. cooked raisins, cooled
1 c. chopped nuts (opt.)

Cream sugar and butter. Add buttermilk alternately with sifted dry ingredients. Mix well. Stir in vanilla, raisins and nuts. Spread in 9 x 12-inch pan. Bake in preheated 350-degree oven for 50 minutes.

Lorraine Pixley, Treas.
Epsilon Gamma No. 1563
Manhattan, Kansas

POTATO AND SPICE CAKE

1 1/2 c. sugar
1 c. cold mashed potatoes
3/4 c. shortening
1 tsp. cinnamon
1/2 tsp. salt
1/2 tsp. nutmeg
3 eggs
1 tsp. soda
1 c. buttermilk
2 c. sifted flour
3/4 c. chopped walnuts

Combine first 6 ingredients; mix thoroughly. Add eggs; mix well. Mix soda with buttermilk; add alternately with flour to egg mixture. Stir in walnuts. Pour into 2 greased 8-inch pans. Bake in preheated 350-degree oven for 50 minutes or until done. Frost with favorite frosting.

Masako Ahlberg, Soc. Dir.
Beta Alpha No. 4068
Dubois, Wyoming

MALMICATION CAKE

1 c. sugar
3/4 c. butter
4 egg whites
1 c. strawberry jam
1 tsp. soda
1 c. sour milk
2 c. flour
1 tsp. allspice
1 tsp. cinnamon
1 tsp. baking powder
1/2 c. raisins

Cream sugar and butter together until light. Add egg whites; beat until fluffy. Blend in jam. Combine soda and milk. Sift dry ingredients together; add alternately with milk to sugar mixture, mixing well after each addition. Blend in raisins. Turn into 2 greased and floured 8-inch round cake pans. Bake in preheated 325-degree oven until cake tests done.

Filling

1/2 c. cream
4 egg yolks
3/4 c. butter
1 c. sugar
1 c. raisins
1 c. chopped pecans
1 c. coconut

Combine cream, egg yolks, butter and sugar in saucepan; cook until thick, stirring and beating constantly. Add remaining ingredients; mix well. Use as filling for cake.

Mildred Burnette, Sec.
Alpha Iota No. 3664
Mount Vernon, Illinois

STRAWBERRY SHORTCUT CAKE

1 c. miniature marshmallows
2 10-oz. packages frozen sliced
   strawberries, thawed
1 3-oz. package strawberry gelatin
2 1/4 c. flour
1 1/2 c. sugar
1/2 c. margarine
3 tbsp. baking powder
1/2 tsp. salt
1 c. milk
1 tsp. vanilla
3 eggs

Sprinkle marshmallows over bottom of greased 13 x 9-inch pan. Combine strawberries with gelatin; set aside. Combine remaining ingredients; blend at low speed until moistened, then beat for 3 minutes. Pour batter evenly over marshmallows; spoon strawberry mixture evenly over batter. Bake in preheated 350-degree oven for 45 to 50 minutes or until golden brown. Serve warm or cold. May serve with whipped cream, if desired.

Florence Sassenberg, Pres.
Alpha Theta No. 3879
Mankato, Minnesota

TRIFLING WITH STRAWBERRY SHORTCAKE

1 3/4 c. milk
1 3 3/4-oz. package instant vanilla
   pudding and pie filling mix
3 tbsp. cream sherry (opt.)
2 pt. fresh strawberries or 1 20-oz.
   bag frozen strawberries
2 tbsp. sugar
1 11 1/2-oz. frozen pound cake,
   defrosted
1 7-oz. aerosol can whipped light cream

Pour milk into bowl. Add pudding mix. Beat about 2 minutes on low speed, gradually adding sherry. Chill until set, about 1 hour. Slice strawberries, reserving 6 whole strawberries for garnish. Sweeten strawberries with sugar. Cut cake into 1/2-inch slices. Set aside 5 slices. Arrange remaining slices in bottom of 2 1/2-quart glass souffle dish or glass bowl. Spoon pudding on top of cake. Cover with sliced strawberries. Stand remaining cake slices in star shape on top of strawberries. Fill spaces between cake with soft cream. Garnish with whole strawberries. Serve at once. Yield: 8 servings.

Photograph for this recipe on page 36.

STRAWBERRY ROLL

4 eggs
1 tsp. vanilla

1 c. sugar
1 c. flour
3/4 tsp. baking powder
1/4 tsp. salt
2 env. Dream Whip, prepared
2 pt. strawberries, sliced and
    sweetened

Beat eggs and vanilla at high speed of mixer until thick and lemon colored. Beat in sugar gradually until fluffy and thick. Add sifted dry ingredients; fold in by hand. Pour into greased and waxed paper-lined 15 x 10 x 1-inch pan, spreading evenly. Bake in preheated 375-degree oven for 12 to 15 minutes. Turn out on large sheet of foil sprinkled with additional sugar. Roll up; let cool for 15 minutes. Unroll; spread with Dream Whip and strawberries. Reroll in foil; chill for 1 hour. Slice and serve.

Betty Duval
Alpha Eta No. 4393
Patterson, Louisiana

TOASTED BUTTER-PECAN CAKE

2 c. chopped pecans
1 1/4 c. butter
2 c. sugar
4 eggs
3 c. sifted flour
2 tsp. baking powder
1/2 tsp. salt
1 c. milk
1 tsp. butter flavoring
3 tsp. vanilla flavoring
1 1-lb. box confectioners' sugar
8 to 10 tbsp. evaporated milk

Combine pecans and 1/4 cup butter. Bake at 350 degrees for 20 to 25 minutes, stirring frequently. Combine remaining butter and sugar; blend in eggs. Sift dry ingredients together; add to creamed mixture alternately with milk. Stir in butter flavoring, 2 teaspoons vanilla flavoring and 1 1/3 cups toasted pecans. Pour into 3 greased and floured 8 or 9-inch layer pans. Bake at 350 degrees for 25 to 30 minutes; cool. Combine remaining toasted pecans with confectioners' sugar, evaporated milk and remaining 1 tea-

spoon vanilla flavoring. Spread between layers and over cake.

Bernice Ball
Eta Rho No. 1459
Fort Worth, Texas

GINGERBREAD

1 3/4 c. sifted all-purpose flour
3/4 c. cornmeal
1 tsp. baking powder
3/4 tsp. salt
3/4 tsp. soda
1 tsp. cinnamon
1 tsp. ginger
1/4 tsp. mace
1/3 c. butter or margarine, softened
1/2 c. (firmly packed) brown sugar
2 eggs
1/2 c. light molasses
3/4 c. buttermilk

Sift together flour, cornmeal, baking powder, salt, soda, cinnamon, ginger and mace. Set aside. Cream butter and brown sugar together. Blend in eggs and molasses. Batter may look curdled. Add dry ingredients; mix thoroughly. Add buttermilk. Beat for 2 to 3 minutes. Pour batter into greased 9-inch square baking pan. Bake in preheated 350-degree oven for 35 to 40 minutes. Serve warm or cold with hard sauce, if desired.

Photograph for this recipe below.

HIGHLAND FLING FROSTING

1   6-oz. package butterscotch morsels
1   8-oz. package cream cheese, softened
1/8 tsp. salt
2 1/4 c. sifted confectioners' sugar

Melt butterscotch morsels over hot, not boiling, water. Blend cream cheese and salt. Stir in melted morsels until smooth. Beat in sugar gradually until of spreading consistency. Yield: Frosting for two 8 or 9-inch cake layers.

Photograph for this recipe above.

HOT CHOCOLATE FUDGE FOR ICE CREAM

1 c. sugar
2 tbsp. cornstarch
1 c. water
Dash of salt
2 sq. chocolate
1 tsp. vanilla

Combine sugar, cornstarch, water, salt and chocolate; bring to a boil. Cover; turn off heat. Let stand until heat is gone from burner. Stir in vanilla. Serve over ice cream while still warm.

Erma R. Kendle
Zeta Phi No. 2593
Junction City, Kansas

CHOCOLATE SUNDAE SAUCE

3/4 c. sugar
1/4 c. cocoa
1   14 1/2-oz. can evaporated milk
2 tbsp. butter
1 tsp. vanilla

Combine sugar and cocoa; blend in milk. Bring to a boil, then simmer for 10 minutes, stirring constantly. Add butter and vanilla. Serve warm or cold. Store in refrigerator.

Leona Luecking, Rec. Sec.
Alpha Omicron No. 1827
West Burlington, Iowa

EASY CHOCOLATE ICING

1   1-lb. box confectioners' sugar
1/2 c. cocoa
1/4 c. butter or margarine
6 tbsp. brewed coffee
1 tsp. vanilla

Combine sugar and cocoa; add butter. Stir in about 4 tablespoons coffee; mix until smooth, adding a small amount of remaining coffee at a time to make of desired consistency. Add vanilla. This recipe ices a 2-layer cake or one 13 x 9-inch cake.

Kay Abbott, Pres.
Beta Theta No. 3791
Durham, North Carolina

HOMEMADE CHOCOLATE SAUCE

1 stick margarine
1/2 c. cocoa
1/2 tsp. salt
1/4 c. light corn syrup
3 c. sugar
1   13-oz. can evaporated milk
1 tsp. vanilla

Blend margarine, cocoa, salt and syrup together in top of double boiler. Add sugar; cook over simmering water, stirring, until thick. Pour in milk and vanilla; stir until sauce is smooth. Serve warm or cold.

Wilma Turnbull, Educational Dir.
Zeta Mu No. 2412
Stockton, Kansas

QUICK FUDGE SAUCE

2 sq. unsweetened chocolate
2 tbsp. margarine
2/3 c. sugar
1/2 c. evaporated milk
1/2 tsp. vanilla

Melt chocolate and margarine in saucepan over low heat. Add sugar and milk; cook until sugar is dissolved and sauce is thickened. Remove from heat; add vanilla. Serve hot or cold.

Donna Wiedeman, Treas.
Rho Tau No. 2932
Sedalia, Missouri

DECORATORS' ICING

1/2 c. Crisco
1/4 c. water
1 lb. powdered sugar
2 tbsp. flour
Dash of salt
1 tsp. vanilla
Food coloring (opt.)

Combine all ingredients in small mixing bowl; beat until smooth and creamy with electric mixer. This frosting may be used for decorating with tube decorator or for frosting cake. Will keep for months in refrigerator if covered tightly.

Sharon Reid
Kappa Nu No. 4415
Newton, Kansas

FRENCH FILLING

1/2 c. milk
3 tbsp. flour
1/4 c. shortening
1/4 c. margarine
1/2 c. sugar
1/4 tsp. vanilla

Stir milk into flour; cook, stirring constantly, until thick. Cool. Combine remaining ingredients; mix until smooth. Combine 2 mixtures; beat for 7 minutes. Fill cupcakes, using paper cone.

Bea Kipila
Beta Zeta No. 2556
Madison, Wisconsin

ORANGE-WALNUT BUTTERCREAM

1/2 c. walnuts
Rind of 1/2 orange
5 tbsp. thawed frozen orange
    juice concentrate
1/2 c. soft butter
2 c. confectioners' sugar

Place walnuts and orange rind in blender container; blend on high speed for 6 seconds or until walnuts are finely chopped. Add orange juice, butter and confectioners' sugar; stir to combine. Cover; blend on high speed for 30 seconds, stopping to stir down once or twice. This makes enough frosting for two 9-inch layers.

Becky Moomaw, Pres.
Eta Omicron No. 4095
Great Bend, Kansas

SOUR CREAM FROSTING

2 c. sour cream
1 c. sugar
1 c. (packed) brown sugar
1 tsp. vanilla
1/2 c. chopped walnuts

Combine sour cream and sugars; cook to soft-ball stage. Add vanilla and walnuts. Beat until thick enough to spread. Recipe makes enough frosting for 13 x 9-inch sheet cake.

Barbara Bunner
Beta Omicron No. 2997
Madison, Wisconsin

STRAWBERRY FROSTING

1/2 c. sliced strawberries
1 c. sugar
1 egg white

Combine all ingredients in small mixer bowl. Beat at high speed for 20 minutes. This makes enough frosting for a large angel food cake.

Joyce Junek, Corr. Sec.
Beta Lambda No. 2679
Milwaukee, Wisconsin

Party Beverages

Regardless of the fun people on hand, the appetizing foods at hand, or the reason for the occasion, every party needs a punch. There are so many recipes for party drinks of every flavor and description — hot and cold, soft or "hard", and sweet, spicy or tangy -- that no convivial get-together, featuring good food and happy people, should be without something equally special to drink. No party beverage recipe is plain, in either its flavor or its appearance, and so it should be chosen carefully to complement the foods with which it will be served, as well as to suit the time of day and the season of the year. Eggnog is an age-old favorite, but would be a poor choice at most wedding receptions, just as a cooling fruit punch or sangria would be at a snow skiing or ice skating party.

Most parties are large enough, and their guests and menus varied enough, for two different punches or beverages. Wedding reception, brunch, and luncheon menus are often made doubly festive by both a champagne punch and an iced coffee and ice cream punch. Fruit punch, champagne, and cappucino coffee all have their place at a New Year's Eve party, while no Christmas gathering is complete without wassail and/or eggnog. Even a small get-together just for late evening dessert seems extra special when the guests have a choice of steaming Irish coffee and a spiced, fruity rum or wine punch.

A pretty punch bowl and matching cups, as well as delicate demitasse cups, cheery Irish coffee mugs, and other special beverage cups add to the gaiety of any party atmosphere. Other decorative touches, such as cinnamon sticks, mint leaf garnishes, specially shaped fruit pieces and ice sculptures also go a long way to please a crowd. ESA members think that a party without its own special beverage or punch truly lacks an important detail. Every cook and homemaker likes to display her creative party-giving skills, and a festive punch is just another special way to do it. Don't forget the punch at your next party.

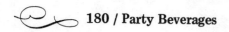

CAFE DIABLE

3 sm. sugar cubes
1/4 c. butter or margarine
1 c. whole coffee beans
Grated rind of 1 orange
Chopped peel of 1 apple
2-in. piece of cinnamon stick
12 cloves
6 tbsp. cognac
6 tbsp. kirsch
6 tbsp. curacao
1 1/4 c. freshly made coffee
Juice of 1 orange

Place sugar cubes and butter in chafing dish or diable pan over direct flame. Melt butter but do not brown. Add coffee beans, orange and apple peel, cinnamon and cloves. Pour in cognac, kirsch and curacao. Stir and heat. Apply lighted match; ignite. When flame dies out, add coffee and orange juice. Let heat to steaming; pour through strainer into demi-tasse cups. Yield: 4 to 6 servings.

Photograph for this recipe on page 179.

FRIENDSHIP TEA

1 c. instant tea
2 c. sugar
2 sm. packages instant lemonade mix
1 14-oz. jar Tang
2 tsp. cinnamon
2 tsp. ground cloves

Combine all ingredients; mix well. Place 2 to 3 tablespoons mixture in cup; fill cup with hot water.

Susie Clesson
Eta Omicron No. 4095
Great Bend, Kansas

HOT SPICED TEA

1 tsp. whole cloves
1 1-in. piece of stick cinnamon
3 qt. water
2 1/2 tbsp. black tea
Juice of 3 oranges
Juice of 1 1/2 lemons

1 c. pineapple juice
1 c. sugar

Tie spices loosely in bag; add to water. Bring to a boil. Tie tea loosely in bag; add to water. Steep for 5 minutes; remove bags. Heat fruit juices and sugar; add to tea. Stir well. Serve hot. Yield: 25 servings.

Mrs. Kay Kesler
Treas., State Chaplain
Beta Chi No. 4196
Anderson, South Carolina

CRANBERRY-CIDER PUNCH

1 1/2 c. water
2 c. sugar
2 sticks cinnamon
2 tsp. whole cloves
2/5 Burgundy
1/8 tsp. salt
1 pt. cranberry juice cocktail
1 qt. apple cider

Bring water, sugar, cinnamon and cloves to a boil. Simmer for 10 minutes; strain. Cool syrup. Combine syrup with remaining ingredients just before serving. Pour into punch bowl with ice.

Veronica Schoenfish, Pres.
Alpha Omicron No. 3217
Cambridge, Nebraska

CRANBERRY-PINEAPPLE PUNCH

1 pkg. Funny Face cherry or raspberry
   drink mix
Lemon juice to taste
1 sm. bottle cranberry juice
1 lg. can pineapple juice
1 sm. can frozen orange juice or Tang
1 lg. bottle lemon-lime drink
1/2 gal. pineapple sherbet

Combine all ingredients except sherbet; chill. Pour into punch bowl; float sherbet on top just before serving.

Ellen Clark
Las Caronas Reg. Coun. Rec. Sec.
Gamma Omicron
Tujunga, California

CREAMY ORANGE DRINK

1 1/4 c. orange juice
1 c. crushed ice
1 env. whipped topping mix

Place all ingredients in a blender; blend until frothy. Yield: 3 servings.

Holli Arnett
Gamma Kappa No. 3265
Northglenn, Colorado

EMERALD PUNCH

1 1/2 c. pineapple juice
1 6-oz. can frozen limeade, thawed
1 tbsp. honey
3 7-oz. bottles Seven-Up
Drop of green food coloring (opt.)

Combine pineapple juice and limeade; add honey. Stir until well blended. Add the Seven-Up slowly and green food coloring. Add ice. Garnish with lime slices. Serve immediately.

Nicola Hoffman, Pres.
Delta Tau No. 3714
Canal Winchester, Ohio

FROZEN STRAWBERRY DAIQUIRI

1 6-oz. can lemonade concentrate
6 oz. light rum
1/2 tsp. vanilla
1 8-oz. package frozen strawberries
1/4 tsp. almond extract

Place all ingredients in a blender; mix. Add cracked ice; whirl until blender jar is full. May add Seven-Up to thin, if desired.

Diane Perkins, Pres.
Beta Zeta No. 2918
Boise, Idaho

GIN FIZZ

4 shots gin
8 shots half and half
1 shot lime or lemon juice

1 shot creme de cacao
2 eggs
4 tbsp. powdered sugar

Combine all ingredients in blender container. Blend for 30 seconds. Add enough ice to reach top of blender. Mix well; serve. Yield: 4 servings.

Mary Ferreira, Scrapbook Chm.
Iota Alpha No. 2961
Fremont, California

BANANA-STRAWBERRY PUNCH

4 bananas, peeled
1 box fresh strawberries, washed and
   capped
1/3 c. sugar
1 qt. chilled extra dry champagne or
   ginger ale
1 pt. pineapple sherbet (opt.)

Combine bananas with strawberries and sugar in electric mixer or blender. Pour into punch bowl; add champagne. Top with mounds of sherbet. Garnish with several whole or halved strawberries and banana slices. This recipe may be doubled to serve 20 to 25 people. Yield: 10-12 punch cup servings.

Photograph for this recipe below.

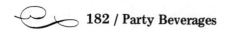

ORANGE J'S

1 6-oz. can frozen orange juice
1 tsp. vanilla
1/4 to 1/2 c. sugar
12 ice cubes
1 c. milk
1 c. water

Combine all ingredients in blender; blend for about 30 seconds or until ice cubes are crushed. Serve immediately.

> Barbara Knotts, Parliamentarian
> Alpha Phi No. 2245
> Nampa, Idaho
> Susan Rostvedt
> Alpha Omega No. 4110
> Bismarck, North Dakota
> Pat Bolin
> Alpha Omicron No. 577
> Enid, Oklahoma

PINEAPPLE-WINE PUNCH

1 46-oz. can pineapple juice, chilled
2 bottles sauturne, chilled
1 pt. brandy
1 6-oz. can frozen lemonade
2 10-oz. packages frozen raspberries
1 25-oz. bottle cold duck

Blend pineapple juice, sauterne, brandy and lemonade. Mix well, gently but thoroughly. Stir in raspberries and liquid. Stir in chilled cold duck before serving. Pour over ice in punch bowl.

> Wanda Johnson, Historian
> Gamma Omega No. 4212
> Grapevine, Texas

SANTA'S SEVEN-UP SURPRISE

1 46-oz. can pineapple juice, chilled
2 6-oz. cans frozen orange juice,
   thawed
1/2 tsp. peppermint extract
10 7-oz. bottles Seven-Up, chilled
2 trays Seven-Up Ice Cubes

Combine pineapple juice and orange juice concentrate in punch bowl; add peppermint extract. Pour in Seven-Up slowly. Add Seven-Up Ice Cubes.

Seven-Up Ice Cubes

Seven-Up
Maraschino cherries

Pour Seven-Up into 2 ice trays; place cherry in each cube. Freeze.

> Ruth Lewis, Publ. Chm.
> Alpha Sigma No. 4298
> Richardson, Texas

SORORITY SPECIAL PUNCH

1 gal. sauterne
1 c. brandy
1 bottle champagne
1 bottle ginger ale
Ice Ring

Remove 1 cup sauterne 24 hours ahead of serving time. Replace with brandy. Chill. Pour sauterne mixture into punch bowl just before serving; add champagne and ginger ale. Serve over Ice Ring.

Ice Ring

1 orange, thinly sliced
1 lemon, thinly sliced

Arrange orange and lemon slices in a ring mold; add enough water to cover fruits. Place in freezer until water is frozen, then add water to rim of mold. Freeze until firm. Unmold; place in punch bowl when ready to serve. Cherries and mint leaves may be added, if desired.

> Pauline Herber, Pres.
> Eta Omega No. 2658
> Watsonville, California

SPARKLING FRUIT REFRESHER

1 6-oz. can frozen orange juice
   concentrate, thawed
1 6-oz. can frozen lemonade
   concentrate, thawed
3 c. cold water
2 drops of red food coloring
1 12-oz. bottle ginger ale, chilled

1 16-oz. package frozen whole
   strawberries, just thawed
1 pt. orange sherbet

Combine concentrates and water in punch
bowl; stir until well blended. Mix in food
coloring and ginger ale. Add strawberries.
Float scoops of sherbet on punch. Serve
immediately. Yield: About 12 servings.

Arliss Morgan, Parliamentarian
Delta Tau No. 4264
Yakima, Washington

FROZEN FRUIT SLUSH

1 sm. can frozen orange juice
1 sm. can frozen lemonade
1 10 1/2-oz. package frozen
   strawberries
1 13 1/2-oz. can crushed pineapple
   and juice
1 c. sugar
Rum to taste (opt.)
2 c. water
3 bananas, sliced

Combine all ingredients; place in freezer for
1 hour. Remove from freezer; stir. Keep in
freezer until 1 hour before serving.

Marilyn Geier, V.P.
Gamma Delta No. 2302
Lincoln, Nebraska

FRUIT SLUSH

1 sm. can frozen lemonade
1 sm. can frozen orange juice
1 lg. package frozen strawberry halves
1 king-size bottle Seven-Up
1 c. sugar
2 bananas, cut in sm. pieces

Thaw lemonade, orange juice and strawberries just enough to mix in large bowl; add
remaining ingredients. Freeze in paper cups.
Thaw for 30 to 40 minutes before serving.
Yield: 12 servings.

Judy Peterson, Publ. Chm.
Alpha Rho No. 4184
Nebraska City, Nebraska

SUZETTE'S BANANA PUNCH

3 1/2 c. sugar
6 c. water
2 c. orange juice
3 c. pineapple juice
Juice of 2 lemons
4 sm. or 3 lg. bananas, well mashed
2 qt. ginger ale

Combine all ingredients except ginger ale;
pour into shallow dish. Freeze for at least 24
hours. Let thaw for 45 minutes. Mash with
potato masher; add chilled ginger ale.

Pandra D. Warren, Pres.
Alpha Sigma No. 3887
Columbia, South Carolina

RECEPTION PUNCH

4 c. sugar
2 c. fresh lemon juice
2 qt. fresh strawberries, washed, capped
   and sliced
2 c. fresh lime juice
1 1 pt. 12-oz. bottle ginger ale

Combine sugar with 1 quart water and 1/4
cup fresh lemon juice. Bring to a boil; boil 3
minutes. Cool. Push strawberries through a
fine sieve. Add to cooled mixture along with
3 quarts cold water, 1 3/4 cups lemon juice
and fresh lime juice. Pour into a punch bowl
over ice. Add ginger ale. Garnish with fresh
mint. Yield: About 9 quarts.

Photograph for this recipe below.

HOLIDAY SLUSH

7 c. hot water
2 sm. cans frozen lemonade
1 sm. can frozen orange juice
2 c. strong tea
1 1/2 c. sugar
1 c. whiskey
Seven-Up or club soda

Combine all ingredients except Seven-Up. Mix well. Freeze. Mix with equal amount of Seven-Up or soda to serve.

Jodee Bainter
Alpha Phi No. 1438
Winner, South Dakota

RUM SLUSHES

1 lg. can frozen orange juice
1 lg. can frozen lemonade
6 c. sugar
2 juice cans rum
9 c. water
4 tbsp. instant tea
Sprite or Seven-Up

Combine all ingredients except Sprite; freeze overnight. Serve by mixing 1/2 slush with 1/2 Sprite or 3/4 slush with 1/4 Sprite. Mix according to how weak or strong you enjoy your drinks.

Peggy Main, V.P.
Delta Beta No. 4323
Savannah, Georgia

SLUSH PUNCH

2 c. sugar
6 c. water
1 46-oz. can pineapple juice
2 12-oz. cans frozen orange juice
   concentrate
Juice of 2 lemons
3 bananas, mashed
2 32-oz. bottles Seven-Up or Sprite
1 10-oz. box frozen strawberries

Bring sugar and water to boil; add juices. Freeze in 2 half-gallon milk cartons. Combine slush and bananas in punch bowl at serving time. Add Seven-Up and strawberries. May add rum or vodka, if desired. Yield: 50 servings.

Marti Plake
Beta Omega No. 4210
Midland, Texas

FRESH RHUBARB PUNCH

2 qt. diced fresh rhubarb
1/4 tsp. salt
3 1/2 c. sugar
1 c. fresh lemon juice
1 c. fresh lime or fresh orange juice
1/2 c. fresh pineapple wedges
1 c. sliced fresh strawberries
Fresh mint leaves

Combine rhubarb, 1 quart water and salt in large saucepan; cover. Bring to a boil; reduce heat. Cook slowly 15 minutes or until rhubarb is tender and mixture is of sauce consistency. Strain mixture. Stir in sugar and lemon juice while mixture is hot. Cool. Add lime juice and 5 cups cold water. Pour into punch bowl over ice. Float pineapple wedges, strawberries and mint leaves over top. Yield: 1 gallon.

Photograph for this recipe below.

NUTRITION LABELING

ESA Women International have included a new and very important feature in this cookbook — A Nutrition Labeling Chart. Commercial food manufacturers have begun to publish nutrition information on food product labels, a practice which ESA members know is invaluable. But, it does the homemaker very little good to know the nutritive value of a can of peaches, for example, if she does not know what part the peaches play in overall nutrition planning.

The US Food and Drug Administration has determined how much of every key nutrient is needed by the average healthy adult. This information is tabulated and well known as the Recommended Daily Dietary Allowance (RDA). The US RDA lists the highest amounts of nutrients for all ages and sexes. Pregnant women, nursing mothers, as well as persons with special dietary needs should consult their doctor for any recommended increases or decreases of the Recommended Daily Dietary Allowance of nutrients in their diet.

UNITED STATES RECOMMENDED DAILY ALLOWANCE CHART

Nutrient	Allowance
Protein	45-65 Grams
Carbohydrates	125 Grams
Vitamin A	5,000 International Units
Thiamine (Vitamin B_1)	1.5 Milligrams
Riboflavin (Vitamin B_2)	1.7 Milligrams
Vitamin B_6	2 Milligrams
Vitamin B_{12}	6 Micrograms
Folic Acid (B Vitamin)	0.4 Milligrams
Pantothenic Acid (B Vitamin)	10 Milligrams
Vitamin C (Ascorbic Acid)	55-60 Milligrams
Vitamin D	400 International Units
Vitamin E	30 International Units
Iron	18 Milligrams
Calcium	1 Gram
Niacin (Nicotinic Acid)	13-20 Milligrams
Magnesium	400 Milligrams
Zinc	15 Milligrams
Copper	2 Milligrams
Phosphorus	1 Gram
Iodine	150 Micrograms
Biotin (Vitamin H)	0.3 Milligrams

IMPORTANT NUTRIENTS YOUR DIET REQUIRES

PROTEIN

Why? Absolutely essential in building, repairing and renewing of all body tissue. Helps body resist infection. Builds enzymes and hormones, helps form and maintain body fluids.

Where? Milk, eggs, lean meats, poultry, fish, soybeans, peanuts, dried peas and beans, grains and cereals.

CARBOHYDRATES

Why?   Provide needed energy for bodily functions, provide warmth, as well as fuel for brain and nerve tissues. Lack of carbohydrates will cause body to use protein for energy rather than for repair and building.

Where?   Sugars: sugar, table syrups, jellies, jams, etc., as well as dried and fresh fruits. Starches: cereals, pasta, rice, corn, dried beans and peas, potatoes, stem and leafy vegetables, and milk.

FATS

Why?   Essential in the use of fat soluble vitamins (A, D, E, K), and fatty acids. Have more than twice the concentrated energy than equal amount of carbohydrate for body energy and warmth.

Where?   Margarine, butter, cooking oil, mayonnaise, vegetable shortening, milk, cream, ice cream, cheese, meat, fish, eggs, poultry, chocolate, coconut, nuts.

VITAMIN A

Why?   Needed for healthy skin and hair, as well as for healthy, infection-resistant mucous membranes.

Where?   Dark green, leafy and yellow vegetables, liver. Deep yellow fruits, such as apricots and cantaloupe. Milk, cheese, eggs, as well as fortified margarine and butter.

THIAMINE (VITAMIN B_1)

Why?   Aids in the release of energy of foods, as well as in normal appetite and digestion. Promotes healthy nervous system.

Where?   Pork, liver, kidney. Dried peas and beans. Whole grain and enriched breads and cereals.

RIBOFLAVIN (VITAMIN B_2)

Why?   Helps to oxidize foods. Promotes healthy eyes and skin, especially around mouth and eyes. Prevents pellagra.

Where?   Meats, especially liver and kidney, as well as milk, cheese, eggs. Dark green leafy vegetables. Enriched bread and cereal products. Almonds, dried peas and beans.

VITAMIN B_6

Why?   Helps protein in building body tissues. Needed for healthy nerves, skin and digestion. Also helps body to use fats and carbohydrates for energy.

Where?   Milk, wheat germ, whole grain and fortified cereals. Liver, kidney, pork and beef.

VITAMIN B_{12}

Why?   Aids body in formation of red blood cells, as well as in regular work of all body cells.

Where?   Lean meats, milk, eggs, fish, cheese, as well as liver and kidney.

FOLIC ACID

Why?   Aids in healthy blood system, as well as intestinal tract. Helps to prevent anemia.

Where?   Green leaves of vegetables and herbs, as well as liver and milk. Wheat germ and soybeans.

PANTOTHENIC ACID

Why?   Aids in proper function of digestive system.

Where?   Liver, kidney and eggs. Peanuts and molasses. Broccoli and other vegetables.

VITAMIN C (ASCORBIC ACID)

Why?   Promotes proper bone and tooth formation. Helps body utilize iron and resist infection. Strengthens blood vessels. Lack of it causes bones to heal slowly, failure of wounds to heal and fragile vessels to bleed easily.

Where? Citrus fruits, cantaloupe and strawberries. Broccoli, kale, green peppers, raw cabbage, sweet potatoes, cauliflower, tomatoes.

VITAMIN D

Why? Builds strong bones and teeth by aiding utilization of calcium and phosphorus.

Where? Fortified milk, fish liver oils, as well as salmon, tuna and sardines. Also eggs.

VITAMIN E

Why? Needed in maintaining red blood cells.

Where? Whole grain cereals, wheat germ, beans and peas, lettuce and eggs.

IRON

Why? Used with protein for hemoglobin production. Forms nucleus of each cell, and helps them to use oxygen.

Where? Kidney and liver, as well as shellfish, lean meats, and eggs. Deep yellow and dark green leafy vegetables. Dried peas, beans and fruits. Potatoes, whole grain cereals and bread. Enriched flour and bread. Dark molasses.

CALCIUM

Why? Builds and renews bones, teeth and other tissues, as well as aids in the proper function of muscles, nerves and heart. Controls normal blood clotting. With protein, aids in oxidation of foods.

Where? Milk and milk products, excluding butter. Dark green vegetables, oysters, clams and sardines.

NIACIN

Why? Helps body to oxidize food. Aids in digestion, and helps to keep nervous system and skin healthy.

Where? Peanuts, liver, tuna, as well as fish, poultry and lean meats. Enriched breads, cereals and peas.

MAGNESIUM

Why? Aids nervous system and sleep.

Where? Almonds, peanuts, raisins and prunes. Vegetables, fruits, milk, fish and meats.

ZINC

Why? Needed for cell formation.

Where? Nuts and leafy green vegetables. Shellfish.

COPPER

Why? Helps body to utilize iron.

Where? Vegetables and meats.

PHOSPHORUS

Why? Maintains normal blood clotting function, as well as builds bones, teeth and nerve tissue. Aids in utilization of sugar and fats.

Where? Oatmeal and whole wheat products. Eggs and cheese, dried beans and peas. Nuts, lean meats, and fish and poultry.

IODINE

Why? Enables thyroid gland to maintain proper body metabolism.

Where? Iodized salt. Saltwater fish and seafood. Milk and vegetables.

BIOTIN (VITAMIN H)

Why? Helps to maintain body cells.

Where? Eggs and liver. Any foods rich in Vitamin B.

SUBSTITUTIONS AND COOKING GUIDES

WHEN YOU'RE MISSING AN INGREDIENT . . .

Substitute 1 teaspoon dried herbs for 1 tablespoon fresh herbs.

Add 1/4 teaspoon baking soda and 1/2 cup buttermilk to equal 1 teaspoon baking powder. The buttermilk will replace 1/2 cup of the liquid indicated in the recipe.

Use 3 tablespoons dry cocoa plus 1 tablespoon butter or margarine instead of 1 square (1 ounce) unsweetened chocolate.

Make custard with 1 whole egg rather than 2 egg yolks.

Mix 1/2 cup evaporated milk with 1/2 cup water (or 1 cup reconstituted nonfat dry milk with 1 tablespoon butter) to replace 1 cup whole milk.

Make 1 cup of sour milk by letting stand for 5 minutes 1 tablespoon lemon juice or vinegar plus sweet milk to make 1 cup.

Substitute 1 package (2 teaspoons) active dry yeast for 1 cake compressed yeast.

Add 1 tablespoon instant minced onion, rehydrated, to replace 1 small fresh onion.

Substitute 1 tablespoon prepared mustard for 1 teaspoon dry mustard.

Use 1/8 teaspoon garlic powder instead of 1 small pressed clove of garlic.

Substitute 2 tablespoons of flour for 1 tablespoon of cornstarch to use as a thickening agent.

Mix 1/2 cup tomato sauce with 1/2 cup of water to make 1 cup tomato juice.

Make catsup or chili with 1 cup tomato sauce plus 1/2 cup sugar and 2 tablespoons vinegar.

CAN SIZE CHART

8 oz. can or jar	1 c.	1 lb. 4 oz. or 1 pt. 2 fl. oz. or No. 2 can or jar	2 1/2 c.
10 1/2 oz. can (picnic can)	1 1/4 c.	1 lb. 13 oz. can or jar or No. 2 1/2 can or jar	3 1/2 c.
12 oz. can (vacuum)	1 1/2 c.		
14-16 oz. or No. 300 can	1 1/4 c.	1 qt. 14 fl. oz. or 3 lb. 3 oz. or 46 oz. can	5 3/4 c.
16-17 oz. can or jar or No. 303 can or jar	2 c.	6 1/2 to 7 1/2 lb. or No. 10 can	12-13 c.

SUBSTITUTIONS

1 square *chocolate* (1 ounce) = 3 or 4 tablespoons cocoa plus 1/2 tablespoon fat.
1 tablespoon *cornstarch* (for thickening) = 2 tablespoons flour (approximately).
1 cup sifted *all-purpose flour* = 1 cup plus 2 tablespoons sifted cake flour.
1 cup sifted *cake flour* = 1 cup minus 2 tablespoons sifted all-purpose flour.
1 teaspoon *baking powder* = 1/4 teaspoon baking soda plus 1/2 teaspoon cream of tartar.
1 cup *bottled milk* = 1/2 cup evaporated milk plus 1/2 cup water.
1 cup *sour milk* = 1 cup sweet milk into which 1 tablespoon vinegar or lemon juice has been stirred; or 1 cup buttermilk.
1 cup *sweet milk* = 1 cup sour milk or buttermilk plus 1/2 teaspoon baking soda.
1 cup *canned tomatoes* = about 1 1/3 cups cut-up fresh tomatoes, simmered 10 minutes.
3/4 cup *cracker crumbs* = 1 cup bread crumbs.
1 cup *cream, sour, heavy* = 1/3 cup butter and 2/3 cup milk in any sour milk recipe.
1 cup *cream, sour, thin* = 3 tablespoons butter and 3/4 cup milk in sour milk recipe.
1 cup *molasses* = 1 cup honey.

METRIC CONVERSION CHARTS FOR THE KITCHEN

VOLUME

1 tsp.	=	4.9 cc
1 tbsp.	=	14.7 cc
1/3 c.	=	28.9 cc
1/8 c.	=	29.5 cc
1/4 c.	=	59.1 cc
1/2 c.	=	118.3 cc
3/4 c.	=	177.5 cc
1 c.	=	236.7 cc
2 c.	=	473.4 cc
1 fl. oz.	=	29.5 cc
4 oz.	=	118.3 cc
8 oz.	=	236.7 cc

1 pt.	=	473.4 cc
1 qt.	=	.946 liters
1 gal.	=	3.7 liters

CONVERSION FACTORS:

Liters	X	1.056	=	Liquid quarts
Quarts	X	0.946	=	Liters
Liters	X	0.264	=	Gallons
Gallons	X	3.785	=	Liters
Fluid ounces	X	29.563	=	Cubic centimeters
Cubic centimeters	X	0.034	=	Fluid ounces
Cups	X	236.575	=	Cubic centimeters
Tablespoons	X	14.797	=	Cubic centimeters
Teaspoons	X	4.932	=	Cubic centimeters
Bushels	X	0.352	=	Hectoliters
Hectoliters	X	2.837	=	Bushels

WEIGHT

1 dry oz.	=	28.3 Grams
1 lb.	=	.454 Kilograms

CONVERSION FACTORS:

Ounces (Avoir.)	X	28.349	=	Grams
Grams	X	0.035	=	Ounces
Pounds	X	0.454	=	Kilograms
Kilograms	X	2.205	=	Pounds

EQUIVALENT CHART

3 tsp. = 1 tbsp.	16 oz. = 1 lb.	4 c. sifted flour = 1 lb.
2 tbsp. = 1/8 c.	1 oz. = 2 tbsp. fat or liquid	1 lb. butter = 2 c. or 4 sticks
4 tbsp. = 1/4 c.	2 c. fat = 1 lb.	2 pt. = 1 qt.
8 tbsp. = 1/2 c.	2 c. = 1 pt.	1 qt. = 4 c.
16 tbsp. = 1 c.	2 c. sugar = 1 lb.	A Few Grains = Less than 1/8 tsp.
5 tbsp. + 1 tsp. = 1/3 c.	5/8 c. = 1/2 c. + 2 tbsp.	Pinch is as much as can be taken
12 tbsp. = 3/4 c.	7/8 c. = 3/4 c. + 2 tbsp.	between tip of finger and thumb.
4 oz. = 1/2 c.	2 2/3 c. powdered sugar = 1 lb.	Speck = Less than 1/8 tsp.
8 oz. = 1 c.	2 2/3 c. brown sugar = 1 lb.	

WHEN YOU NEED APPROXIMATE MEASUREMENTS . . .

1 lemon makes 3 tablespoons juice
1 lemon makes 1 teaspoon grated peel
1 orange makes 1/3 cup juice
1 orange makes about 2 teaspoons grated peel
1 chopped medium onion makes 1/2 cup pieces
1 pound unshelled walnuts makes 1 1/2 to 1 3/4 cups shelled
1 pound unshelled almonds makes 3/4 to 1 cup shelled
8 to 10 egg whites make 1 cup

12 to 14 egg yolks make 1 cup
1 pound shredded American cheese makes 4 cups
1/4 pound crumbled blue cheese makes 1 cup
1 cup unwhipped cream makes 2 cups whipped
4 ounces (1 to 1 1/4 cups) uncooked macaroni makes 2 1/4 cups cooked
7 ounces spaghetti make 4 cups cooked
4 ounces (1 1/2 to 2 cups) uncooked noodles make 2 cups cooked.

MAKE 1 CUP OF FINE CRUMBS WITH . . .

28 saltine crackers
4 slices bread
14 square graham crackers
22 vanilla wafers

Index

COLOR PHOTOGRAPH RECIPES

PHOTOGRAPHY CREDITS: National Peanut Council, Cover; California Strawberry Advisory Board; California Plum Commodity Committee; DIAMOND Walnut Kitchen; Rice Council; National Peanut Council; Knox Gelatine, Inc.; Evaporated Milk Association; The Nestle Company; California Apricot Advisory Board; National Cherry Growers Industries; General Foods Kitchens; The American Spice Trade Association; California Raisin Advisory Board; United Fresh Fruit and Vegetable Association; Processed Apples Institute, Inc.; Washington State Apple Commission; The Quaker Oats Company; National Biscuit Company; Cling Peach Advisory Board; National Dairy Council; Best Foods: A Division of Corn Products Company International; The J. M. Smucker Company; American Dairy Association; Keith Thomas Company; Florida Citrus Commission; Armour and Company; The Borden Company; Beatrice Foods Company; R. D. Bigelow, Inc.; Bernard L. Lewis, Inc.

Recipe on page 131.